Early Modern History

SPONSORS

This encyclopedia project was initiated and guided by the **Yayasan Dana Bakti**

with the support of the **Shangri-la Hotel***, Jakarta.*

It was also made possible thanks to the generous and enlightened support of the following companies:

PT. Makindo
Sinar Mas Group
Bakrie Group
Bank Artha Graha
Satelindo
Telekomindo
Telekomunikasi Indonesia
Indobuildco
Indosat
Inti
Pasifik Satelit Nusantara

Plaza Indonesia Realty
Siemens Indonesia
WES Intratama Consortium
Wahana Tigamas Buana/AT&T
Konsorsium Pramindo Ikat
Artha Telekomindo
Amalgam Indocorpora
Elektrindo Nusantara
PT. Ratelindo
Komselindo

INDONESIAN HERITAGE

Early Modern History

VOLUME EDITOR

Anthony Reid *Research School of Pacific and Asian Studies,*
The Australian National University, Canberra

VOLUME EDITORIAL TEAM

Sian Jay
Senior Editor

Nelani Jinadasa
Designer

T. Durairajoo
Editor

Helen West
Picture Researcher

AUTHORS

Taufik Abdullah - *Indonesian Institute of Sciences
(LIPI), Jakarta*
Ibrahim Alfian - *Department of History,
Gadja Mada University*
Hasan M. Ambary - *National Research Centre for
Archaeology, Jakarta*
Leonard Andaya - *Department of History,
University of Hawaii*
Barbara Watson Andaya - *School of Hawaiian, Asian and
Pacific Studies, University of Hawaii*
Jane Atkinson- *Social Science Division,
Lewis and Clark College, Portland, Oregon*
Leonard Blussé - *Department of History, Leiden University*
Peter Boomgaard - *Royal Institute of Linguistics
and Anthropology (KITLV), Leiden*
Gill Burke - *Research School of Pacific and Asian Studies,
Australian National University*
Peter Carey - *Trinity College, Oxford University*
Helen Creese - *Department of Asian Languages and Studies,
University of Queensland*
Jane Drakard - *Department of History,
Monash University*
John Guy - *Indian and Southeast Asian Department,
Victoria and Albert Museum, London*
Virginia Hooker - *Faculty of Asian Studies,
Australian National University*
Jeyamalar Kathirithamby-Wells - *Netherlands Institute for
Advanced Study in the Humanities and Social Sciences*
Roger Knight - *Department of History, Adelaide University*
Ann Kumar - *Faculty of Asian Studies,
Australian National University*
Ruurdje Laarhoven - *University of Hawaii*

Adrian Lapian - *Indonesian Institute of Sciences (LIPI),
Jakarta*
Lee Kam Hing - *Department of History,
University of Malaya, Kuala Lumpur*
R Z Leirissa - *Department of History, University of Indonesia*
Pierre-Yves Manguin - *Ecole Française d'Extreme-
Orient, Paris*
Luc Nagtegaal - *Royal Institute of Linguistics and
Anthropology (KITLV), Leiden*
Sandra Niessen - *Department of Human Ecology,
University of Alberta*
Onghokham - *Netherlands Institute for Advanced Study
in the Humanities and Social Sciences*
Ian Proudfoot - *Faculty of Asian Studies,
Australian National University*
Willem Remmelink - *Japan-Netherlands Institute, Tokyo*
M.C. Ricklefs - *Research School of Pacific and Asian Studies,
Australian National University*
Peter Ridell - *Centre for Islamic Studies,
Brunel University, London*
Mary Somers-Heidhues - *Göttingen University, Germany*
Supomo Suryohudoyo - *Faculty of Asian Studies,
Australian National University*
Heather Sutherland - *Vrije Universiteit, Amsterdam*
Roger Tol - *Royal Institute of Linguistics and
Anthropology (KITLV), Leiden*
Carl Trocki - *School of Humanities,
Queensland University of Technology*
Alfons van der Kraan - *Department of Economic History,
University of New England, Armidale*
Geoffrey Wade - *Hong Kong*

ARCHIPELAGO PRESS

Contents

INDONESIA:
Early Modern World

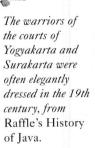

Bhinneka Tunggal Ika — *it is various, and yet it is one. This mystical saying of a 14th century Javanese poet is profoundly appropriate as the motto for the Indonesian state. It is the variety of Indonesia that gives it its common character. Each region replicates, in its own way, the diversities between mountain and valley, upstream and downstream, large (mainland) islands and small ones, forest and coast.*

Plethora of Interrelated Cultures

Until the 20th century, no state had integrated the peoples of even one major island, and yet each of these diverse peoples were in relations of trade, tribute or ritual with a number of others.

The reasons for this plethora of interrelated cultures can be put simply. The physical character of the Indonesian Archipelago made contacts by water easy, but difficult by land. The calm waters of Indonesia's 'Mediterranean' with their regular monsoon winds were ideal for sailing; and most of the Archipelago's inhabitants were close to the sea, a lake or navigable river. Yet the building of roads or permanent tracks was made difficult by mountains, rivers, swamps, and above all, heavy rainfall. Hence the contacts between peoples were the episodic ones that come from trading, raiding, warring and sending tribute by sea; not the imperial subjugation encouraged by the large river-systems of China, India, and Egypt; the plains of Russia and central Asia, or the road-crossed open land of central Europe and central America.

Defining a Place — 'Indonesia'

This book is concerned with the territory which has become universally familiar since 1945 as Indonesia. Both Dutch imperialists and Indonesian nationalists found a natural unity in the 17,508 islands of the Archipelago, though nothing but the diplomatic convenience of late 19th century colonial officials can explain the lines drawn across the middle of Borneo and New Guinea, and until 1975, down the middle of Timor. The lines were drawn when the world was being divided up among sovereign states which could no longer tolerate any messy corners for which some such state was not responsible. But it would only be much later that the highlanders of the Baliem Valley in Irian, the islanders of the Aru Archipelago, the swidden cultivators of central Borneo, or even the peasants of central Java, knew that they had all become Indonesians.

The term Indonesia, adopted by some European ethnographers in the 1880s and by nationalists in the 1920s, is used in this book to refer to people who themselves had no concept of a common identity. The transformation of myriad Archipelago peoples into Indonesians is one of the astonishing stories of the 20th century, which falls wholly outside the scope of this book. While there are dangers of doing violence to the real autonomy of various states and systems by using the common term 'Indonesians' for them before 1900, some outsiders, such as Francois Pyrard in 1619, already thought that the trading peoples of the coasts 'differ nowise in features, colour, dress, language or customs — in fact they are the same people'. Europeans called them by designations like 'Indian Islanders', 'East Indians', and later 'Malays', while Arabs saw them as 'Jawi' from 'below the winds'. Their material culture was fashioned by

Boats were the main mode of transport in Indonesia. A Dayak of Borneo on a boat as depicted by Van Pers, Nederlandsch Oost-Indie Typen *(The Hague, 1853-62).*

similar environmental problems, and most enjoyed a diet dominated by rice (or sago) and fish.

Moreover, the hundreds of ethno-cultural groups and states which occupied the Archipelago were held together by important networks. The relative fertility and sophistication of Java gave it a central role in supplying both foodstuffs and manufactures to the other islands around the Java Sea, and the myths of the latter often acknowledged some debt of civilisation to Java. The major Eurasian trade route which developed strongly from around 1400 for cloves, nutmegs and sandalwood, extended through the Strait of Melaka and the Java and Banda Seas as far as Maluku and Timor, and some traders even went further east for birds of paradise, pearls and slaves. Along this route, from Aceh to Aru, Timor and Ternate, the lingua franca of trade from at least the 15th century was Malay — the language of the great entrepots of Sriwijaya, Pasai, and Melaka. With it, along the same route, came Islam. Making its first major advance in the port of Pasai in the 1290s, Islam became established in the 'age of commerce' between the 15th and mid-17th centuries as the faith of all the important trading states of the Archipelago. In the period 1570 to 1650 a distinctive literary culture took shape in the Malay language, one of the five great literary traditions of the Islamic world, producing literature both sacred and profane that was read from Aceh to Ternate. Although those who participated in this culture were a small urban and commercial elite, their influence and wide dispersion ensured even more firmly than the Dutch who followed them that the islands would have a common destiny.

No history can give equal time to all those who lived in the period in question. The majority of Indonesians lived outside the towns and trade routes where they could be observed by foreigners, and have left us no writings of their own as witness to their lives. Try as we may to compensate, kings leave their mark more firmly on the past than simple cultivators. The uplanders, including virtually all Batak, Dayak, Toraja, Irianese and people of Nias and Pasemah, remain outside the historical record until 'discovered' in the late 19th century. It is highly unlikely, nevertheless, that they lived the unchanging lives beloved of tourist brochures. Whenever oral histories or other data enables us to glimpse the interior, we see warfare, migrations and technological adaptations which altered the lives of each generation as profoundly as those on the coast.

Defining a Time — 'Early Modern'

To periodise history is to impose some necessarily controversial retrospective coherence on it. Colonial writers tended to see the periods in wholly foreign terms — Portuguese, VOC, colonial, Japanese. The Indonesian National History now used in Indonesian schools preferred to label its six volumes: Prehistory, Ancient Period (to 1600), the Muslim States (c.1600-1800), 19th century, Nationalist Movement (1900-42), and Post 1942. In this volume we have chosen the increasingly popular neutral 'early modern' to emphasise that Indonesia is an equal part of world history. By early modern we mean the period in which Indonesian states interacted intensively with the rest of the world as part of a process of global modernisation and unification which involved commercialisation, writing, linear views of time, and ceaseless technological change. Specific dates can be misleading since these changes affected different places at different times, but the volume essentially embraces the 15th to the 19th centuries.

The end of the period is defined by the destruction around 1900 of the last autonomous political systems — those of Aceh, Bali-Lombok, the

An extremely rare aquatint of the Dutch Governor's Mansion in Surabaya, from Voyage autour du monde ..., *engraved by Sigismond Himeley and published by Arthus Bertrand in Paris, 1835.*

«« The Balinese kris is characteristically ornate. The handle takes the form of a raksasa or guardian demon, a popular Balinese motif. Kris in Bali were closely associated with the ritual self-sacrifice known as puputan.

Kain simbut, a simple batik found in west Java. These kain simbut were in common use until the 1930s and they were intriguing for the way that they seem to 'foreshadow' many of the elements in the most complex and ritually significant Javanese court batiks.

Batak, Bugis, Toraja and others — even though in other parts of the Archipelago Dutch rule had begun to fashion a multiracial 'Indische' society much earlier. Because the development of that new society in the Dutch-ruled towns of the 19th century is in many ways the first act of the modern transformation of Indonesia, it is not given full attention in this volume.

The beginning of the 'early modern' is more difficult to determine. Many have seen the arrival of Portuguese vessels after 1500 as the definitive linking of Indonesia into a world system of commercial and military competition. The last of the Hindu-Javanese states also crumbles in the period between 1470 (the conventional date for the Muslim conquest of Majapahit) and 1527 (the last evidence of successor Hindu States in East Java). Others note that the Portuguese were absorbed into an ongoing Asian trade system, which was radically changed only by the monopolies established by the Dutch East India Company (VOC) after 1620. My own view is that the shift to a period in which cosmopolitan port-cities set the pattern for Indonesian life begins before the Portuguese, and has nothing to do with

A Senenan, or royal tournament, of central Java in the 19th century, as depicted by Van Rees, Nederlandsch-Indie (1883). These activities occupied a large proportion of people's time in early modern Indonesia.

them. In the 15th century an efficient Eurasian seaborne trading system became established, stimulated first by the Chinese state-trading expeditions under Zheng He in 1405-33, and then by the rapid rise in shipments of Malukan spices and pepper along the Muslim route to the Mediterranean. This burgeoning commerce gave rise to a series of Muslim port-states along the trade artery from Pasai and Pidië in north Sumatra, through Palembang, to Cirebon, Demak, Japara and Gresik in Java, and Banda and Ternate in Maluku. While these states dominated their interiors only after 1500, their rise is part of the early modern story.

The sources also change with these port states. In the classic or ancient period of Hindu-Buddhist states, our primary sources are inscriptions in copper or stone, the physical remains of temples and puzzling reports in Chinese sources. The Muslim states begin to provide us with chronicles, even if few of the copies which come down to us are much older than 1800. Their inherent sense of history as progress, with the Muslim present conceived as an advance on the pagan past, is part of the modern mind-set. Along with this came a sense of enquiry and comparison, as external contacts bring technological, aesthetic and intellectual novelties, some of which are adopted or adapted. Indonesia's geography and cash-crops exposed it more than most parts of the world to these stimuli, and ensured that Europe's early modern period was also Indonesia's.

The Problem of Colonialism

The role of the European in Indonesia is very prone to distortion. In purely factual terms it was as follows. The insatiable demand for Indonesia's spices in the 15th-17th centuries provoked the Portuguese to round the Cape of Good Hope in 1498, and to conquer the chief Southeast Asian entrepot of Melaka in 1511. The Portuguese held out against other Europeans until 1596, and competed on equal terms with Muslim traders to ship the spices westward. Apart from Melaka they had direct influence only in Maluku, the source of the spices. In 1580 the Portuguese crown was merged with the Spanish, and Hispanic interventions in spice-rich Maluku were thereafter mounted primarily from Spanish Manila.

The Dutch arrived as enemies of the Catholic powers in 1596, soon followed by the weaker English, French and Danes. The Dutch quickly sent more ships to the East than the other Europeans combined, reaching a peak of 257 ships answering to VOC (Dutch East Indies Company) control in Asian waters in the 1660s. This unique concentration of naval power enabled the Dutch Company to conquer and fortify Jakarta (renamed Batavia) in 1619, nutmeg-growing Banda in 1621, Ternate in the 1620s, Portuguese Melaka in 1641, Makasar in 1660-69 and Banten in 1682. Although the arrival of the northern Europeans had at first boosted the local economies, the VOC's success in monopolising

the supply of Malukan spices and dominating many other items of long-distance commerce had an undoubted dampening effect on Indonesian commerce from about 1650, and removed the economic basis of the major maritime states. While the 17th century VOC ruled only a tiny proportion (less than three per cent) of Indonesians, it had considerable indirect influence on their lives through its economic muscle, and may have begun to insulate them to some extent from the global economic and scientific innovations.

In the 18th century the VOC was in a slow decline commercially, but shifted its interests to the production of coffee and sugar in Java, which required ever greater interference in Javanese politics. After a century of constant warfare on behalf of its client kings, the Company became the strongest military force in Java, and directly governed the Preanger from 1723, and the northern *pesisir* from 1755. Outside Java, however, its economic power was increasingly eroded by English, American, Chinese, Bugis, and French traders. War with England after 1794 virtually ended Dutch power in the Outer Islands, though in Java itself the revolutionary regime of Daendels and then the English interregnum under Stamford Raffles (1811–16) introduced for the first time something like direct colonial authority. After their authority was restored in 1816 by the new superpower, England, the Dutch slowly conquered the whole Archipelago, completing it in a vigorous burst of activity in 1898-1905.

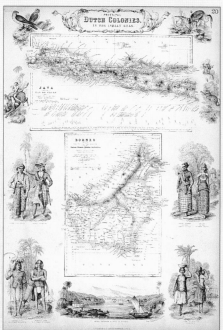

This hardly constitutes '350 years of colonial rule' as was claimed, first by chauvinist colonial writers, and then by nationalists eager to maximise the extent of oppression. Ambonese and Betawi (the polyglot native population of Jakarta) may have been under Dutch rule for just over three centuries and many Javanese for two, but elsewhere there are few places where Netherlands rule was effective for more than a century. This book shows that Indonesian societies were dynamic throughout the early modern period, and seeks to give the European role no more than its due.

Three kinds of distortion have to be guarded against. The issue of perspective is easiest to deal with. Those who look at Indonesia from Europe may have a disproportionate interest in Europeans. Sources are a more serious problem, since the Europeans wrote much more copiously than Indonesians, and preserved their writings in archives and in publications easier to read today than are the Javanese *kidung* and Malay *hikayat*. So we must frequently read Indonesian history through European sources. Most difficult of all is the problem of determining which themes in Indonesia's rich past are relevant for today. Some of the early nationalist histories found themselves exaggerating the Dutch factor in their search for a unifying thread in this period. Indonesians who fought against the Dutch seemed more relevant than those who fought against each other, or even those who pioneered new modes of thought and expression.

In these pages the authors hope to convey their enthusiasm for the diversity, colour and autonomy of early modern history.

Chronology

Java

Sumatra

	Java	Sumatra

Century 15

1389 : Death of Hayam Wuruk begins the decline of the Majapahit Empire.
1400 : Rise of Gresik, Jepara and Demak as important Muslim ports.
1400-53 : Frequent Majapahit missions to China, and in 1412 to Japan and Korea.

1419 : Date on gravestone of Malik Ibrahim at Gresik.

1478 (Saka 1400) : Conventional date for Demak-led Muslim conquest of Majapahit.

1356-75 : Adityavarman establishes Tantric Buddhist kingship in Minangkabau.
1400-39 : Pasai sending frequent missions to China.
1405-34 : Females rule in Pasai.
1405 : Chinese imperial intervention in Palembang, to 'pacify' local Chinese.
From **1419** : Palembang sends missions to China and to Ryukyu.
c. 1400 : Melaka established as Muslim port to rival Pasai. Pidië and Aru established as enclave Muslim ports.
1459-77 : Melaka under Sultan Mansur Shah, concentrates Melaka Straits trade.

Century 16

1504-46 : Demak under Sultan Trenggana dominates Central Java and the *pesisir*.
1512 : Jepara's abortive naval attack on Melaka.
1522 : Portuguese seal treaty with Sundakelapa.
1527 : Sunan Gunung Jati conquers Sundakelapa and renames it Ja(ya)karta.
1527 : Demise of Hindu polity at Kediri. Trenggana aspires to succession as ruler of Java.
1546 : Sultan Trenggana killed while crusading at Panarukan. Division and decline of Demak.
1552 : Sultan Hasanuddin develops Banten as pepper-port, and conquers Pajajaran.
1584 : Senopati takes control of Mataram, and extends its sway in south-central Java.

1509 : Portuguese ships begin to call at Pasai and Pidië, and attempt invervention.
1514-30 : Sultan Ali Mughayat Syah raises Aceh to dominate North Sumatra, and later conquers Pasai and Pidië (1520-24).
1537 : Series of Acehnese attacks on Portuguese Melaka begin.
1539-71 : Aceh becomes major link in Muslim spice and pepper route to Middle East.
1563-8 : Aceh obtains military assistance from Turkey.
1530-50 : Demak domination of Palembang.
1540s : Aceh wars against Batak 'kingdom'. Islam spreads to Minangkabau.

Century 17

1601 : Death of Senapati of Mataram.
1602 : English establish post at Banten.
1609-24 : Ranamanggala becomes regent of Banten. Tougher state control of pepper trade.
1613 : Sultan Agung succeeds to Mataram throne. Begins aggresive policy towards *pesisir*.
1628-9 : Sultan Agung's attempts to take Batavia defeated.
1636-8 : Banten sends mission to Mecca to obtain title of Sultan.
1646-77 : Amangkurat I of Mataram begins troubled reign by massacring *ulama*.
1651-82 : Sultan Abdulfatah Ageng brings Banten to commercial height.

The Dutch, English and French frequent Aceh as major pepper centre.
Flowering of Islamic Malay literature in Aceh.
1607-36 : Sultan Iskandar Muda brings Aceh to peak of power. Controls pepper and tin supplies.
1620s : The Dutch and English begin buying pepper from Palembang and Jambi.
1629 : Disastrous failure of massive Aceh assault on Portuguese Melaka.
1637-41 : Sultan Iskandar Thani, and his adviser Raniri, enforce Islamic law in Aceh to unprecedented degree.
1641-99 : System of queens in Aceh.

Century 18

1703 : Pakubuwana I ascends Kartasura throne as client of the VOC.
1740 : Massacre of Chinese at Batavia.
1743 : Javanese capital moves 12 kilometres east to Surakarta.
1746 : Pangeran Mangkubumi rebels against Pakubuwana II and VOC.
1749 : Death of Susuhunan, VOC declares his son as Pakubuwana III.
1755 : Giyanti Treaty recognises Mangkubumi as Sultan of Yogyakarta and Pakubuwana as Susuhunan at Surakarta.
1757 : Rebel Mas Said recognised as autonomous Mangkunegaran ruler.

1699-1726 : Arab dynasty in Aceh.
1710 : Tin mining begins in Bangka.
1727 : 'Bugis' dynasty in Aceh; civil war (1735) celebrated in the *Hikayat Pocut Mohammed*.
1750s : Chinese miners begin more intensive exploitation of Bangka tin.
1762 : English trade from Madras to Aceh leads to founding of British factory in Banda Aceh.
1780s : Lebai Dappah opens new pepper-growing frontier on Aceh's west coast.
1795-1823 : Reign of Jauhar al-Alam in Aceh marked by civil war involving British factions in Pinang.

Century 19

1808 : Pangeran Dipanagara begins role as visionary focus of dissent in central Java.
1808-11 : Marshall Daendels inaugurates intensive rule of Java.
1825 : Java War against Dutch erupts.
1830 : Capture of Dipanagara.
1830-33 : Governor-General Bosch inaugurates highly profitable *cultuurstelsel*.
1851 : 'Dokter-Jawa' school established.
1850s-60s : Raden Ngabei Ronggawarsita writes the last great Javanese court texts in Surakarta.
1851 : Raden Saleh returns from Europe.
1860s : First railways built.
1870 : Agrarian Law — decline of *cultuurstelsel*.

1803 : Return of three Minangkabau pilgrims from Mecca, initiating the Padri movement.
1815 : End of Minangkabau dynasty.
1804-21 : Sultan Mahmud Badaruddin of Palembang resists Dutch and English.
1820s : Islamisation of Mandailing.
1823 : Palembang sultanate ended by Dutch.
1837 : Dutch capture of Bonjol.
1838 : Dominance of Tuanku Ibrahim in Aceh.
1862 : Ludwig Nommensen's mission to the Toba Batak, begins conversion to Protestant Christanity.
1873 : Dutch attack on Aceh begins 40-year war.

Borneo and East

1400 : Bugis-Makasar states, and new writing systems, develop.
1400 : Muslim contact with Maluku, initially perhaps at Bacan.

From around **1407** : Javanese buying cloves and nutmeg promotes Muslim port-states, notably Ternate and Banda.

1511-48 : King of Gowa, Tuniparisi' Kallona, establishes Makasar state.
From **1512** : Malukans welcome Portuguese as alternative buyers of spice.
Islamisation of Banjarmasin and Hulu Sungei (Kalimantan).
1570 : Portuguese kill Sultan Hairun of Ternate, bringing to power his militantly Islamic son Babullah (1570-84).
Luwu the first Bugis state to accept Islam.
1593-1637 : Karaeng Matoaya as ruler of Tallo' and chancellor of Gowa lays basis for Makasar's success.

1600-10 : Makasar (kings of Gowa and Tallo') accepts Islam, and begins expansion.
Conversion of Ambonese Catholics to Dutch-style Calvinism following Dutch victory of 1606.
Muslim resistance to VOC in Ambon, led by Kakiali (1633-43) and Telukabesi (1643-6).
1660 : Arung Palaka leads Bugis revolt against Makasar.
1660 : Expulsion of Portuguese from Makasar, at VOC demand, begins its decline.
1666-9 : Bugis/VOC defeat of Makasar.
1683 : Ternate, a vassal of VOC, dominates South Sulawesi.
1672-96 : Arung Palaka as king of Bone.

1726 : Wajo exile Arung Sengkang (La Madukelleng) conquers Pasir and Kutai (Kalimantan). Returns to rouse Wajo against Bone rule (1735).
1739 : Karaeng Bontolongkasa seizes throne of Gowa in opposition to VOC, soon crushed by VOC/Bone forces.
Chinese (Hakka) miners begin mining gold in west Kalimantan, founding powerful kongsis such as Lanfang (1777).
1779 : Dutch depose Tidore ruler, leading to rebellion of Nuku against VOC, with English encouragements.

1815 : Eruption of Mount Tambora in Sumbawa the largest in recent history.
1817 : Anti-Dutch rebellion of Pattimura on Saparua, in Ambonese Archipelago.
1838 : Civil war and reunification of Lombok under Anak Agung Gde Jilantik.
1849 : Lombok's subsequent conquest of Karangasem.
1859-63 : Dutch end Banjarmasin sultanate and rule South Kalimantan directly.
Queen of Bone, We Pancaitana dominates South Sulawesi and resists Dutch until 1859 defeat.
1850-54 : Dutch overcome and suppress last Chinese mining kongsis.

European/Dutch in Archipelago

1509 : Portuguese first reach Pasai.
1510 : Portuguese Afonso d'Albuquerque conquers Goa and Melaka (1511).
1512 : Portuguese mission from Melaka under Serrão reaches Ambon.
1522 : Portuguese factory built in Ternate.
1550s : Portuguese establish smooth trading relations with Banten and Palembang.
1574 : Portuguese expelled from Ternate, and take refuge in Tidore.
1579 : Sir Francis Drake of England visits Ternate.
1595-7 : First Dutch expedition to East under Cornelis de Houtman trades at Banten.

1601-3 : First English voyage under John Lancaster visits Aceh.
1605 : VOC captures Portuguese fort at Ambon.
1615 : Dutch post at Japara initiates troubled relations with Sultan Agung.
1619-23 : Jan Pieterszoon Coen as Governor General of VOC, establishes town at Batavia.
1621 : Coen conquers Banda Archipelago.
1623 : 'Amboina massacre'.
1641 : VOC conquers Melaka.
1677 : VOC conquers Surabaya and acquires Priangan.
1682 : VOC conquers Banten, forcing British to shift pepper base to Bengkulu.

1730-67 : Sustained malaria epidemic in Batavia as result of fish-ponds, causing roughly half of those newly arriving in city to die within a year.
1740 : Massacre of Chinese in Batavia.
1743 : VOC obtains full sovereignty over Surabaya, west Madura, Japara etc.
1745 : Governor General van Imhoff establishes country residence at Buitenzorg (Bogor).
1755 : VOC's sovereignty over whole pesisir.
1750-61 : VOC administration begins move to a healthier area (Weltevreden (Pasar Senen)) under Governor General Mossel.
1781-4 : British occupy Padang.
1796-1816 : British occupy Maluku.

1808-11 : Marshall Daendels rules Java for Napoleon.
1811-16 : British occupy Java, with Thomas Stamford Raffles as Governor.
1819 : Raffles signs Treaty with Sultan Jauhar al-Alam of Aceh guaranteeing defence of Aceh.
1818-23 : Raffles as Lt. Governor of Bengkulu.
1824 : London treaty transfers Bengkulu.
1830-37 : Dutch direct rule over West Sumatra.
1848-9 : Dutch conquest of Buleleng (Bali).
1871 : Sumatra treaty; Dutch attack Aceh.
1894 : Dutch conquer Lombok.
1896-1909 : Systematic conquest of Archipelago by Dutch.

Outside World

1402-24 : Ming Emperor Yongle sends missions under Zheng He to Southeast Asia and beyond. Energetic Chinese external policy.
1453 : Turkish capture of Constantinople.
1470s : Portuguese explore West Coast of Africa.
1492 : Christopher Columbus seeking route to Asian spices for Spain, discovers West Indies.
1493 : Pope Alexander VI publishes bull dividing new world of discoveries between Spain and Portugal.
1494 : Treaty of Tordesillas ratified.
1498 : Vasco da Gama reaches India for Portugal.

1517 : Martin Luther posts his 95 theses, beginning Protestant Reformation.
1519-56 : Charles V as Emperor establishes peak of Spanish global power.
1519 : Spanish conquest of Mexico.
1521 : Spanish expedition under Magellan reaches Philippines and circumnavigates globe.
1520-66 : Sultan Suleiman 'the magnificent' establishes Turkish naval power.
1567 : Ming Emperor licenses private trade to Southeast Asia.
1572 : Revolt of Netherlands against Spain.
1585 : Spanish capture of Antwerp shifts commercial centre of Europe to Amsterdam.

1600 : Japan unified under Tokugawa shogunate.
1602 : VOC formed in Amsterdam with sole rights to send Dutch ships eastward.
1609-21 : Dutch-Spanish peace.
1635 : Closing of Japan.
1638 : Foreign trade restricted to Dutch and Chinese at Nagasaki.
1642-60 : England disrupted by Civil War.
1644 : Ming Dynasty replaced by Qing (Manchu).
1600-87 : Muslim Golconda dominates Southeast India, trades with Archipelago.
1646-83 : Anti-Ming rebels in Taiwan and Xiamen dominate Chinese-Southeast Asia trade.

1769-72 : French expedition under Pierre Poivre breaks Dutch clove monopoly by obtaining plants from Maluku and planting in Mauritius.
1776 : American revolution frees New England shipping to operate outside monopolies.
1780-84 : Fourth Dutch-English War cuts Holland off from Indies.
1786 : British establish entrepot at Penang, partly to gather Indonesian produce.
1789 : French Revolution.
1795 : French revolutionary troops conquer Netherlands, placing it at war with England, which quickly occupies Cape of Good Hope and Ceylon.

1808 : Louis Napoleon placed on throne of (French-occupied) Netherlands.
1814-15 : Defeat of Napoleon sealed at Congress of Vienna.
1819 : Raffles establishes British colony at Singapore.
1824 : London Treaty exchanges English territory and claims in Sumatra for Dutch territory in the Malay Peninsula.
1841 : James Brooke's Sarawak 'kingdom' rouses Dutch fears.
1842 : Treaty of Nanking ends opium war.
1859 : Telegraph links Batavia to world.
1869 : Opening of Suez Canal.

During the period under consideration (15th to 19th centuries), Indonesia consisted of a great diversity of states and peoples with their own sets of customs, beliefs and practices. These lithographs, published by P.A. van der Lith (1875), provide some idea of the way cultural diversity was expressed in the manner different people dressed.

Despite this diversity, there was an underlying coherence to the region based on three factors: a common Austronesian cultural root of almost all the

The elephant became an important symbol of kingship in both Sumatra and Java. Several hundred elephants took part in the Sultan of Aceh's funeral procession in 1641.

Pepper was developed as a cash crop by various Sumatran cultivators during the 15th to 19th centuries and became Indonesia's most important export commodity.

The rulers of 18th century Palembang employed Chinese labour to mine the high grade tin ore that was sold to the Dutch as a trade monopoly.

The interior peoples of Borneo, and other islands, were important suppliers of rare trade goods to the coastal states.

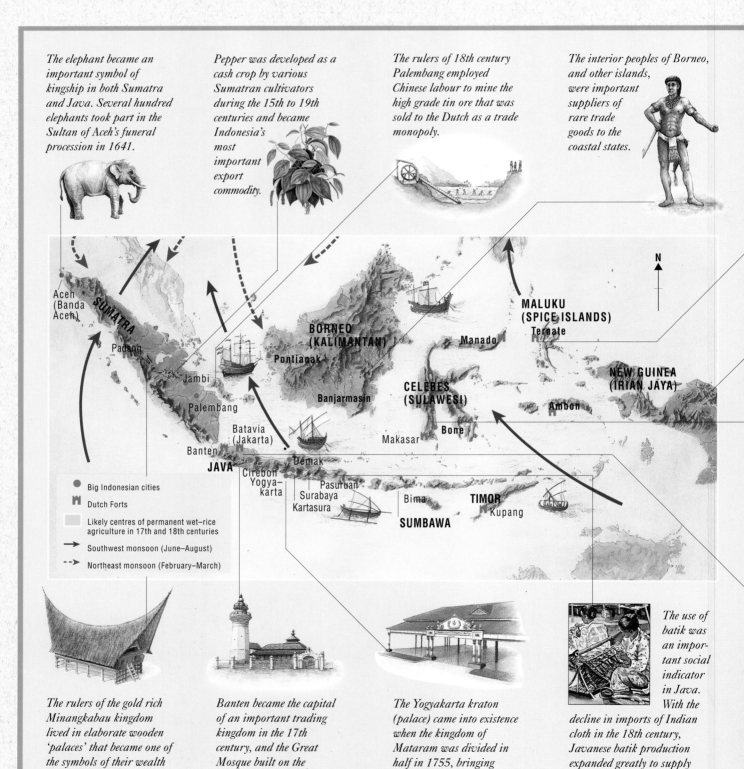

SUMATRA
Aceh (Banda Aceh)
Padang
Jambi
Palembang

BORNEO (KALIMANTAN)
Pontianak
Banjarmasin

MALUKU (SPICE ISLANDS)
Ternate
Manado

CELEBES (SULAWESI)
Makasar
Bone

NEW GUINEA (IRIAN JAYA)
Ambon

Batavia (Jakarta)
Banten
JAVA
Cirebon
Yogyakarta
Demak
Pasuruan
Surabaya
Kartasura
Bima
TIMOR
Kupang
SUMBAWA

- ● Big Indonesian cities
- ⛫ Dutch Forts
- ▮ Likely centres of permanent wet–rice agriculture in 17th and 18th centuries
- → Southwest monsoon (June–August)
- ⇢ Northeast monsoon (February–March)

N

The rulers of the gold rich Minangkabau kingdom lived in elaborate wooden 'palaces' that became one of the symbols of their wealth and power.

Banten became the capital of an important trading kingdom in the 17th century, and the Great Mosque built on the proceeds of trade still stands as a monument to its past.

The Yogyakarta kraton (palace) came into existence when the kingdom of Mataram was divided in half in 1755, bringing peace to Java, though at great cost.

The use of batik was an important social indicator in Java. With the decline in imports of Indian cloth in the 18th century, Javanese batik production expanded greatly to supply many of the peoples of the outer islands.

populations; a similar wet tropical environment governed by the alternation of winds; and relatively easy communication by river and sea. Within that environment were also crucial dividing lines: fertile and poor areas; deep ocean trenches to the east and west of Sulawesi with very different flora and fauna on either side; and contrasts between a wet climate in the west, and a much drier one in the east.

The valuable spices of Maluku which were traded as early as 1700 BC, brought Indians, Chinese, Arabs, and eventually Europeans to the islands.

Feathers from the beautiful birds of paradise were highly valued as trade items in the island trade network.

Maritime trade has been important in the region for over 2,000 years. The Bugis of South Sulawesi controlled a large share of the trade in the region throughout the 18th and 19th centuries.

The stadhuis or city hall in Batavia represented Dutch power as a law court, administrative centre and prison.

THE ISLAND WORLD AND ITS PEOPLE

The pattern of Indonesian history owes much to its environment of forest, mountain and water. As an island world athwart some of the world's key trade routes, it was accessible to, yet distinct from, the great civilisations of Eurasia. Because Sumatra and Borneo were difficult to tame through agriculture, Indonesia was not subject to mass migrations, and its population remained relatively low — about nine million in 1600, still below 13 million in 1800, but at least 30 million (three-quarters in Java) by 1900.

Indonesia's position between the Asian and Australian continents provides reliable northeasterly winds between November and March, and southwesterly ones between June and September. The monsoon pattern enabled sailors to reach China or India in one monsoon and return on the other. It also created the seasonal pattern of wet and dry which governed agriculture. The constant rainfall in the west produced dense forest with little game and difficult conditions for the slash and burn agriculture which was the first step to taming the forests. Only pockets like the north coasts of Aceh and west Java, and the highland valleys populated by Minangkabau and Batak, encouraged agriculture at an early stage. In eastern Java and the islands further east, on the other hand, there is a marked dry season from May to September, making for more open forest and easier conditions for burning-off, crop-ripening, and hunting.

At the dawn of the early modern era, then, it was in some river valleys of central and east Java, Bali, Lombok, south Sulawesi, and parts of north and central Sumatra that agriculture became developed and populations dense enough to support states. Populations also concentrated around river mouths in the west, and small islands in the east, strategically located for trade and fishing. Elsewhere, the pattern until the last two centuries was dense forest, which scattered populations exploited for sago, honey, game and export commodities, while tilling the soil in small enclaves around its edges.

Speakers of Austronesian (Malayo-Polynesian) languages who now dominate the Archipelago, except for Irian and parts of Maluku, arrived within the last 3,000 years on journeys that linguists believe began in Taiwan. Seafarers and rice-growers, they spread these skills through the Archipelago, either absorbing or marginalising the earlier inhabitants. Having had a common root less than 3,000 years ago, their languages retain many similarities with each other and with the lingua franca of at least the last 600 years — Malay (the basis of Bahasa Indonesia).

Forests and the Advance of Agriculture

The Indonesian Archipelago remained densely forested throughout the early modern period. Nevertheless, the gradual growth of population, made possible by intensified rice agriculture and new food plants from America, created large pockets of permanent rice fields on the one hand, and grasslands on the other.

➳ Many varieties of banana grow through-out Indonesia and are an important source of carbohydrate. From an original watercolour by Bertha Hoola van Nooten, 1880.

➳ Cloves were endemic to only five islands in Maluku. Before they became an international trade commodity they were traded with other nearby islands for sago, the staple in this region.

Chilies were introduced to Indonesia in the early 16th century from the Americas. An early record mentions them being grown in Indonesia soon after they were imported.

Forest and Agricultural Products

Indonesia's agricultural past is closely connected with rice and spices, a factor that has masked many changes in Indonesian agricultural practice and diet. Rice was indeed the most important staple crop in the western part of the Archi-pelago in the period between 1200 and 1800. Spices such as cloves, mace, and nutmeg from the eastern islands, and pepper from a wide area, dominated plant exports to China, India, the Middle East and to Europe during most of this period. However, the commercial cultivation of sugar, coffee, tea, tobacco and rubber gradually caused them to diminish in importance in the 19th and 20th centuries.

In the 13th century most of the Archipelago was still covered with forests. Occasionally, other types of vegetation were encountered as certain areas were too wet, dry, acid or steep for trees to take root, or because forest fires or human intervention had removed the forest cover. Concentrations of human settlements could be found along the coasts and in the more fertile river valleys, particularly in Java.

In western Indonesia, rice was the main food crop of the sedentary populations. It was grown on irrigated or rain fed *sawah* (bunded fields), or, in the upland areas, on 'dry' fields (ladang, *huma*, *gaga* and *tegal*). In many parts of eastern Indonesia, sago, bananas, and roots and tubers (taro and yams) were the main locally grown vegetable foodstuffs.

Cereals such as rice, (foxtail) millets, sorghum and Job's tears were less important. At that time, sago (from various palm species) was no doubt largely or even entirely a wild product. This was initially the case with many important export products such as nutmeg and mace from Banda, cloves from Maluku, sandalwood from Timor, and camphor and benzoin from Sumatra, although all these were partly cultivated by the 17th century. Rice and pepper from Java were the only truly agricultural export products of importance in terms of bulk before the spice boom of the 16th century.

In addition to the starchy staple foods such as cereals, roots and tubers, and sago, there were also wide varieties of fruit for vitamins, and several species of beans for proteins available to Indonesians. Finally, Indonesia had a number of non–food crops at their disposal, of which cotton and indigo were the most important.

Changes in Agricultural Production

Between 1200 and 1800, many of these features changed considerably. First there was the slow, gradual shrinking of the forests, often hardly perceptible to the contemporary observer, but in the long run highly significant. This was caused by the expansion of subsistence agriculture, due to the gradual rise in population. On a more restricted scale, wooded areas gave way to commercial crops.

In some areas, such as the central Batak area around Lake Toba, and on Sumba, Sumbawa and Timor in the east, and Kedu in Java, extensive grasslands developed at least by the 18th century. The reasons for this are obscure. Some of them may have been deliberately created to facilitate the raising of horses and cattle for which these regions are now famous. Some of these areas experienced the pressure of population on land early on, with Batak genealogies, for example, revealing a history of migration from impoverished Samosir island (in Lake Toba) over a period of four or five centuries. In the earlier literature, excessive pressure on land by shifting cultivators was held responsible for the 'green deserts' of *alang-alang*, *glagah* (both tall grasses) and ferns encountered in many places. The shifting cultivators may have played a role in some areas, but natural fires caused by prolonged droughts, and fires lit by hunters were probably also to blame. Finally, the exploitation of the forests themselves, particularly for the acquisition of timber, for the construction of ships and houses, and other valuable kinds of woods (cassia, sandalwood and sappan) led to a loss of forested areas. In Java, large quantities of teak were cut in the 17th and 18th centuries for the VOC settlement of Batavia and for the VOC shipyards on Java's northeast coast. It seems likely that the loss of forest cover reached its highest average rate here during the period under consideration.

Second, new food crops were introduced after 1500 when Spaniards and Portuguese brought 'exotic' seeds and cuttings from America. It is

EXPORT PRODUCTS AND CASH CROPS, 1200–1700			
Expansion of cash crops		**Export products to India, China, Middle East and Europe**	
Products	**Areas**	**Products**	**Areas**
rice	Sumatra, Java, Bali	camphor, benzoin	Sumatra
pepper	Sumatra, Kalimantan	rice, pepper	Java
coffee	Sumatra, Java	sandalwood	Timor
sugar, tobacco	Java	cloves	Maluku
cloves	Ambon	nutmeg, mace	Banda
nutmeg, mace	Banda		

RICE
Rice was the staple food for most of western Indonesia between the 13th and 19th centuries. After harvesting, the rice was threshed and winnowed before being pounded. These tasks were invariably undertaken by women, as depicted in this print by C.W. Meiling, after Auguste van Pers (The Hague, 1853-62).

important to mention the crops that deeply influenced local agricultural practices and dietary habits. Nowadays, it would be difficult to imagine Indonesian cuisine without chilies and peanuts. Maize, sweet potato and cassava influenced both agricultural practice and diet though cassava did not become a major food resource until after 1850. Maize began to revolutionise Indonesian agriculture from the time it entered Maluku in the 16th century. It not only took the place of other less high yielding cereals such as millet, sorghum and Job's tears, but it also moved into upland areas where no food crops had been grown before, thereby paving the way for higher population densities. On a smaller scale, sweet potatoes replaced indigenous roots and tubers, due to higher yields per unit of land.

Third, cash crops for export expanded considerably. Cloves came increasingly from cultivated trees, of which large numbers had been planted in Ambon and nearby islands where the plant was previously unknown. In the Banda islands nutmeg and mace were also harvested, predominantly from planted trees. Pepper, by 1200 only grown in Java, conquered large parts of Sumatra and also came to be grown successfully in Borneo. Sugar cultivation in Java expanded soon after the founding of Batavia (1619) in the area surrounding the city. Coffee was new to Indonesia. Introduced around 1700, it expanded fairly rapidly in Java and Sumatra, particularly in the late 18th century. Another new plant was tobacco, which became an important local crop, often soon after its introduction. It was mostly grown for domestic consumption but was also exported in some quantities.

Finally, the spread of rice cultivation should be mentioned. This was largely due to population growth. Although the population grew very slowly by modern standards, over a period of six centuries the cumulative increase was nevertheless impressive, at least locally. This applies, for instance, to many regions of Java, to Bali and to the Minangkabau area in Sumatra. Some local areas started to specialise in rice cultivation in order to provision nearby ports and regions specialising in cash crops. The hinterlands of Aceh, Batavia and Makasar in the 17th and 18th centuries are examples. One often encounters a transition from 'dry' to 'wet' rice, partly also caused by population growth, partly stimulated by rulers who wanted a more sedentary population and higher tax returns. Furthermore, rice cultivation also spread to areas in eastern Indonesia where it had been absent or marginal before.

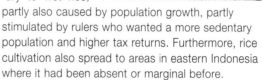

Coffee was first planted in Indonesia as an experimental crop at Cirebon, West Java, in 1699, and Javanese coffee was already on the market in Amsterdam as early as 1712. Today, coffee is grown throughout Indonesia, mostly in smallholder plots and home gardens. In some regions it remains a relatively minor cash crop, but in other areas, such as Timor, it constitutes a major export commodity.

Rice fields had to be guarded from birds and animals, and dangau (temporary huts) like that depicted (left), were used by the guards, who were most often small boys. Strings with pennants attached were used to scare away birds.

Breaking in a wet–rice field in Java. Between 1600–1800 more land was brought under the plough to feed the steadily increasing population.

Food, Feasting and Famines

*T*he reliablility of food supply for the Indonesian people prior to 1800 is unclear. However, the quantity and quality of the diet varied between societies, between classes, and between periods. Meals for most people were often frugal and monotonous, even in normal times, although occasionally feasts brought some variation. Many periods, however, were not normal, and all societies repeatedly went through times of scarcity or even famine.

A BANDA FEAST, c. 1598

'... a piece of banana leaf is laid down before each person and on this they put their bread which they call sago. Next when everyone has his own leafy place, lots of rice cooked with meat sauce is brought out, which they consume with such pleasure that they seem to taste Jupiter's brains. The country folks are very vigorous eaters: they snatch whole handful of rice and throw it in their mouths. While thus eating and eating, a few warriors of good family jump into their midst and give amazing displays of combat...'.

De Bry, 1598

Uneven Distribution — Climatic Variability

Calculating average calorie consumption per person per day for the whole of Indonesia in the period between 1400 and 1800 would not make much sense, even if it were possible. The food intake of hunter-gatherers differed in quantity and quality from that of shifting cultivators, who, in turn, had other consumption patterns compared to sedentary peasants. Furthermore, there were differences according to class or hereditary rank within these societies, particularly within peasant societies. Kings and aristocrats ate better than most commoners, who, in turn, were better fed than slaves and bond-debtors. City dwellers had a different calorie intake from villagers.

Moreover, food consumption was unevenly distributed over the year and the decade. All types of societies were annually confronted with a 'lean season'. In areas like Java and Bali with a monsoon climate where, usually, pronounced dry and wet seasons alternate regularly, the most difficult period

Ritual and life cycle ceremonies were the usual occasions for feasts. The participants in this Javanese wedding procession (after W. Barrington d' Almeida from The Illustrated London News, *1896) could look forward to the welcome addition of meat to an otherwise rather frugal and monotonous diet.*

occurred at the end of the dry season. In a normal year, most people would survive such a lean season. However, many years were not normal. A prolonged drought, a long period of heavy rains and floods, or, in the worst possible case, a combination of a very wet and a very dry season, would cause harvest failures and high food prices. Occasionally, such abnormal conditions would occur during a number of years in a row, with disastrous consequences. In Java, the best documented area of Indonesia, the

famines resulting from such conditions were usually regional affairs, but in exceptional cases the effects could be felt in large parts of the island. People in the humid rain forest zone without a pronounced dry period had different, though comparable problems (Sumatra and Borneo). Even there, prolonged droughts could lead to harvest failures, and if there was no dry spell at all, shifting cultivators were unable to fire their fields prior to cultivation, which resulted in lower yields.

Epidemics and Natural Disasters

Climatic variability was not the only threat. Epidemics and epizootics (livestock epidemics) frequently accompanied periods of adverse weather conditions, leading not only to a direct increase in mortality, but also indirectly intensifying the effects of the climatic deviation by causing a lack of sufficient healthy people and animals to work the fields. Epidemics and epizootics could also make their appearance under normal weather conditions. If these epidemics decimated and/or weakened the population sufficiently, the effect on the harvest would be similar to that of rainfall anomalies. Pests and plagues could also severely damage the crops, either independently or in combination with droughts or very wet periods. The Sultan of Banten ordered his male subjects to kill 10 rats each within 30 days when these vermin infested the rice crop in 1676.

The combined effects of climatic extremes, epidemics, and pests and plagues could create a series of setbacks which might dominate an entire area for a long time. This was the case in Java between 1647 and 1662, when a series of droughts, rats and cattle mortality led to harvest failures which, combined with epidemics, caused very high mortality rates. High mortality owing to a series of long droughts, occasional periods of heavy rain, smallpox and 'hot' fevers were reported from Banda and Maluku during the period 1651 to 1661. So-called 'acts of God', such as volcanic eruptions, earthquakes, typhoons and tsunamis, could also be devastating. The eruption of Mount Tambora on Sumbawa in 1815 may serve as an example. It immediately killed tens of thousands of people from Sumbawa, Lombok and Bali. Because it also destroyed large numbers of cattle and rice fields, thereby causing harvest failures and famine for many years to come, the number of indirect victims was even larger.

Wars and Raids

Frequently occurring wars and raids were often equally, or even more disruptive, not so much due to large numbers of battle victims (as a rule few people were killed in battle) but by the fact that many able bodied men were drafted for a long time, leaving their fields untended, by the destruction of standing crops and villages, and by the diseases that broke out in the army owing to faulty logistics. This could be observed, for instance, in Java in 1618, when the wars of Mataram were the cause of harvest failures. In 1624–7 the effects of the war operations were amplified by bad weather conditions and epidemics, causing not only harvest failures but also famine in central Java. Similar conditions obtained in 1674–8, although in this case harvest failures partly preceded warfare. Therefore, 'abnormal' times seem to have recurred with sad regularity. Nevertheless, it is likely that in 'normal' times the majority of the people had enough to eat, albeit that their daily diet was rather frugal, usually rice with salt or salted fish, some greens, and, after 1500, chilies. Although there was an impressive variety of fruit and pulses in many areas, the average peasant seems to have sold these products rather than eaten them.

Feasts

Life in most of the societies mentioned, however, was punctuated by feasts (*selamatan*), which were islands of abundance and variety in a sea of monotony. On these occasions, buffaloes, cattle, pigs (in non-Muslim societies), sheep, goats, and chickens were slaughtered. The reasons for feasting, their frequency, and the degree of lavishness of these ritual meals varied between classes and from one society to another. Of all societies, Javanese may have been the most 'festive'. Apart from the three large Muslim court festivals, in which the population of the court towns participated, most feasts were village or family affairs. Some were linked to the agricultural cycle, such as the 'cleaning of the village', but most ritual meals were related to life-cycle phenomena, such as marriage, birth, the dropping of the umbilical cord, 'setting down on earth' (35 days after the birth of a child), circumcision, and death. Outside Java, many societies held ritual meals at burials, during shamanistic sessions for the retrieval of wandering souls, and at festivities commemorating important ancestors. These feasts were often important status markers, also functioning as levelling mechanisms. In this way, feasts redistributed some of the wealth of the better-off, thereby relieving the monotony of the common man's dull fare.

« Volcanic eruptions such as that on Gammaconorre on Gilolo (now Halmahera) in 1673, depicted here by Valentyn in 1724, could destroy crops and homes and lead to starvation. It is estimated that the eruption of Mount Tambora on Sumbawa in 1815 led to the deaths of 44,000 people.

The selamatan is still an important aspect of Indonesian life. This photo depicts a Bugis feast in Sulawesi.

THE FISH MARKET AT BATAVIA …
as observed by J. Nieuhof in 1662. Jacob Cornelisz van Neck, captain of the second Dutch fleet to the Archipelago, which arrived in 1598, was struck by the fact that the Javanese ate predominantly rice and fish. Fishing, either off-shore, in rivers or ponds, produced the largest share of the everyday protein intake of many Indonesians.

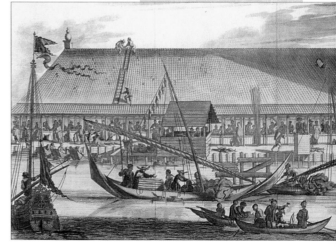

Fruit of the Forest

Among Indonesia's important resources are its rain forests. For two thousand years these forests were famed as a source of quality products used as medicines, fumigants and dyes. Resins, aromatic woods and animal products were sold to Indian, Chinese and Middle Eastern merchants in a trade which sustained entrepots such as Sriwijaya. Indeed Indonesia's place in international trade originated in the early demand for forest products, rather than the spices and pepper for which the islands were principally renowned in the 16th and 17th centuries.

» *It is now illegal to hunt rhinoceros in Indonesia. The demand for their powdered horn for use as an aphrodisiac nearly led to their extinction by the 20th century.*

» *Rattan and bamboo have always been, and still are, important forest products, being used throughout the Archipelago to make a variety of everyday utensils.*

A Cornucopia of Products

The names of forest products, and the regions in which they were thought to grow, dominate early Chinese and Arab accounts of the Archipelago. Aromatic woods, used for incense, included sandalwood, which grows from east Java to Timor; lac extracted from rattan; and *gaharu*, also known as eaglewood (*Aquilaria sp.*) and aloeswood. The rotted wood of this species, mainly *Aquilaria malaccensis*, yields a resin used as a perfume or incense, and was also widely believed to cure chills. It was collected mainly from southeast Sumatra and the eastern Archipelago.

Gums and resins were procured from other local trees and shrubs. Benzoin, or *kemenyan* derived from the *Styrax benzoin*, was used for incense and as a fumigant as well as for medicinal purposes. The camphor tree found in Sumatra, Kalimantan and the Malay Peninsula, yielded a highly prized resin which was used to cure ailments ranging from toothache to stomach complaints. Dragons blood, a gum found in rattan palms from Sumatra, Kalimantan and the

Malay Peninsula, was used for medicines and dyes; while dammar was the name given to the sap or resin found in several tree species growing in local forests. An export item from early times, dammar was used, among other things, for varnish and sealing wax. Red sappan wood from Java and north Sumatra, and gambier, from east Sumatra, were used as dyes.

The Animal Products

The rain forest also yielded animal products for export. Bees wax and honey, birds' nests and insect secretions known as lac were all collected for sale from the forests. Hunters trapped elephants for ivory and rhinoceros for their precious horns, supposedly efficacious as an aphrodisiac. A musky secretion extracted from the glands of the civet cat, or *musang*, was exported for perfume. Birds' nests, parrots and birds of paradise from eastern Indonesia, decorative tail feathers and hornbill casques were among the avian merchandise collected from the rain forests for sale in foreign lands.

International Trade

The Indonesian islands were both a source of forest products, and a hub of international trade. Some products were collected by various ethnic groups in forest areas, but exported through a particular entrepot famous for that product. Many of the woods and resins mentioned here were collected from forests throughout the Archipelago for sale in the ports which straddled the trade routes between China and India. Sriwijaya, Barus, Pasai, Melaka and

BIRDS' NESTS

The Chinese formerly provided a ready market for the nests of cave swiftlets which were gathered by local people, in Sulawesi and on the south coast of Java, for example. The nests are made from the saliva of the birds and when soaked produce a gelatinous base used in cooking. This engraving from the *Illustrated London News* (1863) shows how precarious the task could be.

Today Indonesia produces 60 per cent of the total world production of edible birds' nests, most of the produce being obtained from Java.

camphor and the port of Barus in north Sumatra that the resin was known in Chinese and Indonesian sources as 'Camphor Barus' and to the Arabs as 'Fansuri', derived from Fansur, another name for the region. Arab geographies from the 9th century AD mention Fansur (Bansur) as a source of the highest quality camphor and there is evidence to suggest that direct trading expeditions were made from the middle eastern ports to northwest Sumatra in search of resins.

The Forest-Port Relationship

The forests were a very different world from the coastal ports where goods were assembled for sale. The inhabitants of each of these separate terrains regarded the other with unease. In many cases it was the inland inhabitants of the Archipelago, those who themselves dwelt in the forests or on the edge of the forests who hunted and collected the jungle produce. In northwest Sumatra, for instance, Dairi Bataks inhabited the regions where the best camphor trees grow, and it was they who harvested the camphor in the hills of Kelasan and carried it down to intermediate villages on the edge of the coastal plain near Barus. There the goods might be sold to middlemen if the hill people felt that conditions on the coast were unsafe. In turn Malay inhabitants of the coast (*pesisir*) tended to regard the jungle as a dangerous and mysterious place.

Rites

Extraction of raw materials such as camphor, honey and bees wax were specialised procedures around which particular rités and attitudes developed. Camphor gathering, for example, was a secret process, conducted by experts who used an esoteric camphor language, and were skilled in divining which trees would yield the precious resin. Batak stories attribute magical and potent properties to camphor wood and tell of camphor trees which possessed the power of speech.

Riau all flourished by supplying inter–Asian trade and doubling as safe harbours for shipping passing between China and western Asia.

Resins, such as frankincense and myrrh, originating in the Middle East and destined for China, were also trans–shipped to China in local vessels. By the 6th century AD, Indonesian pine resin and benzoin had been inserted in this trade as substitutes for the 'Persian' products demanded in China. Sumatran camphor was already well known to Chinese apothecaries and it was not long before local pine resin and benzoin became valued items in the China trade in their own right.

Region-Product Links

Certain regions of the Archipelago came to be closely linked with the natural products which grew there. Northwest Sumatra, in particular, was famed as a source of benzoin and the highest quality camphor. So consistent was the association between

DAMMAR

Dammar (Mal. *damar*) is the name given to resin. Resins are clear, volatile, organic liquids produced by certain trees and plants, usually as a result of injury to the bark caused by wind, fire, lightning or human agency. Dammar is used for purposes of varnish, pharmaceutical products, and cosmetics.

Dragon's blood is a general term applied to a number of red resins obtained from a variety of palms. Calamus draco or Dragon's blood palm, from Kohler's Medizinal Pflanzen, *1887 (above). The resins were used in drugs and dyes. The resin of the rattan palm* Daemonorops didymophyllus *is still used by the Dayak of Central Kalimantan to stain the rattan used to weave their colourful mats and baskets.*

ʻʻ *Hunting birds of paradise for their decorative feathers, coloured lithograph by J. Moynet, after A.K. Wallace, from* Le Tour du Monde.

« *Hornbill casques were exported to China where they were carved into elaborate ornaments.*

Civet cats were hunted for the musky secretion produced by their genital glands, which was exported for use in the perfume industry.

Mining and Metalwork

*T*he rich mineral resources of the Indonesian Archipelago have been mined by indigenous and migrant labour for many centuries. Five islands provided most of Indonesia's mineral wealth before the present century — Sumatra, Kalimantan, Sulawesi, Bangka and Belitung. From these sites came gold, diamonds, iron, silver and tin. Other minerals found there and elsewhere in the Archipelago included oil, sulphur, nickel, coal and copper; but these did not begin to be significantly exploited until the beginning of the 20th century.

Chinese labour was used to mine the tin of Bangka, and many Chinese were also skilled smiths, setting up business in major ports and towns. A Chinese smith in Batavia, as depicted by Lemercier (1853–55).

 Indonesian smiths produced high quality bronze instruments under the patronage of the Javanese courts.

A tin mine in Bangka. While the labourers (in queues) are loosening the soil with pacul, a chain–pallet pump removes water from the mine.

Metalwork

Metalwork in Indonesia is a skilled art with a long history. Goldsmiths, armourers, bronze founders, black-smiths, and jewellers used complex processes and skill to manufacture kris and other damascened weapons, gamelan instruments, dress ornaments, sirih boxes, lamps and numerous other items, the manufacture of which flourished under royal patronage from Hindu-Buddhist times through to the 19th century.

Gold

A Sanskrit inscription of 732 AD mentions Sumatra's gold mines, and the Tang Annals (618–906 AD) list gold and silver amongst the riches produced there. Most of this gold was alluvial and was recovered by panning and sieving. Aceh tradition credits Indian migrants with the new technologies of sinking shafts and building tunnels for underground lode mining.

By the 17th century the practice of underground mining was long established, and there were said to be about 1,200 different mines in the Minangkabau hills. Output was brought by sea to Aceh and, with gold from mines in Bukit Barisan, gave Aceh the reputation as the richest city in the region. In Lebong (upper Bengkulu), gold mining continued more or less continuously. From the 17th century much of it was being sold to the Dutch East India Company. Subsequently, the Dutch went into Sumatran mining on their own. They reactivated the Salida mine near Padang in 1737, producing gold and silver. The rich deposits at Lembong Donok and Lembong Tandai were more fully exploited in the 19th century, playing so dominant a role that they overshadowed all other gold mining. Kalimantan was the other major source of gold, particularly the Bajang mountains, the Bawang–Belankang ranges in west Kalimantan and

TECHNOLOGICAL INNOVATIONS

Generally, the technology of mining, prospecting, refining and smelting, were less developed in Indonesia than in contemporary China, or Europe. Methods were labour intensive. However, tin mining did produce two important technological innovations. Firstly the pump-and-wheel technique for draining the mines, and secondly, the 'Bangka Drill' means of obtaining ore.

MINERALS DEPOSITS IN INDONESIA (17th TO 20th CENTURIES)

the coastal swamps between Pontianak and Sambas. These gold workings were operated by indigenous people under the auspices of local Malay rulers. In the 1740s the Panembahan of Mempawah invited a small group of Chinese to mine gold in the Duri valley. Gradually small colonies of Chinese grew and prospered along the rivers. The gold was won by sluicing from relatively shallow pits. In 1812 Stamford Raffles calculated that Kalimantan produced 350,000 ounces, an exaggeration, but production was certainly over 100,000 ounces. Some of this remained with local rulers, some was exported to Java for ornament making, but most was exported to China.

Diamonds

Diamonds were found only in Kalimantan and were highly valued by the rulers there, who originally prohibited their export. However, by 1604 the Dutch were trading with the diamond diggers of southeast Kalimantan and in the 18th century the Sultan of Banjarmasin signed a contract to supply precious stones to the VOC. Diamond mining in the southeast was in the hands of the Malay population, and in the west the mines were operated by Chinese. Operations were small scale. Mining teams rarely exceeded 18, and digging rarely reached below 20 feet. Paydirt was puddled, sifted through a screen and panned, a method that recovered even the smallest stones. Polishing and cutting the stones was also done locally. Martapura was a centre for diamond cutting for centuries and Kalimantan diamonds gained a reputation for brilliance and purity. Stones weighing 10 to 13 carats were sometimes sold in Batavia and diamonds of 30 to 40 carats were unusual.

Iron

In prehistoric times iron was a precious metal, used for weapons and agricultural implements. Trade in iron had become large-scale by the 12th century, both in smelted ore and in manufactured products. William Marsden (1783) believed that Minangkabau craftsmen had been supplying arms for Aceh and the rest of northern Sumatra 'from the earliest times', using the iron mined from Gunung Besi near Batu Sangkar. Sulawesi iron, rich in nickel, was exported to Java, where it was mixed with 'ordinary' iron for kris manufacture. Kalimantan was another source of ore, especially the island of Karimata off its

southwest coast. The seizure of Sukadana by Mataram (Java) in 1622 was probably intended to secure control of this source of iron. Karimata ores were 'brown iron', ferromanganese, producing a hard steel, but low grade surface ores were also abundant in Borneo. These continued to be worked as isolated local operations into the 19th century. Upland peoples retained a knowledge of smelting long after iron production in other areas had gone into decline.

Tin

Indonesia's tin is mainly found on the islands of Bangka and Belitung. Bangka ores are high grade, producing tin of purest quality. Tin mining did not really begin here until the 18th century. The Dutch had already been attempting to control the tin trade from the Malayan Peninsula to China in the 17th century, and in 1722 the Sultan of Palembang gave the VOC a trade monopoly in Bangka. The first mines were in the Mentok area; the alluvial deposits mined from small pits using techniques developed on the Malay Peninsula. Later, shallow diggings developed; often with conduits arranged to wash topsoil away. From the late 1730s the rulers of Palembang began bringing Chinese miners to Bangka. Initially production was spasmodic and declined after reaching a high point of 35,837 pikuls in 1785. Shortly thereafter the Dutch assumed control of mining. Tin production was in a slump during the turbulent time which followed, but picked up steadily in the 19th century.

A view of the Dutch mines at Sildasi Tampang, on the west coast of Sumatra, which were operated without interruption from 1669 to 1737 (Heydt, 1744).

Gold panners in Batang Gadis, West Sumatra. These gold panners are using traditional sluices and coconut husks to hold nuggets.

Goldsmiths produced intricate jewellery throughout the Archipelago. These examples surrounding an old picture card, are from Ambon, illustrated by Valentyn in 1724.

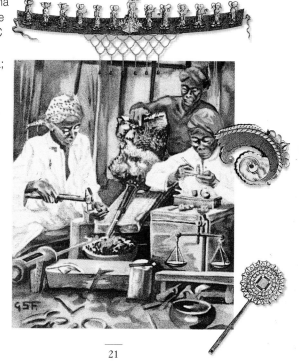

Ceramics: Local Innovation and External Trade

*E*arthenware ceramics represent one of the most ancient craft traditions of Indonesia. The development of this tradition in the period 1200 to 1800 AD was in part influenced by the presence of imported glazed ceramics from China and mainland Southeast Asia, and these trade wares were in turn designed to meet Indonesian taste and needs.

These 15th century Vietnamese tiles on the outer wall of the Great Mosque at Demak are said to have come from the site of the capital of the kingdom of Majapahit (13th–15th centuries). Despite claims that the use of tiles on mosques and tombs was copied from the Near East, there is evidence that tiles were used in pre-Islamic Indonesia.

Vessel (kendi) of polished earthenware, c. 15th century. East Javanese kendi developed a bulging spout and squat body.

Indonesian Earthenwares

Archaeological evidence dating from 3,500 BC testifies to the prehistoric origins of an Indonesian pottery tradition. The most abundant type of pottery found throughout the Archipelago is made up of unglazed earthenware objects produced for domestic use. They consist primarily of hand made earthenware vessels, unglazed and subjected to low temperature straw firings. However, evidence exists of glazed earthenwares. The Majapahit potters of the 14th century possessed the technical ability to produce low-fired lead glaze. They seemed to have used the technique mainly for colouring decorative objects, possibly for use on walls.

A variety of different quality goods were produced, ranging from coarse utilitarian cooking pots and stoves, to highly burnished drinking vessels. Polished earthenwares have been excavated from a number of funerary sites in both western and eastern Indonesia and shards from domestic wares have been widely retrieved from controlled excavations. Relief sculptures on the 9th century monument of Candi Lara Jonggrang at Prambanan depict a variety of vessels, a number of which resemble known ceramic types; the spouted *kundika* (an early prototype of the *kendi*) on the pavilion is most probably a local earthenware. These techniques and types of earthenware were produced by many communities in Southeast Asia. However, it is clear that within this larger tradition of pottery making, numerous local traditions thrived. Locally produced and readily replenished supplies of earthenware jars and cooking pots formed the staple of this production.

In those parts of Indonesia where suitable clay was found, villages specialising in pottery production

EARTHENWARE PRODUCTION
Traditionally, most pottery has been made by women, a tradition continued in Kampung Dukuh, West Java. Villagers say that they were originally pottery specialists during the golden age of the kingdom of Banten, the capital of which lies ten kilometres away. They used the paddle and anvil technique shown here (left). Firing was done by piling rice straw around the pots and setting it alight (below). This has been typical of Indonesian pottery since the introduction of this technology several thousand years ago.

developed, and the potters produced wares for the surrounding area, sometimes up to a 100 kilometre radius. If these potting villages were near important trade centres, their wares were often exported to other communities. Pots produced in Java, for example, were shipped from the north coast ports to Kalimantan and Maluku.

Earthenware vessels are ideal for storing drinking water, as the porous body has a natural cooling action on its contents. An early example of a spouted drinking vessel of this type was found at Melolo, a prehistoric burial site in Sumba, and now in the National Museum in Jakarta. It probably dates from the first millenium AD. It has a highly polished finish, with incised decorations, and only one orifice at the tip of the spout. It could only be filled by completely submerging it, and may have been for ritual rather than everyday use. It provides a good example of the high quality workmanship being produced in Indonesia. The abundant supply and relative cheapness of imported glazed wares, particularly Chinese imports, hindered development of a vibrant and innovative local tradition. With the emergence of a reliable supply of quality ceramics from China by around the 12th century, and later from Thailand and Vietnam, the economic imperative to generate local wares was diminished. Unglazed earthenwares continued to be produced locally to satisfy domestic needs, while the needs for prestige and ritual ceramics was fulfilled by imported glazed wares.

Imported Ceramics

Glazed Chinese ceramics from the early centuries AD have been reported from sites in western Indonesia, but their provenance is not secure, and it is with the iron- or copper-glazed wares of the 8th and 9th century that archaeologically documented examples appear. Shards of this ware have been recovered during excavations in the vicinity of the temple of Prambanan in Central Java, an association suggesting a prestigious role for these imported wares.

The bulk of the Asian ceramic trade, for which the Indonesian islands provided a major market, consisted of a great variety of forms and vessel types, decorated in an equally diverse range of glazes. The study of their distribution contributes to an understanding of the character, scale and duration of the economic fortunes of particular regions and shifting patterns of maritime trade in Southeast Asia. Their use in burial rituals also reveal aspects of traditional religious practices. For example, considerable quantities of covered boxes from Thailand, in pristine condition, have been discovered in graves in southern Sulawesi. They appear to have been imported expressly for use as funerary goods. In other communities, such as the Iban of Borneo, imported ceramics were appropriated for ceremonial and ritual use, and acquired added meanings and value through this process of acculturation.

Locally Inspired Imports

Over time a creative dialogue developed between local and imported ceramics. Whereas it might be assumed that local wares would come to imitate the more prestigious imports (as occurred with some types of wares in Cambodia and Thailand), in Java the ubiquitous *kendi* evolved into a distinctive local form. The glazed stoneware and porcelain versions later produced in Vietnam, China and Thailand appear to have been made to satisfy demand for this favoured form in Java, reflecting the power of indigenous market preference. Vietnamese *kendis* of this type most directly follow the earthenware model.

Other instances of high quality glazed imports following local earthenware models reinforce this view of the Asian ceramic trade being characterised by a high degree of market specialisation. For example, in the Red River delta region of northern Vietnam a group of underglazed decorated tiles were expressly produced for use in the monuments and palaces of the Majapahit kingdom of eastern Java. The inspiration for these glazed tiles is to be found in the moulded terracotta plaques used in Majapahit architecture. Vietnamese tiles survive from the Majapahit region and from the north coast mosques of Demak and Kudus, where a number of these tiles were later installed, continuing a tradition of employing foreign ceramics in Indonesian architectural decoration.

Minaret at Kudus, decorated with imported glazed ceramics, mainly Chinese, late European, and one Vietnamese.

«« Decorative earthenware plaque with parrot in centre. Probably 14th century Majapahit, Candi Gunung Gangsir, East Java.

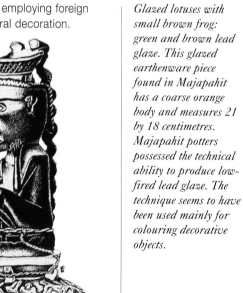

Glazed lotuses with small brown frog: green and brown lead glaze. This glazed earthenware piece found in Majapahit has a coarse orange body and measures 21 by 18 centimetres. Majapahit potters possessed the technical ability to produce low-fired lead glaze. The technique seems to have been used mainly for colouring decorative objects.

Earthenware sculpture from Banten palace site, 16th-18th centuries. Rooftop decoration in bird form. Clay birds were popular decorations in Java, 14th-16th centuries.

Chinese jar with a wooden stopper in the form of a Toba Batak priest figure. 15th century Dehua ware, Fujian, adapted as a magic potion jar, Sumatra.

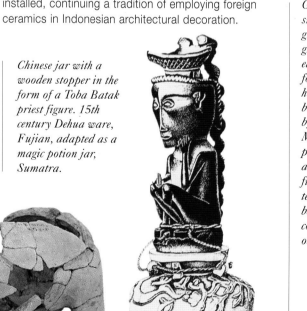

Earthenware coin bank from the site of the Banten palace, 16th-18th centuries. A four-footed animal, perhaps a monkey, with eyes of broken Chinese porcelain.

Textiles: Embellishments of Life, Death and Status

*T*he capacity of Indonesian society to absorb imported textiles kept pace with the 'flood of cloth' that entered the island world through foreign and Asian traders coming to purchase cloves, nutmegs and pepper. Indonesians used the exotic cloths not only as body-coverings, a commodity with utilitarian value, but also as a measure of value and power in all sorts of social transactions.

» Women in various parts of Flores and Lembata still use drop spindles to spin their home-grown cotton. Their ancestors wove ikat cloths like those they wear today, and produce for export around the eastern Archipelago.

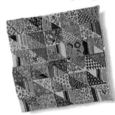

This batik from Cirebon reveals the relationship between batik and Indian chintz. Some of the motifs display Chinese, Indian and Javanese inspiration.

Simple backstrap looms like this one in Iliape, Lembata, Nusa Tenggara Timur, have been used for centuries by the women of the eastern islands to weave their dark-coloured ikat cloths.

The Centrality of Cloth

Cloth functioned in a multitude of ways, as a status symbol separating royalty and commoner, as an ethnic marker distinguishing one community from another, and as a sign of regional affluence differentiating the wealthier lowlanders and coastal traders from the inland horticulturists and forest dwellers. Cloth also figured in the dynamics of politics and economics, in that the accumulation of textiles was recognised as a measure of one's wealth, class, status, and power. People received wages in cloth, paid taxes in cloth, and squared debts in cloth. The underlying consumption pattern pervading Indonesian communities everywhere was cloth centred.

Local Textile Production

Although the weaving of tree fibres and manufacture of barkcloth probably preceded the use of cotton and silk to clothe Indonesians, these latter fibres were already widely used by the 16th century. Silkworms were nurtured for their product in Aceh and south Sulawesi, while cotton was grown in most of the areas with a long enough dry season — notably eastern Java, Bali, Lombok, Sumbawa, Flores, Buton, South Sulawesi and Selayar. The women of the Archipelago spun the cotton or silk (and still prepared tree-bark fibre in some upland areas), fixed their own dyes from indigo and other plant or mineral based colourings, and wove the cloth on backstrap looms. The dryer cotton growing areas in the east exported cloth to the rest of the Archipelago, the striped *lurik* of Java and *ikat* varieties similar to those still woven in Flores being the most popular. When available, however, the much brighter colours and bold designs of Indian cloths were highly valued.

A Flood of Indian Imports

The spice boom of the 15th and 16th centuries brought unprecedented wealth into Indonesia, and allowed its inhabitants to indulge in buying soft, expensive silks from China and brilliant cottons from India. The Indian textiles, *kumitir, cahutar, kemer-kendit, makhmal* and *berem* mentioned in the 15th century *kidung* tales, were imported alongside Chinese brocade, pongees, satins and taffetas, and filled a large part of the Indonesian market from the 15th to the 18th centuries.

Dutch Intervention

The demand for pepper and spices escalated in Europe in the 16th and 17th centuries. Dutch merchants set out for Asia from 1596 bringing coins, precious metals and trade goods from Europe. When they started to participate in the vibrant commercial world of the Indonesian Archipelago they also discovered that the people valued highly imported Indian textiles. They further realised that trading in foreign cloths was at least twice as profitable as trading in Indonesian cloths. Merchants of the Dutch East India Company (VOC) soon established themselves on the Indian coast at Coromandel, Surat and Bengal in order to buy hundreds of thousands of pieces of cloth every year over the next two centuries. These textiles flooded the markets of the Archipelago.

In order to protect their trade and profits, the management of the VOC in Batavia,

INDIAN TRADE TEXTILE, 18th CENTURY

The detail is of a fine luxury chintz with designs resembling those known from imported Indian patola and Indonesian batik. The picture shows hand painting and multiple dye baths creating the several shades of blue, red, black, mustard yellow, brown and black.

Within the squares one recognises the circle motifs and eight pointed star designs prominent in the trade-patola cloth. The light blue lines seen under a magnifier turn out to be a series of parallel slanted small stripes. The contours of many flowers are drawn in Indian ink. The cloth is folded double with the holes in the border allowing the continuation of the pattern throughout the width of the cloth to show through. This complexity of the design and intricate technique places it in the category of superior luxury trade chintz.

PEPPER AND THE SHIP CLOTHS OF LAMPUNG

The sharp rise in Indonesian imports from India was a significant indicator of improved buying power based on pepper exports. In Lampung, in South Sumatra, the 'ship cloth' evolved during this period for ritual and ceremony. The *palepai* from Krui, and the *tampan* of wider geographical distribution in the south and southwest, carried the ship motif, often decorated with the tree-of-life, flanked by elephants or horses — all symbols of prosperity. The dark granular pattern in which the designs were picked on these cloths are reminiscent of the region's ubiquitous pepper grain. With the decline of Lampung's prosperity by the beginning of the 19th century, the manufacture of 'ship cloths', too, gradually declined and disappeared.

Jeyamalar Kathirithamby–Wells

endeavoured to enforce a monopoly on the buying of spices and the selling of textiles in the Archipelago.

Textile Types

Over 200 cloth types and varieties were involved in the Dutch controlled textile trade in Indonesia. Cloths could vary in material, in size and thickness, in price, and usage. This bewildering diversity can be simplified by grouping the textiles into five broader categories: chintz, checked and striped, luxury, muslin, and plain textiles.

Ordering, Shipping and Distributing Cloth through the VOC

VOC production orders for the Indian trade textiles were annually coordinated in Batavia: orders came from Europe, from Japan and from branch offices throughout Indonesia. The largest demand in the islands was for textiles from Coromandel followed by those from Surat and finally Bengal. Valuable textiles were separately wrapped in paper at the production sites. Two textiles, *bafta* and *cannekin*, were identifiable by a golden seal on the back of the wrapping. Expensive textiles of silk or fine chintz were usually wrapped in cheap cloth or oiled paper with a pleasant fragrance, and placed in chests of scented wood. Ordinary textiles were baled.

Indonesians treasured the precious cloths and stored them in special places and containers such as handwoven baskets, decorated boxes of palm and pandanus leaves, carved and inlaid chests and in earthenware vessels. People bought the imported textiles from various sources; from the Company stores, the market place, at auctions, from itinerant merchants, from 'smugglers,' and from the VOC personnel. A continuous roll of cloth, or a bolt from Europe could be measured by a standard length such as the Dutch *ell*. In the case of the India–Indonesia textile trade, however, cloths were traded in pieces rather than in lengths. These pieces were linked in the actual weaving during which dividers or borders were indicated where the individual pieces

or 'daughter cloths' could be cut from a 'mother cloth'. Cloth was sold directly by the VOC as well as through Indian, Chinese and Indonesian traders. The Company as a wholesaler usually sold bales of cloth. Pieces were only sold in the company stores or at auctions.

Decreasing Imports: Substitution

The VOC's import of Indian pieces of textiles decreased steadily from about 300,000 pieces a year in the 1650s to 100,000 by the 1780s. The likely cause of the decrease was import substitution by the Indonesians. For example, the popular Coromandel chintz was replaced by Javanese batik, beginning in the 17th century and becoming dominant by the middle of the 18th. Similarly, the women weavers in Makasar and its nearby islands marketed their striped and checked textiles through Bugis traders in competition with the VOC traders. Local traders could not be fully controlled by the Dutch because of the speed of the Indonesian vessels, which sailed in large numbers and were well armed. These fleets provided the much needed cloths throughout the island world. It was this strong import–substitution counter movement which eventually ended the Dutch monopoly of imported textiles.

The VOC letters ordering cloth to be sent from India included tiny pieces of sample cloth such as these found in Dutch archives. They included, for example, small checked blue and white Chelas (right), blue and white checked Chelas from Poplia (centre), and blue, red, green and white Borad Berms (left). These samples demonstrate how 'daughter' cloths were cut from larger pieces.

The main market at Banten (Java). The market was the central organising principle of trade. This everyday market sold foodstuffs such as rice, vegetables, fruit and fish, and was also the venue for selling livestock, cloth, pepper and other goods, de Bry (1598).

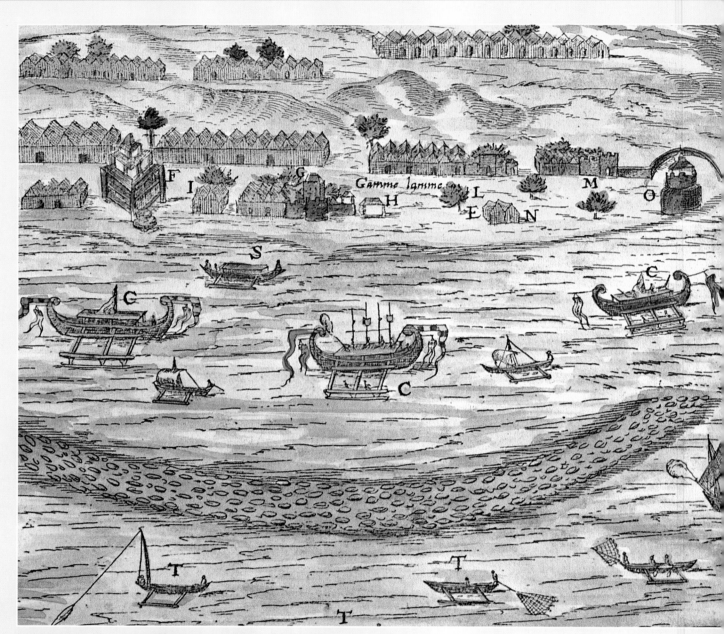

DESCRIPTION OF THE STATE OF GAMA LAMA ON TERNATE

The painting depicts Indonesian and European vessels at the clove port of Ternate, c. 1600.

A: Two Dutch ships anchored offshore.

B: Kora-kora, royal Malukan boats coming to enquire of the Dutch who they were and of what name.

C: Naval kora-kora.

E: Public meeting place, usually under a tree, the sun being too hot.

F: Mosque.

G: Royal palace built of stone.

H: Hut housing the cannon which Capt. Francis Drake once threw overboard when buffeted by a violent storm and which was later retrieved by the local inhabitants.

I: Dwelling officially given by the king to the Dutch who stayed behind.

L & M: St. Paul's Monastery, built by the Portuguese.

N: Home of the royal interpreter.

O: Tower with armament of cannon.

V: Cargo boat for inter-island transport of goods.

THE STIMULI OF TRADE AND RELIGION

The Indonesian Archipelago is one of nature's marketplaces. Almost everywhere accessible by boat, it also enjoyed an annual alternation of northeast and southwest monsoons. Sailors could take their vessels to China, India or Maluku on one favourable monsoon and return on the other. Whenever there was tolerable order on the sea routes between the eastern and western ends of Eurasia, these were preferred to overland routes by Indian and Arab traders, Buddhist missionaries, and pilgrims. From about the end of the 14th century the sea routes were always busier than the land, giving rise to ever growing numbers of ships and traders from all over Eurasia in the harbours of Sumatra, Java, Kalimantan and the Malay Peninsula.

Traders regularly stayed for four to six months in the islands while they waited for the favourable wind to journey onward or return home. Although a small number of Arabs and others had previously sailed all the way to China on a voyage of several years, a more efficient system of entrepots was established by the 15th century. Ports such as Pasai and later Aceh in North Sumatra, Melaka, Pahang and Patani on the Peninsula, and Banten, Demak and Gresik in Java became the exchange points for goods on the different routes. Other entrepots developed throughout the Archipelago to funnel goods to these major centres.

The 'age of commerce' which transformed Southeast Asia began in the 15th century under the influence of a rising demand for spices from Europe and an amazing burst of expansive energy in China. But it was Muslim traders for the most part who carried the spices and other goods between Southeast Asia and these growing markets. Arab, Persian and Indian merchants spread their faith with their trade from the Middle East to Gujarat, South India, the Indonesian Archipelago and beyond. The arrival of the Portuguese in pursuit of Malukan cloves and nutmeg in 1509 was a consequence of the rapidly growing tempo of this trade, not its cause.

The trade which flowed so strongly around the Archipelago from the 15th to the mid-17th century brought new wealth and firearms to the rulers of the ports. It brought new kinds of cloth, ceramics, tools and other luxuries which stimulated experimentation in dress and life–style. Above all it brought new ideas — new ways of making ships, guns, forts and palaces; new ways of perceiving the state, the family, the self and morality; and a radically new religious faith in the form of Islam.

People of the Sea

*T*he world economic boom of the 15th and 16th centuries brought about a substantial increase in Asian maritime trade. The harbour polities of Insular Southeast Asia, particularly those that lay astride the major maritime trade routes of the Straits of Melaka and the Java Sea, contributed their share to this period of economic growth by fostering a vigorous local shipbuilding industry.

A late 16th century war galley of Banten, from Lodewijcks, The First Dutch Expedition..., *Amsterdam, 1598.*

Maritime Traders

For some 2,000 years the people of western Indonesia participated in the maritime trade networks of Asia, and developed a series of shipbuilding traditions. They earned, among contemporary Asians and Europeans alike, a well deserved reputation as experienced seafarers who made the best use of a maritime environment. Fishing had long provided one major source of proteins for the people of the region and no doubt contributed to their familiarity with navigation. During the last centuries of the first millennium BC, local and regional maritime trade and exchange networks expanded into long distance overseas commerce that brought ships and traders to harbours as far apart as southern China in the East, and to the Persian Gulf, the Red Sea and Madagascar in the Indian Ocean.

Jong

Until the 13th or 14th centuries, Indonesian trade was carried in large stitched-plank ships, known from both written sources and recent archaeological excavations. In the 15th and 16th centuries, these stitched–plank vessels were no longer built. By then, large–scale trade was carried out in ships known in Malay or Javanese as *jong*, a local term that gave birth to the word 'junk' in European languages (later to be used only for Chinese ships). These *jong* were built along the coasts of Java and southern

*An early 16th century Portuguese artist's rendering of Indonesian ships (*Lopo Homen Atlas, *1518).*

Vessels of the Java coast as represented in Lodewijcks The First Dutch Expedition *(Amsterdam, 1598).*

Kalimantan, where timber (teak or ironwood) was readily available in the large quantities that were necessary to build such huge ships. And they were huge sailing vessels, even by contemporary European standards. When, late in the 15th century, the Portuguese newcomers to the Indonesian scene first met them at sea, they were surprised to find that they carried much larger tonnages than their own ships. Malay and Javanese *jong* that hauled 350 to 500 tons of merchandise are regularly described by Portuguese sources, with a few hundred people aboard, including crew and a large number of petty merchants. Merchandise was carried under the deck in individual compartments (*petak*) separated by bamboo matting.

In keeping with the earlier stitched-plank tradition, these *jong* were assembled without the use of iron. Wooden dowels had by then replaced the earlier fibre lashings to keep the planks fastened together, and the shell was in turn dowelled to the sturdy frames. They carried multiple masts, and as many lug sails of fibre matting, including a typical bowsprit sail. One other feature inherited from earlier times was the multiple sheathing of the hull; as one layer of planking became old, one or two additional layers were superimposed on the first. The *jong* were steered by means of a pair of side rudders, exactly like the Bugis *pinisi* that were still built in the 1970s in Sulawesi, ships that are true descendants of the 16th century *jong,* albeit on a small scale.

War Fleets

These large *jong* however were to disappear in the second half of the 16th century, due to a combination of economic and political factors. In the early 16th century harbour states such as Japara, Banten, Bintan, Johor, Lingga, Indragiri or Aru all kept modest fleets of long craft of the *lancang, kelulus* or *penjajap* type ready to launch attacks on rival powers. However, in marked coincidence with the vanishing long distance trading fleets of

REMAINS OF A 15th CENTURY TRADING SHIP

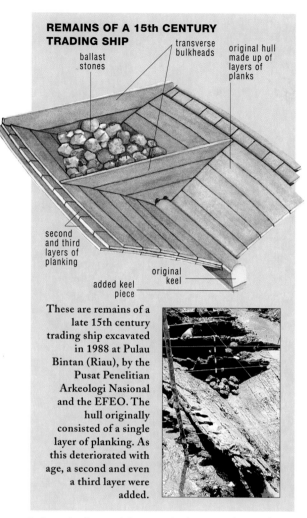

ballast stones

transverse bulkheads

original hull made up of layers of planks

second and third layers of planking

original keel

added keel piece

These are remains of a late 15th century trading ship excavated in 1988 at Pulau Bintan (Riau), by the Pusat Penelitian Arkeologi Nasional and the EFEO. The hull originally consisted of a single layer of planking. As this deteriorated with age, a second and even a third layer were added.

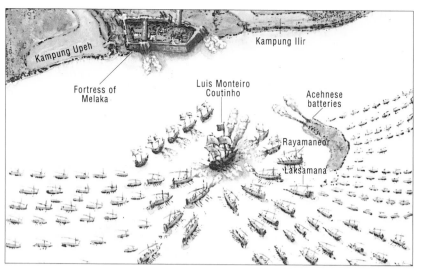

Kampung Upeh

Kampung Ilir

Fortress of Melaka

Luis Monteiro Coutinho

Acehnese batteries

Rayamaneor

Laksamana

The siege of Melaka by the war fleet of Aceh, after an early 17th century drawing by Godinho de Eredia, in the collection of the National Library, Lisbon.

Indonesia, these states acquired an ever increasing capacity to fight at sea, and by the end of the century were launching impressive war fleets of much larger and better armed vessels. Aceh is the most revealing of all cases because of the sheer size and power of its fleets and the frequency of its attacks by sea, mainly on the Portuguese.

In the second half of the century, Aceh was already capable of swiftly sending war fleets comprising 300 or more long vessels, including a majority of middle sized ones, and up to 50 large *ghali*. The latter were new ships for the region, as their foreign name implies, galley type craft built according to Mediterranean standards learnt from Portuguese renegades and Turkish shipwrights. They were built in such a way as to allow them to carry and shoot the large cannon necessary for battles at sea. Dozens of such battles are recorded in 16th century sources, both among sultanates and between the Muslim powers, mainly Aceh and Johor, and the Portuguese, on whom they kept a constant pressure. The largest of these galleys was built in the 1620s for Sultan Iskandar Muda of Aceh; she was 100 metres in length, had three masts and carried a crew of 700. According to the Portuguese who succeeded in capturing and taking her to Goa, her name was 'Terror of the Universe' (probably a free translation of *Cakra Dunia*), and she was bigger than anything they had known so far. These war fleets served the expansionist policies of the sultans of

Aceh or Banten in their search for pepper. The capital and energy spent on building, maintaining and renewing these huge and profusely armed war fleets cannot but have placed considerable strain on the capacities of these two fast growing powers to maintain their own trading fleets.

Long distance maritime commerce ended up being farmed out, and fell into the hands of Gujarati merchants in Aceh and the Chinese in Banten, whose large trading vessels took over the Indonesian *jong*'s share of the trade.

A New Shipbuilding Tradition

A new shipbuilding tradition appeared in the region during those times, probably due to the steady interchange with China and its merchants. This so-called South China Sea shipbuilding tradition mixed Southeast Asian and Chinese technical features; iron nails and axial rudders were introduced and the sails probably were of the Chinese type. Wrecks belonging to this tradition have recently been excavated and studied by archaeologists in Indonesia and elsewhere in Southeast Asia.

The disappearance from the local scene of the large ocean-going *jong*, however, does not mean that there was not a significant fleet of lesser coasters (under 100 tons). These comprised smaller junks or other round bottomed vessels, and a great number of multi-purpose long vessels (*balang, lancang, kelulus, penjajap, kora-kora, orembai*, etc.) that could serve in war as well as in peace. These swift vessels, most of which could be propelled by sail or oars, plied the interstitial networks, collecting cargo for accumulation in the main ports. They were suitable for the internal seas of Indonesia, with its many narrow straits and dense archipelagos, and its changing local winds and often strong currents. These, together with the fishing fleets, kept the local shipbuilding traditions alive until modern times, when fleets of small to medium sized Madurese, Butonese and Bugis ships became the last witnesses to the earlier grandeur of Indonesian shippers.

An early 17th century rendering by Godinho de Eredia of a Malay junk, from L. Janssen, Malaca, l'Inde méridionale et le Cathay, *Bruxelles 1881.*

Ship cloth, a ceremonial cloth of the Paminggir people of Lampung, Sumatra. Ships are a frequent motif in Indonesian textile art, a reflection of their prominent role in coastal societies.

The Lure of Spices

*T*he fact that the most valuable of the spices in international trade came from Maluku, the furthest extremity of the 'known' world, did much to lock a major part of the Archipelago into a trading network. But the spices would also prove vulnerable to monopoly in the hands of well organised Europeans.

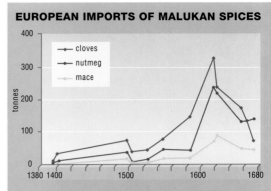

EUROPEAN IMPORTS OF MALUKAN SPICES

European imports of cloves and nutmeg increased rapidly around 1400. Thereafter growth was steady, apart from the major disruption caused by the Portuguese attack on established trade routes in the Indian Ocean.

Data from Anthony' Reid's article in Modern Asian Studies

The Spices

The lure of cloves, nutmeg, and mace was a major stimulus in the development of international trade in Southeast Asia. The clove tree (*Eugenia aromatica, Kuntze*) was endemic to Ternate, Tidore, Moti, Makian, and Bacan. Nutmeg and its red filament — mace — come from the nutmeg tree (*Myristica fragrans, Linn*) which was endemic to the islands of Banda. After 1550 trees were transplanted to other parts of the Archipelago, and later to the world.

The earliest evidence of the spice trade comes from the Mesopotamian site of Terqa in present day Syria, where archaeological excavations have revealed a store of cloves in the pantry of an ordinary household dating back to 1700 BC. A Han emperor in China (third century BC) required his courtiers to have cloves in their mouths when addressing him. Though a number of pre-14th century Chinese . sources identify the origin of the cloves in Maluku, only one dated about 1350 actually refers to Chinese junks sailing directly from China to the area. The collection and transport of spices from Maluku to the western half of the Archipelago were principally in the hands of Malays, Javanese, and Bandanese.

Entrepots

In the heyday of the southeast Sumatran state of Sriwijaya (7th to 11th centuries), spices from Maluku became one of Sriwijaya's main export items. A major change occurred in the late 14th century when the northeast Javanese coastal towns with their ruling Chinese, Arab, and Javanese elite, became the major points of a vibrant inter-Archipelago trade network which linked the spice islands to the rest of the world. Melaka, founded at the beginning of the 15th century, continued the tradition of serving as the principal distribution centre for spices in the international marketplace.

A woman drying cloves in Tidore. Europe was enamoured with the clove because of the extravagant claims of its efficacy. The sweet smelling essence distilled from it was said to strengthen vision. Rubbing the powder on the forehead relieved head colds, and added to food and drink it stimulated the appetite and cleared the bladder and intestines. An added inducement was the belief that when drunk with milk it enhanced coitus.

Dutch merchants at Nera negotiating with the local governor for the purchase of nutmeg, c.1600, de Bry (1601).

The European Demand for Spice

From Melaka the spices were transported by Muslim traders by sea to Bassorah on the Persian Gulf and then north to Damascus or Aleppo in the Mediterranean. When this land route was disrupted by the Turks in the 15th century, the trade shifted to the Red Sea. The major nodes of this trade network were, therefore, the Muslim kingdom of Melaka, the Muslim Gujarati traders of Cambay in northwest India, and the Muslim Mamelukes of Egypt.

From the eastern Mediterranean the spices were brought to the northern Italian ports and then transshipped to the rest of Europe. Although the Red Sea route was on a more direct line from the west coast of India to the Mediterranean, the price of spices in Europe continued to remain high because of the high cost of transfers and portages. Christian Europe's desire to remove its dependence on its religious enemies and to acquire cheaper spices became a major motivation in its search for a sea route to Asia.

The Portuguese Involvement

The arrival of the Portuguese in the spice islands in 1511 was the beginning of European involvement in the spice trade. They introduced new methods of harvesting cloves. Whereas the Malukans would simply break off branches and bring them to the harbour to a passing trader, the Portuguese made the Malukans separate the cloves from the branches and leaves, dry, and bag them. Since European traders arrived regularly throughout the year, the Malukans were assured of an ongoing trade. This was a factor in their willingness to initiate changes in production to accommodate the European traders.

Although Portuguese participation had increased the profitability of the spice trade, they were not essential for its survival. The eviction of the Portuguese from Ternate in 1575 had little economic impact on the kingdom, and in fact the 1570s and the 1580s marked a resurgence in the spice trade. A 1584 Spanish document reported the economic vitality of Ternate, where ordinarily some 1,000 Javanese, Sangleys (Chinese from the Philippines), and Acehnese came to trade. In response to increasing demand, the Ternatens resumed their voyages to east Seram and to the Seram and Goram Laut Archipelago to sell their cloves.

The Arrival of the Dutch

The Dutch pursued a similar policy in attempting to monopolise the sale of cloves from Ternate. But, like the Portuguese, they realised the futility of enforcing a monopoly without local cooperation. In 1652–53, the Dutch introduced a policy of *extirpatie* (eradication) of all spice trees in Maluku in order to control

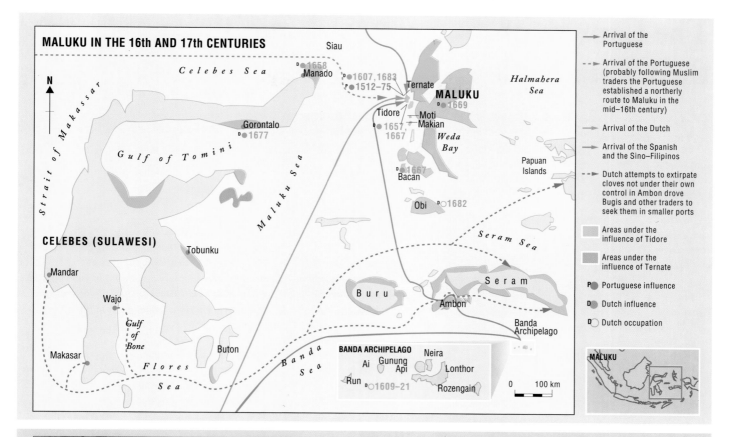

MALUKU IN THE 16th AND 17th CENTURIES

Map labels:

Siau
Celebes Sea
Manado D 1658
1607, 1683 P
1512–75 P
Ternate
MALUKU
D 1669
Halmahera Sea
Tidore
Moti
Makian
Gorontalo D 1677
1657 D
1667
Weda Bay
Gulf of Tomini
Strait of Makassar
N
Maluku Sea
Papuan Islands
D 1667
Bacan
Obi D 1682
Seram Sea
CELEBES (SULAWESI)
Tobunku
Seram
Mandar
Buru
Wajo
Gulf of Bone
Ambon
Banda Archipelago
Makasar
Buton
Flores Sea
Banda Sea

BANDA ARCHIPELAGO
Ai Gunung Api Neira
Run D○1609–21 Lonthor
Rozengain

0   100 km

MALUKU

Legend:
→ Arrival of the Portuguese
⇢ Arrival of the Portuguese (probably following Muslim traders the Portuguese established a northerly route to Maluku in the mid-16th century)
→ Arrival of the Dutch
→ Arrival of the Spanish and the Sino–Filipinos
⇢ Dutch attempts to extirpate cloves not under their own control in Ambon drove Bugis and other traders to seek them in smaller ports
▢ Areas under the influence of Tidore
▢ Areas under the influence of Ternate
P● Portuguese influence
D● Dutch influence
D○ Dutch occupation

THE ARRIVAL OF THE DUTCH AND THE KING OF TERNATE AT THE CITADEL OF TIDORE IN 1605

L: The rowing-boats in which the Dutch reached the shore.

M: Ships belonging to the King of Ternate, who, with almost 500 Dutch at his disposal, implored them to let him help them if need demanded it.

N: A village in the northern part of the state, which the Dutch set fire to and destroyed.

O: The King of Ternate, with his people drawn up in battle array.

P–Q: The Dutch advance in order of battle against Tidore.

R: The spot where the King of Ternate sat with his men to await the outcome of the assault.

S: The fortification hastily thrown up consisting of big storage jars piled up together and packed with soil.

From 'An Account of the Voyage of Admiral Jacob von Neck from Holland to the East Indies in 1600-03 and the Voyages of Johan Herman von Bree from 1602-04'. First published 1606 by de Bry.

production and maintain high prices in Europe. They limited the growing of nutmeg trees to Banda and clove trees to Ambon. Even with this drastic measure spices continued to reach the outside world via the Bugis, Makasar, and Mandar traders of south Sulawesi. They went with their light boats, known as *padewakang*, from Sulawesi to east Seram and neighbouring archipelagoes and the Papuan islands, where they obtained spices and brought them to Pasir, Sulu, and Manila. Other traders went from northern Maluku to the Goram Archipelago, and then on to Java and the Malay world.

The *extirpatie* policy was too difficult to implement, and there were too many ways in which spices could be traded outside the purview of the Dutch East India Company. What led to the decline in the importance of the spice trade was not the failure of any particular European or indigenous policy, but the changing demands in the market place. Profits of the VOC fell when European demand for spices declined as the 18th century progressed.

As Portugal had found in the 16th century, the costs of maintaining a commercial empire with its fleets, forts, and factories, and enforcing a monopoly on spice trading, were huge. Moreover, in subsequent centuries spice trees earlier smuggled out of Maluku were beginning to produce and supply the world market. By then the 'Trinity of Spices' had already ceased to exercise a lure on the imagination of the Europeans.

The five islands of Maluku from right (north) to left–Ternate, Tidore, Moti, Makian and Bacan, by W.J. Blaeu (c. 1630).

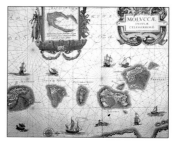

The Growth of the China Trade

*W*hile maritime links between the trade ports of Indonesia and China can be traced back to well before the 13th century, it was the attack on Java by the naval forces of the Mongol rulers of China in 1293 that was to usher in a new age — an age marked by an increased intensity in commercial, cultural and military interaction between China and the polities of Indonesia.

An early 17th century rendering by Gondinho de Eredia of a Chinese armed junk.

↗ *Chinese map of Southeast Asia from 'A Geographical Treatise on all within the circuit of the seas', published in 1848 by Xu Jiyü.*

» *Chinese porcelain, like this 16th century Jiangxi plate, found in Jailolo, North Maluku, were traded with Indonesia for spices and other products of the Archipelago.*

↘↘ *Melaka in the 16th century, by João de Barros (Lisbon, 1552). The capture of Melaka in 1511 by the Portuguese introduced a new force to the maritime trade in this region.*

Combining Trade and Diplomacy

The rise of the state of Majapahit in Java in the late 13th century shaped new external trading patterns and networks in the region. At the same time, the Mongol incursions appear to have resulted in a greater role for Chinese copper cash in the Javanese economy as well as the introduction of Chinese shipbuilding techniques in the region. By the 14th century, so the *Nagarakrtagama,* a Majapahit chronicle informs us, merchants from India, Cambodia, China, Dai Viet, Champa and Siam were crowding to Java. An increased demand for luxury items in 14th–century Majapahit fuelled the import of Chinese silks and porcelain, while at the same time the increasing power of the Javanese state allowed it to secure the aromatics and spices necessary to fund these imports.

Chinese texts provide us with contemporary accounts of the diplomatic trade missions from the polities of Indonesia to China during the late 14th and early 15th centuries. Missions from an 'Eastern King' and a 'Western King' of Java are recorded, as are envoy traders sent by 'Maharaja Palembang' of San-fo-qi, and by various kings of Samudra. The missions from Java were led by persons entitled 'Arya' or 'Patih' though many of them bore Chinese names.

They traded aromatics, spices, horses and exotic fauna to China, and took silks, porcelain and iron back to Java and Sumatra. The missions despatched by China to Southeast Asia through this period included envoys as well as traders who brought with them the famed porcelains of China and silks of diverse varieties.

The Zheng He Voyages

At the beginning of the 15th century, the Yongle Emperor of the Ming dynasty in China initiated a series of policies intended to bolster his own position and expand Ming influence beyond China's borders.

These policies included the sending of eunuch admirals, the most famous of whom was a Muslim named Zheng He (Cheng Ho), to the maritime polities of Asia and the Middle East. Numerous voyages extending over the period 1405-33 took Chinese troops and traders to the ports of Java, Palembang, Melaka, Aru, Samudra and Aceh, and into the Indian Ocean. It has been contended that these voyages were the initial impetus which gave rise to Southeast Asia's 'age of commerce' over the next several centuries. A 15th–century Chinese text *Ying-yai Sheng-lan* (Wonderful Views of the Ocean's Shores), which records places visited on these voyages, notes that Chinese ships trading with Java at that time came first to Tuban, then proceeded to Gresik, after which they sailed on to Surabaya and to

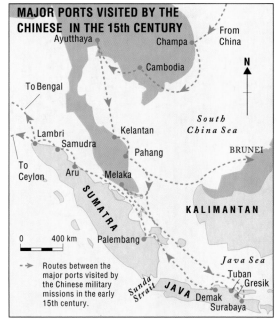

MAJOR PORTS VISITED BY THE CHINESE IN THE 15TH CENTURY

Ayutthaya
From China
Champa
Cambodia
To Bengal
Kelantan
Lambri
Samudra
Pahang
To Ceylon
Aru
Melaka
SUMATRA
South China Sea
BRUNEI
KALIMANTAN
0   400 km
Palembang

→ Routes between the major ports visited by the Chinese military missions in the early 15th century.

Java Sea
Tuban
Gresik
Sunda Strait   JAVA
Demak
Surabaya

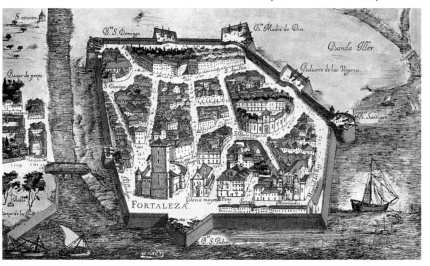

Majapahit, 'where the king of the country lives'. Java provided the Chinese traders with sappan wood, diamonds, steel and turtle shells. In the same work, it is noted of Palembang that 'ships from every place come here', and that aromatics such as gum benzoin, as well as luxuries such as ivory were eagerly sought commodities of the area.

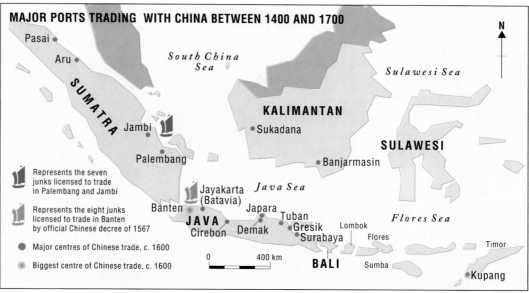

MAJOR PORTS TRADING WITH CHINA BETWEEN 1400 AND 1700

N

Pasai
Aru
South China Sea
Sulawesi Sea
SUMATRA
Jambi
KALIMANTAN
•Sukadana
SULAWESI
Palembang
•Banjarmasin

Represents the seven junks licensed to trade in Palembang and Jambi

Represents the eight junks licensed to trade in Banten by official Chinese decree of 1567

● Major centres of Chinese trade, c. 1600

● Biggest centre of Chinese trade, c. 1600

Jayakarta (Batavia)
Banten
JAVA
Cirebon
Demak
Japara
Tuban
Gresik
Surabaya
Java Sea
Lombok
Flores
Flores Sea
Timor
0   400 km
BALI
Sumba
Kupang

The eunuch-led naval expeditions ended in the 1430s and official Chinese missions to the Archipelago dwindled swiftly thereafter. Javanese envoys, however, continued to arrive frequently in China until the second half of the century. The economic benefits that could be gained by such missions are underlined by the fact that in 1443, the Chinese emperor had to instruct the ruler of Java, to limit such missions to one every three years. 'Official' diplomatic trading missions between China and the Indonesian polities ceased before 1500, and Chinese trade with Southeast Asia was increasingly taken over by private merchants operating from the ports of Fujian and Guangdong. These private traders sailed with the monsoon winds to most of the major ports of the Archipelago to trade their porcelain, silks and iron for pepper and other spices. Such private trade was facilitated by the presence of Chinese persons in many of the major ports of Indonesia. By the early 15th century there were at least 1,000 Chinese families in Tuban and Gresik in Java, and several thousand Chinese residents of Palembang.

In addition, by the early 15th century, major Sumatran ports such as Palembang and Samudra were also in trade contact with Vietnam and Ryukyu (modern Okinawa), while Ryukyuans are noted as trading porcelain with Java in the middle of that century. In 1412 an official mission from Majapahit, led by an enterprising Chinese merchant, even reached Japan and Korea. Vietnamese ceramic exports to the Archipelago surged in the late 15th century, particularly after Vietnam's capture of the ports of Champa. The wall tiles in the mosque at Demak, and those excavated at Trowulan in East Java, were produced in Vietnam.

The Rise of the Northern Javanese Ports

The decline of Majapahit ushered in a period of less centralised political power, with more trade ports and a wider dispersal of trade goods throughout the Archipelago. By 1500 the northern coast of Java was dotted with port-polities governed by Muslim rulers. Demak appears to have been one of the major of these ports. Some of the accounts detailing the rise of Demak, Japara, Gresik and Cirebon suggest the involvement of Chinese Muslim maritime traders in the establishment and early activities of

these ports, as well as close family and trading links between the ports.

Two other major changes affected maritime trade in this period. The Portuguese capture of Melaka in 1511 introduced a new force in Asian trade, while the lifting of Chinese prohibitions on private maritime trade in 1567 provided a new impetus to trade links between the merchants of the Archipelago and those in China.

CHINESE PORCELAIN PLATE, 17th CENTURY
This Chinese plate was probably manufactured in Jiangxi, southeast China. The design is thought to depict an expedition launched by the first emperor of the Qin dynasty in 219 BC. The expedition sought the 'The Isles of Fortune' off the Kiangsi coast, where the palaces of the gods rise above fields in which grow the sacred mushrooms of immortality. The plate was found in Ternate, Maluku, once an important spice trading port.

New Ports and New Trade Patterns

The 17th century saw the rise of further new ports and the introduction of new commodities. The Chinese text *Dong-xi-yang Kao* (Account of the Eastern and Western Oceans), published in 1618, notes many details of the Indonesian China trade. Banten is recorded as the main port of Java, while Palembang, Jambi and Aceh are listed as the most prominent ports of Sumatra. Sukadana, Banjarmasin and Timor are also noted as sources of Chinese imports. Apart from the usual aromatics like sandalwood, and spices, such as aloes, cloves, and pepper which the Archipelago had long supplied, these ports also exported to China items such as rhinoceros hides, ox skins, diamonds, rattan, and even coconuts.

Banten, which had been growing as a centre for the pepper trade since the 16th century had attracted a large number of Chinese traders, mainly from Fujian. The community which developed there brought Banten into a wide ranging Hokkien trade network that extended to Ayutthaya, Manila, China and even Nagasaki. The arrival of the Dutch, however, heralded the end of Banten's dominance and the opening of a new chapter in the history of Indonesian trade.

A copy of an early European rendering of Zheng He (Cheng Ho), the most famous eunuch admiral sent by the Ming Emperor to the maritime polities of Asia.

The Pepper Empires of Sunda and Sumatra

*B*lack pepper (Piper nigrum) played an important role in trade and civilisation in the early modern era. Though Indian pepper had entered the international market as early as Roman times, the demand for this spice soared in post-Mediaeval Europe for use as a flavouring and for preserving meat.

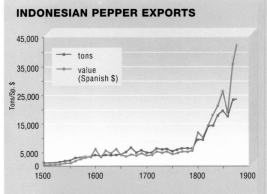

INDONESIAN PEPPER EXPORTS

This graph represents estimates of Southeast Asian (in practice almost entirely Indonesian) pepper exports between 1500 and 1900, both in terms of quantity (tons) and value (hundreds of Spanish/Mexican dollars). Until about 1820 pepper was Indonesia's most important export, and its fluctuations gave a good indication of the pattern of trade in general. Exports rose rapidly until 1600, and peaked in 1670 before a long 18th century period of stagnation, when the Dutch and English Companies controlled most of the Archipelago's pepper at fixed low prices.

Source: Bulbeck, Reid, Tan and Wu, Southeast Asian Exports in the Long Term (forthcoming)

Pepper Production

In maritime Southeast Asia, pepper was first recorded in 1187 in Java by Zhou Chufei. Unlike the finer spices from Maluku, *Piper nigrum* from India spread rapidly and extensively from the 14th century throughout the foothills and coastal regions from north Sumatra to west Java. In 1382 a single Javanese mission to China is recorded as having carried some 45 tons of pepper.

The easy integration of pepper into existing dry-rice or shifting cultivation (*ladang*) resulted in its ready adoption as a cash crop by the Acehnese, Sundanese, Batak, Pasemah, Rejang, and Lampung peoples, as well as migrant Minangkabau in Jambi, Indragiri and Palembang. In these areas, pepper was cultivated in newly cleared forest land. After an initial crop of paddy, the pepper vines were planted and, at the end of their three to 12 year productive cycle, the ground reverted to fallow. Ideally the same ground was not cultivated until after forest regeneration some 20 to 30 years later.

The easy adaptation of pepper to subsistence food production and its value as an exchange commodity for cloth, salt and other luxuries were incentives for the evolution of new techniques in forest farming. It included the widespread use of *Erythrina corallodendron* (the coral tree) as an effective prop and shade for the vines. This tree, through its nitrogen fixing properties, reduced soil deterioration normally associated with pepper cultivation, and thus eased the pressure for constant clearing of primary forest for crop renewal.

The Pressure of Demand

By the 17th century, however, the strength of demand began to jeopardise the fine-tuning of forest farming to export production. Permanent plantations of pepper vines

superseded ecologically adapted forest farms. By the beginning of the 19th century large areas, notably in Lampung where population was boosted by migration from Java, were laid to waste by spreading *Imperata cylindrica (lalang* or *alang-alang)*. The increasing pressure under which pepper cultivation was brought bears testimony to its commercial success. It dictated the political economy of the area for over four centuries. Apart from serving as a catalyst for the commercial revolution in the Mediterranean world centred at Venice, pepper brought spectacular changes to Southeast Asian society. Muslim exports to the Middle East and the Mediterranean, and Chinese imports for increasing consumption by a rising population, enabled Indonesia to dominate production, far outstripping Malabar. European consumption of pepper is calculated to have increased by 50 to 100 per cent in the first 60 years of the 16th century and 150 per cent in the next 70 years. Indonesia exported some 6,000 tonnes a year by the 1670s, most of it originating from west Java and Sumatra. The high price pepper earned in the international market during 1616-41 aided the political expansion of the Aceh and Banten sultanates. Conversely, the decline in price during the last quarter of the century corresponded to the destabilisation of these sultanates.

Southeast Asia's taste for Chinese and Indian manufactures was sharpened by the availability of pepper as an exchange commodity. Economic growth brought pronounced socio-political changes, forcing egalitarian chiefdoms into hierarchically oriented systems which evolved into petty kingdoms such as Inderapura and Mukomuko, in West Sumatra. These subsequently locked into the expanding circle of Aceh's and Banten's political

Pepper vines growing in an old ladang.

MAIN AREAS OF PEPPER CULTIVATION IN WEST JAVA AND SUMATRA, c. 1500-1900

Banda Aceh
Pedir
ACEH   Pasai
Langkat
Serdang
Susoh
BATAK   Batubara
Singkil   Asahan
Melaka
Tapanuli
Natal
Airbangis   MINANGKABAU
Pasaman   Siak Sri Inderapura
Tiku   Pelalawan
Padang   Pariaman
Painan   Indragiri
Airhaji   Jambi
Inderapura   REJANG
Mukomuko
Palembang
Bengkulu
Silebar   PASEMAH
Manna   LAMPUNG
Krui
Banten
Batavia
Sunda Strait   Cirebon
PRIANGAN

0   200 km   N

Pepper Cultivation

influence. Jambi, Inderagiri and Palembang remained independent but were less successful politically than Aceh and Banten.

In the main, indigenous powers protected local markets from the thrust of European monopoly control and promoted the inflow of silver by insisting on cash payments instead of barter for pepper. At the same time, the controls and institutional changes they enforced within the organisational structure of production and marketing laid the foundations for later colonial economic policies such as forced cultivation, export monopoly and crop extirpation as mechanisms for price control. The pepper economy in Sumatra and Java mediated the region's transition into the modern era, enabling the indigenous economy to accommodate to expanding global trade.

Pepper and Islam

Apart from reinforcing established ties with China, the enhanced purchasing power of the pepper region brought it closer to the Muslim world. Islam gained a firm footing as a state religion. Islamic fervour supported expanding networks of commercial patronage, intellectual and cultural influence and new technologies of arms and shipping. Aceh's political links with Turkey were matched by the spiritual inspiration Banten drew from Mecca. With wealth from pepper and increased shipping, the rulers of both kingdoms looked to improved technologies from the west for long distance commercial ventures in junks of larger tonnage. In Banten, the ruler, Sultan Abdul-fath Abdulfattah Agung (1651-82) engaged Portuguese and English pilots on vessels marketing pepper as far afield as Persia, China and Japan. The wealth from pepper financed the architectural splendour of the Bait al-Rahman mosque in Aceh, the royal pleasure garden at Tirtayasa (Banten), sumptuous feasts, extensive harems, war fleets and

elephant herds, and, no less, the reception and patronage of Islamic scholars.

Vulnerable Prosperity

It was in connection with the pepper economy that rulers in Sumatra and west Java established their initial links with Europeans. Chinese entrepreneurs served the expanding pepper economy by financing production and commodity transportation. The pepper economy became the spring board for Chinese economic penetration, immigration and settlement.

The cash earnings from pepper, however, laid society open to the evils of arms, opium and gambling, and destabilised the indigenous economy. Under colonial authority, cash-crop production, modelled after pepper, became the basis for economic control over most of Sumatra and Java. By the mid-19th century other commodities such as coffee and tin outstripped pepper in the world economy. But for west Java and Sumatra, the development of the pepper economy was synonymous with an era of power and prosperity.

A typical field house of a shifting cultivator in Lampung, where farmers planted pepper in their ladang as a secondary crop, after they had finished harvesting their rice. They were then able to sell the pepper harvest as a cash crop. In places like west and south Sumatra, west Java and south Kalimantan, pepper cultivation spread in lightly populated areas of shifting cultivation. In these regions pepper could be planted without necessarily foregoing staple food crops.

The Spread of Islam and Islamic Kingship

*W*ith the spread of Islam throughout the Archipelago, from around 1300 to 1650, a new concept of kingship took hold. An 11th century tombstone at Leran (on the north coast of Java) suggests that Muslim traders were involved in local trading networks at a time when Hinduistic culture was still dominant.

The Chinese quarter and Dutch trading houses (not shown here) were placed outside the confines of the main town, as were the Indians' residences.

The close relationship between the mosque, the market, and the palace (kraton) in Banten, may have given birth to its dynamic and cosmopolitan coastal (*pesisir*) culture during the 16th century.

Interior view of the tomb complex in Leran. The oldest dated tombstone of Java is on the far right.

The mosque at Japara as depicted in Reistogt Naar en Door Oostïndiën *by Wouter Schouten, first published in 1676, and reprinted in 1780. The engraver may have exaggerated the Chinese features of this mosque (since destroyed), although Chinese influence was considerable in Japara's heyday as a commercial centre in the late 15th and early 16th centuries.*

Conversion of the Earliest Islamic States

Firmer evidence of the spread of Islam comes with the formation of Islamic centres of power. Every such political organisation had to make itself known to its neighbours and to its own people, in order to establish its legitimacy and provide cultural account-ability for the change of religion. In doing so, each Islamic centre of power provided a record of its existence and its historical experiences. Most of the myths of conversion, mythologised versions of collective memories, are stories about the intricate relation between religion and the rulers. The *Hikayat Raja–Raja Pasai*, for example, tells how a local ruler dreamed that he met the Prophet Muhammad, who told him, in his dream, that a certain *ulama*, Syekh Ismail, would come from Arabia. The ruler came to the shore the next day and met the *ulama*, who taught him the Islamic statement of belief. After his conversion he was installed as king and assumed a new name, Sultan Malik al–Saleh. This mythical story is corroborated by his tombstone at the Samudra–Pasai burial complex. The inscription carved on it states not only the name of the king and the date of his death (1297), but also an exhortation on the temporality of life and the eternity of the world to come. These inscriptions are generally considered to be the earliest Islamic reflections on reality to be found in the Archipelago. The various myths of conversion rarely fail to mention the existence of a kind of network of conversion. A particular centre of power would usually be treated and honoured as the sender of the Islamic message in the myth of conversion of the recipient. For example, it was an *ulama* from Pasai, who was a resident in the compound of the merchants of Pasai in Patani, according to the *Hikayat Patani*, who finally managed to persuade the King of Patani to convert to the Islamic religion. By doing so he would be freed from his incurable disease. In the intricate network of local collective memories, Pasai is treated with much respect by most of the newly emerging Islamic centres of power. The 16th century *Sejarah Melayu* (Malay Annals) relates that Melaka, the biggest entrepot which attracted *ulama* from all over the Islamic world, looked up to Pasai on religious matters. In the tradition of Javanese *wali,* or saints, Pasai is also mentioned as a centre of learning, as well as the point of embarkation for the Holy Land.

de Bry (1598)

The Conversion of Javanese Rulers

Javanese tradition presents a different picture of conversion to that found in Malay or Makasarese accounts elsewhere. It puts more emphasis on the role of the travelling *maulana,* some of whom were later recognised as *wali*. It is on the one hand a story of how men of religion tried to find social niches in the dominant Hinduistic religious culture and the political hegemony of the Majapahit empire, and, on the other, of the manner in which intellectual encounters took place. While engaging in trade, some of them began to settle and establish religious schools or *pesantren* which, as time went by, managed to attract students from the surrounding areas. Such is the story of Malik Ibrahim, later to be remembered as the Sunan Giri, after his place of burial, who was an important trader, an influential teacher, and a local ruler. Another *wali* who played the same role was Sunan Gunung Jati in Cirebon. He was the conqueror of the Hindu kingdom of Pajajaran, in West Java, founder of the sultanate of Banten, and victor against the Portuguese in the struggle for control of present day Jakarta.

Kraton and Pesantren

It was an alliance of the Islamic principalities, under the spiritual leadership of Sunan Kudus, the 'ruling–priest' of Kudus, that finally conquered the empire of Majapahit in the early 16th century. Demak emerged as the new hegemonic power. The hegemony of Islamic maritime power, however, did not last long. In the early 17th century Mataram, an agrarian kingdom, became the dominant power. The close relationship between the mosque and its *pesantren*, the market, and the *kraton* (palace) may have given birth to the dynamic and cosmopolitan *pesisir* (coastal) culture, but it was the same political culture that made Java a special case in the history of Islamic kingship in Southeast Asia. The *pesantren* was not only a religious school, as the stories of the *wali* show, it was also potentially a small political centre. In the Javanese concentric political system, whereby the central *kraton* was surrounded by smaller ones, the *pesantren* could also be regarded as a potential challenger to the centre. Since the emergence of Mataram, the *kraton* and the *pesantren*, or the ideas they respectively upheld, have been engaged in an unending dialogue in their search for a harmonious cosmic order.

Islamic Kingship

The testimony of the 14th century Arab traveller, Ibn Batuta, on the Sultanate of Samudra–Pasai, about the sultan who made war on the heathen population and who regularly discussed Islamic doctrine with foreign–born religious scholars, is a very familiar picture in the tradition of Islamic kingship in the Indonesian Archipelago. The ability to attract religious scholars and the willingness to send religious preachers were usually taken as signs of the sultan's wealth and power. The divergent types of cultural encounters that preceded the foundation of the sultanates may determine the nature of their political traditions, but they shared similar ideas of what Islamic kingship should be. It was conceived to be a sacred institution based on a patterned person–to–person relationship between individuals. As such it should be ruled by a proper person, who was supposed to have certain noble qualities. Having a just ruler, wise judges (*kadhi*), honest ministers and loyal subjects were the core ideals of any kingship. Most sultanates perceived the ruler as being 'the leader of the Muslims' or 'the shadow of God on earth', and hence as the peak of both religious and political authorities. The ideal king was, as Syaikh Nuruddin ar Raniri, the great 17th century scholar, describes Sultan Iskandar Muda of Aceh in his encyclopaedia Bustan-us-Salatin, one who 'built the (central) mosque, and several mosques in every town, ...enforced Islam by ordering people to pray five times a day, to fast during the Ramadhan month and to perform *sunnat* [recommended] fasting, and by forbidding them to drink *arak* (alcohol) and to gamble'.

The dynamic Islamic sultanates of the 16th to 18th centuries were, however, structurally weak. They were very much dependent on the personalities and the abilities of their respective rulers to control the competing elites. Moreover, these sultanates lived in unstable relations with their neighbours, whether these were the hierarchic relations of suzerain and vassal, an alliance, or a state of enmity. When western commercial powers posed unprecedented challenges, the existing political system simply failed to function properly.

HIKAYAT RAJA RAJA PASAI

This is the oldest known history written in the Malay language. Believed to have been composed in the 15th century, it relates the coming of Islam to the now–vanished kingdom of Pasai on the north coast of Sumatra. This manuscript (OR.14350, ff. 45r–46r), now in the British Library, is the oldest known example of a manuscript written in the Malay language. It was probably copied from an older text in Semarang in 1797.

The Governor of Banten (centre) in council with the kadhi (wise judges) (left) in 1596, from Begin Ende Voortgangh *(Amsterdam, 1645–6), by Issac Commelin.*

The Wali Sanga: Apostles of Java

*A*ny reconstruction of the early history of Islam in Java, before 1600, has to cope with a paucity of concrete evidence and the prominence of semi-legendary pious traditions which have grown up around the so-called 'nine apostles' (Wali Sanga), most of whom are associated with particular revered graves — holy (keramat) places. These traditions give the wali the primary role in the spread of Islam along the north coast (pesisir) from Gresik to Demak to Cirebon and Banten, through a mixture of inner strength, miraculous powers, and warfare.

The tomb of Sunan Giri near Gresik, East Java.

Carved white stone screen surrounding tomb of Sunan Kudus who was the defender of the kingdom of Demak.

One of the guardians responsible for the care of the tomb of Sunan Gunung Jati, outside the town of Cirebon.

The Mesjid Agung of Demak, reputedly built at the behest of the walis in the 16th century.

The Wali

A coalition of these *wali*, led by Raden Patah, King of Demak, is also usually said to be responsible for the military defeat and destruction of Hindu Majapahit in the Javanese year 1400 (1478), though 1527 is now believed by historians a more likely date for the end of the Majapahit kingdom.

The word *wali* comes from the Arabic and has wide currency throughout the Islamic world. It is usually translated as 'saint'. In the Javanese case, one might also think of the *wali* as 'apostles', since the famous *Wali Sanga* or nine *wali* are regarded as the principal agents of Java's conversion to Islam. Their careers span the 15th and 16th centuries.

In his comparison of Javanese and Moroccan styles of Islam, the famous anthropologist Clifford Geertz uses the figure of one of the most important *wali*, Sunan Kalijaga, to personify significant continuities and congruences with pre-Islamic cultural and intellectual preferences, seeing him as a man of meditation and contemplation, indifferent to the material world and exemplifying a representation of the old Yogic tradition. But the careers of the *wali*, though known only in broad outline, were generally characterised by a good deal of engagement with the world, and indeed often led to the foundation of

hereditary political dynasties. Even the 'unworldly' Sunan Kalijaga founded such a dynasty at Adilangu or Kadilangu near Demak, which maintained a semi-independent status as late as the first half of the 19th century.

In Java, of course, a period of withdrawal from the world to meditate and undertake asceticism, such as was undertaken by Sunan Kalijaga, is often seen as a prelude to the acquisition of power upon returning. The expansion of the politico-military power of the Sultanate of Demak in the first half of the 16th century was associated with another famous *wali*, Sunan Gunung Jati, who was also involved in the foundation of two major sultanates in Northwest Java, Banten and Cirebon, which continued to exist for centuries after the end of Demak's existence as an independent state. Sunan Gunung Jati is buried in a royal cemetery five kilometres north of Cirebon, and his grave, like those of the other *wali*, such as Sunan Muria, buried on Mount Muria near Kudus, is a major place of pilgrimage. *Wali*, in Java as in other parts of the Islamic world, are widely believed (despite the questionable theology associated with this belief) to possess *baraka, (or berkah* in the Javanese rendering), meaning 'blessings', which can be obtained from their tombs.

Giri and Kudus

The town of Giri, near Gresik in East Java, also a major place of pilgrimage, was founded by another famous *wali*, Sunan Giri, and was

a centre for the promulgation of Islam to Lombok, Sulawesi, Kalimantan, Maluku and Ternate. The *Babad Tanah Jawi,* the oldest Javanese document recounting the *walis'* lives relates how, when Giri was attacked by the armies of Majapahit, the last great pre-Islamic kingdom, Sunan Giri happened to be writing. On hearing the news of the Majapahit attack he threw down his pen and prayed to God for succour. His pen was turned into a kris which without human agency attacked and routed the Majapahit troops. This story illustrates well both the spiritual and the worldly potency of the *wali*. Giri occupies an important place in the Javanese tradition; the main figure of the well-known Serat Centini, Sheikh Among Raga, is a descendant of the Giri *wali* dynasty, and his name harks back to pre-Islamic religious beliefs.

Giri and Kudus on the north coast and Tembayat in Central Java continued as small states ruled by the descendants of *wali* until they were extinguished by the rising power of Mataram, founded by Senapati, whose grave at Kota Gede near Yogyakarta is a place of pilgrimage. Under Mataram's famous ruler, Agung (1613-1646), the kingdom expanded rapidly conquering Tuban, Gresik, Surabaya and Pasuruan in an attempt to dominate coastal trade. Though Agung introduced the Javanese Islamic calendar and obtained the title of sultan from Mecca, he and his successors would not brook any challenges from independent *wali* dynasties. Such challenges could be formidable, as in the involvement of the revered Pangeran Rama of Kajoran, a member of the Tembayat line, in the rebellion of the 1670s associated with the Madurese prince Trunajaya. Tembayat was the last *wali* foundation to be conquered by Mataram, in 1719, but like the *wali* families of Kudus and Giri, the Tembayat family also married into the Mataram royal house, being incorporated into the right-hand branch of the dynastic genealogy. The Mataram court sent offerings to the burial-places of *wali*, and to places associated with strong pre-Islamic Javanese beliefs, such as the south coast, where the *labuhan* to Lara Kidul is made, and Mount Lawu, associated with Sunan Lawu. Dipanagara claims in his autobiography that his decision to lead the Java War was influenced by the appearance to him of both Sunan Kalijaga and Nyai Lara Kidul.

Syncretism

In 1964 Mangaradja Parlindungan's controversial book *Tuanku Rao* presented in modern Indonesian (laced with English and other languages) what purported to be a lost Peranakan Chinese chronicle of the rise of Muslim power in Java, which claimed that some of the *wali* as well as other early Muslim rulers were Muslim Chinese some of whose ancestors had been associated with the Zheng He voyages. Some scholars were impressed at the confirmation this brought to other fragmentary evidence, though doubts remained about the source's authenticity. Meanwhile some Indonesian Muslim leaders reacted with outrage, the colonial period having produced a sense of polarisation whereby Islam and Chineseness were seen as antithetic to each other, so that Parlindungan's evidence was interpreted as a slight upon Islam. Whether or not Parlindungan's new evidence is accepted, there is no doubt that there was a very strong Chinese input to the *pesisir* in this period and in succeeding centuries, as may be seen in the architecture, such as the Sam Po Kong or 'Gedung Batu' complex at Semarang, with its syncretism of Chinese and Javanese cult figures, or the mosques of Cirebon and Madura, the principal mosque of Sumenep being perhaps the most strikingly Chinese in form. The coastal towns also had connections with other parts of present-day Indonesia and Southeast Asia, such as Palembang and Champa, both of which are associated with the Islamisation of Java.

Another famous figure included in some lists of *wali* is Sheikh Siti Jenar, who is known for taking the position of the 10th century Persian mystic al-Halla, that is, that it is possible for humans to achieve identity with God. Just as was al-Hallaj, Siti Jenar was also sentenced to death, in this case by a synod of the other *wali*. However, the Babad account of supernatural occurrences associated with his death suggests that its author felt some sympathy for Siti Jenar's claims. The *wali* have remained powerful exemplars in all succeeding centuries through numerous representations of their lives and teachings, first in manuscript and subsequently in print and even film.

The tomb complex of Sunan Bayat at Klaten. The split gateways (candi bentar) are an architectural legacy of Indonesia's pre-Islamic era.

⌐⌐ *The tombstone of one of the associates of Sunan Gunung Jati, near Cirebon.*

Soko Tunggal: a three-branched tree trunk that supported the original structure of Sunan Bonang's tomb. The detail is a carved motif of an ascetic's dwelling on a mountain. Early wali portrayed themselves as ascetics who were associated with mountain meditation spots. Their tombs are often in such locations.

Portuguese and Spanish Influence

*T*he Portuguese and Spanish legacy is still evident in maps, not only in geographical names such as Flores and New Guinea, but also in lusitanised and hispanicised versions and spellings of indigenous toponyms like Borneo, Celebes, Seram, Makasar, Manado, Sumatra, Ternate, Tidore, and Timor.

Gateway to the Portuguese fort at Melaka. From the Journal of a Voyage in 1811-1812, *engraved by J. Clarke, (1814).*

➶ *A Topaz and his wife as sketched by Johan Nieuhof in Batavia in the 1650s. In Batavia these Portuguese-speaking 'Topaz' were converted to Calvinism and tended to assimilate to the larger category of Mardijkers (from* merdeka *or free), the freed Christianised former slaves of Europeans.*

➵➵*A 16th century Portuguese ship.*

The assault and capture of Tidore fortress and two Portuguese ships by the Dutch, de Bry (1606).

Portuguese Expansion

For the Indonesian Archipelago the colonial period began in 1511 after the Portuguese capture of Melaka. The Portuguese advance was indeed very rapid. Following Vasco da Gama's first Indian landfall in 1498, they quickly established forts all around the Indian Ocean.

Soon after the conquest of Melaka, ships were sent to Maluku where they were allowed by the Sultan of Ternate to build a *feitoria (factory)* which later became a fortress.

Indonesian rivalries and political fragmentation contributed to the early Portuguese victories, but much had to do also with superior technology in shipbuilding and naval warfare. As a rule Asian trading vessels had been unarmed, and it was the first time the local population were confronted with *Feringgi* (Franks, as Europeans were known at the time) who demanded monopoly rights with the force of arms.

After the fall of Melaka, however, local rulers improved on their inadequate warships and weaponry, and in time they succeeded in developing their fighting capabilities at sea, sometimes helped by Portuguese renegades. In the 1520s an Islamic counter-offensive began, and although Melaka remained in Portuguese hands until conquered by the Dutch VOC in 1641, further Portuguese expansion came to a halt. Portuguese Melaka, to a certain extent, had a flourishing market, but it never could control the Archipelago's trade and shipping. Aceh and Johor in particular became serious competitors, and further south the sultanate of Banten was growing in importance.

Likewise, in the eastern region the Portuguese scored initial success in Maluku by acquiring monopoly rights from the Sultan of Ternate for the trade in spices. Their presence strength-ened the position of the sultan, especially over his chief rival, Tidore. With superior Portuguese support Ternate could claim tribute from local rulers. But Portuguese attempts to wrest political supremacy eventually resulted in their expulsion from the area by Sultan Baabullah in 1575.

Spanish Expansion

In 1571 the Spaniards gained a foothold in Manila in their own pursuit of the riches of 'India' by the westward route via the Americas. For much of the 16th century Spain and Portugal had been in dispute about the *Questão das Molucas*, but in 1580 the King of Spain also became King of Portugal, and when the Portuguese were expelled from Ternate and had to withdraw to Ambon, they appealed for help from Manila. Several expeditions sent by the Spaniards to Ternate failed. However, in 1606 they managed to occupy and rebuild the old Portuguese fortress now locally known as Kastela (from Castile).

The Spaniards had to maintain a precarious existence as the Sultan of Ternate was backed by the VOC who had arrived in 1599. When in 1663 the Spaniards abandoned their fort in Ternate, the only settlement remaining was in Siau (held since 1624) in the Sangir Archipelago. Since the Dutch were bound by treaty with Spain, the conquest of Siau was accomplished by the Sultan of Ternate with VOC support, '...in such a manner that peace be maintained between the Netherlands and Spain, except, when the Castilians desire the contrary...'. In November 1677 the island was taken, and the Spaniards left for Manila.

Trade

The main attraction for Portuguese and Spanish expeditions to the Archipelago was trade. Maluku produced cloves and nutmegs, while Solor and Timor had sandalwood. Trade with the Solor and Timor

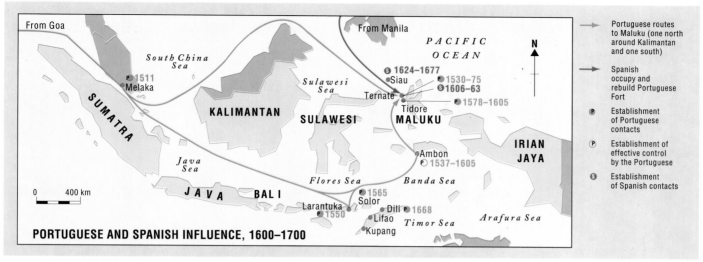

PORTUGUESE AND SPANISH INFLUENCE, 1600–1700

Legend:
- Portuguese routes to Maluku (one north around Kalimantan and one south)
- Spanish occupy and rebuild Portuguese Fort
- Ⓟ Establishment of Portuguese contacts
- Ⓟ Establishment of effective control by the Portuguese
- Ⓢ Establishment of Spanish contacts

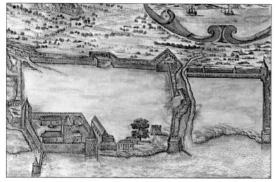

region was conducted by *casados*, married Portuguese settlers from whom many mestizo communities in the region arose. In the course of time a special community was born, the Tupassi (*Topaz*), or 'Black Portuguese' in Dutch sources. They were also known as 'Larantuqueiros' — people from Larantuka on the east coast of Flores where they had gathered since 1600. Earlier, the most important settlement was around the fortress which the Dominican priests had built on the island of Solor in 1566. However, the Topaz were often at odds with the Dominicans, and soon they developed their own political organisation based at Larantuka. William Dampier who visited the Topaz settlement in Lifao on the north coast of Timor (1699), reported that they were '...a sort of Indians, of a copper-colour, with black lank hair. They speak Portuguese, and are of the Romish religion, but they take the liberty to eat flesh when they please. They value themselves on the account of their religion and descent from the Portuguese; and would be very angry if a man should say they are not Portuguese...'.

Power lay in the hands of two families: Da Costa and d'Hornay, the latter descendants from a VOC deserter. Even after the Portuguese government finally included Solor and Timor in the *Estado da India* in 1702, the Larantuqueiros were the virtual masters of the area. In fact Topaz pressure became so serious that the Portuguese captain-general had to leave Lifao and find shelter further east at Dili (1769).

Meanwhile, both the Topaz and the Portuguese had to face the Dutch who had also been attracted by the sandalwood trade. The Dominican fort in Solor

was taken by the VOC. In 1653 the Dutch had established themselves at Kupang in the western part of Timor. In 1854 a treaty was negotiated (ratified in 1859) whereby the Dutch gained sovereignty over the Larantuqueiros in exchange for 200,000 guilders and Dutch recognition of the Portuguese colony in east Timor.

Missionaries

Much has been written about Iberian activities in converting the people of occupied territories. According to C. R. Boxer, 'If trade followed the flag in the British empire, the missionary was close behind the merchant in the Portuguese empire'. However, in Indonesia it was not until three decades later that serious efforts were made in this respect, especially with the arrival of Jesuits, the most famous among them St. Francis Xavier who arrived in Ambon in 1546. The Dominicans claimed to have converted about 100,000 people in the Solor area, but when the VOC took over their fort in 1613 they counted only 2,450 Catholic families. Many Catholic families in Maluku and Siau, however, left with the Spaniards for the Philippines, while those who remained had to 'reform' to Protestantism by order of the VOC officials. Only in the second half of the 19th century did liberal governments in the Netherlands allow Catholic missionaries to work in the Archipelago, and the flourishing Christian communities of Flores and neighbouring islands were more a product of Dutch prosetylisation as a consequence of this policy.

More widespread than Portuguese rule and Catholicism was the use of the Portuguese language. Indeed, until well into the 18th century, Portuguese in its local variety, became the *lingua franca* alongside Malay.

« *The Spanish Fort of Gamma Lama on Ternate (Argensola, 1706).*

⩗ *The Portuguese church in old Batavia owed its name to the sermons held in Portuguese and is a living testimony of Iberian involvement in the area during the 16th and 17th centuries (Heydt, 1744).*

The Dutch had the better of their battles against their Spanish and Portuguese rivals. This scene shows the battle with the Spanish fleet of 28 ships. The battle resulted in a victory for the Dutch in January 1602, by Van der Aa.

Crescent and Cross in Global Conflict

*O*ne of the reasons Islam and Christianity became great rivals in 16th century Indonesia was that they had much in common. Whereas the Indian religions (Hinduism and Buddhism) had mingled with each other and with local beliefs, the 'religions of the book' drew clearer lines between who was within the faith and who was outside. Their contest for the loyalties of Indonesians transformed the religious landscape of the Archipelago.

❶ *Sultan Suleyman receiving a visitor.*

❷ *Sultan Suleyman with his troops at the Battle of Mohacs.*

❸ *Sultan Suleyman. Sultan of the Ottoman Empire from 1520 to 1566, who undertook bold military campaigns that enlarged his realm. His fleet also made contacts with the Acehnese.*

Anti-Portuguese Drive

Portugal and Spain forged their national identities by crusading against the 'Moros' (Moroccan Muslims) who had built an Islamic civilisation in Andalusia, in Spain. Their discovery of sea routes to Southeast Asia was a continuation of that long crusade. By taking the spice trade to Europe, and out of the hands of the Muslims, they hoped to go on serving God (as they saw it) and themselves at the same time. They would also strike a blow in the vulnerable rear of Ottoman Turkey, which had emerged as the great Muslim threat to Catholic Europe.

Portuguese attacks on Muslim shipping and ports in the Melaka Straits and surrounding waters led to a coalition among the different sultanates in the region who united to repel the Christian threat. The establishment of the aggressively anti-Portuguese sultanates of Aceh (North Sumatra) and Banten (West Java) in the 1520s was a direct response to Portuguese attempts to dominate the weaker small ports in these regions. In Maluku, where the Portuguese pioneers of 1512 were warmly welcomed as allies in the frequent, petty wars of the region, the conflicts between rival federations of villages gradually assumed the character of religious wars between supporters of the Portuguese, who often became Catholic, and supporters of the Malay and Javanese traders, who just as frequently became Muslim. An Ambonese Muslim account, the *Hikayat Tanah Hitu,* described how 'After some time quarrels arose, and we fought with them. We attacked each other, overcame each other as if there would be no end to the holy war'.

New Pepper Route

Muslim merchants shifted their trade to the stronger sultanates where they could be protected against the Portuguese. Instead of the older trading system which had carried pepper and cloves in stages from Maluku, through coastal Java, Melaka, and India to Arabia and Egypt, Muslim shippers by the 1530s had developed a route avoiding the Portuguese strongholds of Melaka and Cochin on the coast of India. They took spices to Banten and then along the west coast of Sumatra to Aceh. From there large Gujarati, Arab and Aceh vessels crossed the Indian Ocean directly to the Red Sea. By the 1560s Aceh pepper ships were bringing more pepper to Egypt and Arabia than the Portuguese were to Europe, and Turkey sent out several military missions to help Aceh in its wars against Portuguese occupied Melaka.

TURKISH HELP FOR 'A MEASURE OF PEPPER'

When a large Dutch force succeeded in conquering the royal palace of Aceh in 1874, they found there an enormous shattered cannon decorated with a Turkish star motif. Venerated as *Lada Secupak* (a measure of pepper), this cannon had for three centuries symbolised Aceh's special link with Turkey.

Popular stories in Aceh associated this name with a mission sent to Turkey with three shiploads of pepper, supplies, and money for the support of the Islamic holy places. But the envoys had such difficulty reaching Istanbul and gaining access to the sultan that they had to consume or sell all this themselves, so that only a small bamboo measure of pepper remained. When this was apologetically offered to the Khalif, he graciously honoured the envoys and sent them back to Aceh, according to the stories, with the great cannon warriors and gunsmiths.

Though legendary in Aceh, this mission is well documented in Turkish. Portuguese and Venetian sources, as well as Raniri's Malay *Bustan al–Salatin.* After the Ottomans had conquered Egypt (1517), they become protectors of both the holy cities of Mecca and Medina and the Indian Ocean spice route. The first Turkish fleet was sent into the Indian Ocean to combat the Portuguese in 1538, and contacts were made with Aceh's crusading Sultan Al'ad–din Ri'ayat Shah al–Kahar (1537–71). In 1566, probably not for the first time, al–Kahar sent an embassy to Istanbul to plead for military help, complaining that the Portuguese had sunk pilgrim ships taking Muslims to Mecca. Some Turkish ships, cannon, gunsmiths and soldiers were certainly sent to Aceh in 1568, and played a role in Acehnese attacks on Portuguese Melaka in 1568 and 1570.

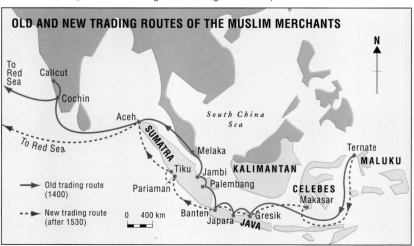

OLD AND NEW TRADING ROUTES OF THE MUSLIM MERCHANTS

To Red Sea — Calicut — Cochin — Aceh — To Red Sea — Tiku — Pariaman — *SUMATRA* — Melaka — Jambi — Palembang — *KALIMANTAN* — *South China Sea* — Ternate *MALUKU* — *CELEBES* — Makasar — Banten — Japara — *JAVA* — Gresik

→ Old trading route (1400)

--▶ New trading route (after 1530)

0   400 km

Muslim–Christian Rivalry

The global conflict between the forces of Islam led by Turkey and those of Catholicism led by Hapsburg Spain reached its peak in the late 16th century both in Southeast Asia and in the Mediterranean. With help from a varied group of other Muslims, Aceh frequently laid siege to Portuguese Melaka. This crusading mentality on both sides transformed Southeast Asian kings who happened to be Muslims into sultans for whom Islam was the principal test of loyalty. Internally too they sought to ensure Islamic observance, since non-Muslims were perceived as potential allies of the Portuguese enemy. All over the Archipelago sharper lines began to be drawn between Islam and its enemies. In Maluku, unprovoked Portuguese brutality in murdering their erstwhile ally Sultan Hairun of Ternate in 1570 galvanised an unprecedented united Muslim counterattack under Hairun's son Babullah. In south Sulawesi the long flirtation of the Makasarese elite with both Islam and Christianity had to be resolved and Islam was formally adopted in 1603.

The rise of Dutch naval power after 1600 ended this Muslim–Christian polarisation, as the Europeans now fought each other more implacably than they fought the Muslims. Moreover, the Muslim shipping line between Aceh and the Arabian ports ended in the 1620s, and Turkey became only a memory. Pan–Islamic solidarity would not again be so important until the late 19th century. The brief period of intense Muslim–Christian rivalry nevertheless galvanised the major Archipelago states to a high point of Islamic self-awareness and observance.

A number of Indonesian rulers or their sons made the pilgrimage to Mecca — all had learned Muslim *ulama* at their courts, and many patronised elaborate processions for Islamic feasts such as Idh al-Adh. In Aceh throughout the first half of the 17th century,

SAINT FRANCIS XAVIER

Despite their militant stance against Islam, the Portuguese did little positively to propagate Christianity in Indonesia, except among their local born wives and children. Only with the arrival in 1545 of Francis Xavier (1506–52), a Spanish Basque who was one of the five original founders of the Society of Jesus–better known as the Jesuits, the intellectual arm of the Catholic counter-reformation— did this change. Francis was the first and greatest of the Jesuit missionaries in Asia, and laid the foundation of Indonesian, as well as Japanese and Sri Lankan, Christianity. He spent several months in Melaka in 1545 preparing himself for a mission to Makasar (South Sulawesi), and there translated into Malay the principal Catholic prayers and commandments. Instead of Makasar he went to Maluku, where he drew thousands to Christianity in Ambon, Ternate and Morotai by his heroic devotion. He also brought Christianity to Japan, and died attempting to do the same in China. The Saint's many miracles became legendary (though he made no reference to them himself). On one occasion in Maluku he was reported to have calmed a tumultous sea by holding the crucifix, but then lost it in the water. Sometime later a crab appeared on the beach holding the crucifix aloft to present to Xavier. In 1547 he was back in Melaka which was threatened by a combined assault from Aceh and Johor. Saint Francis is said to have galvanised the defence, and then prophesied correctly the victory of a small Melakan fleet which sailed north to confront the attacking Muslims.

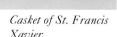

Casket of St. Francis Xavier.

and in Banten under Sultan Ageng (1651-82), there was an Islamic court imposing *shari'a* penalties for theft and adultery. The extreme example of the self-consciously Muslim ruler was Sultan Iskandar Thani of Aceh (1637-41). With the Gujarati born scholar Nuruddin ar-Raniri at his side, he imposed a complete *shari'a* system, banned Chinese traders from Aceh, executed dozens of Portuguese who refused to embrace Islam, and condemned to death for apostasy (*murtad*) those supporters of the mystical ideas of Hamzah Fansuri and Syamsuddin whom Raniri judged heretical.

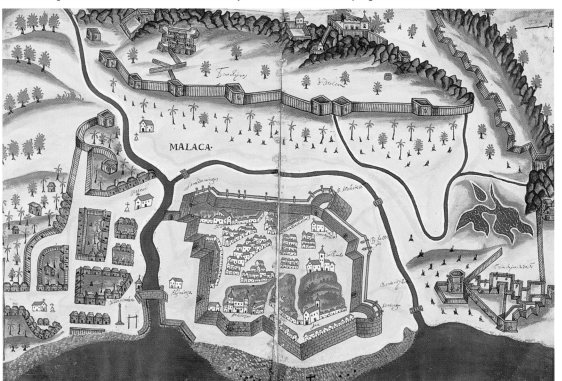

The Acehnese seige of Portuguese Melaka in 1629. The illustration (British Library MS 197 f. 382) shows the stockades and artillery dominating the Portuguese fort. Sultan Iskandar Muda of Aceh had despatched 'the finest fleet that had ever been seen in Asia, full of great and small cannon'. It was made up of 20,000 men and 236 vessels. Although they besieged the fort for three months by land, erecting stockades and cannon, they were unable to prevent the supply of the city by sea. With the arrival of a large Portuguese fleet, the siege was lifted.

Women and the World of Commerce

Women in Indonesia have traditionally enjoyed a relatively high status, and from early times played an important role in the economy. This was reinforced by a generally bilateral kinship system that encouraged female inheritance, and by the male–female complementarity that lay behind much of indigenous ritual.

Women and Agriculture

Women's opportunities lessened as the economy became more commercialised from the late 18th century, but their prominence in small trading and marketing is still a feature of Indonesian society.

One of the reasons for the economic independence of Indonesian women has been their role as horticulturists. Furthermore, in a number of Indonesian societies, such as Minangkabau in central Sumatra, land was inherited through the female line. Female labour was also essential in rice production, a staple food through most of Indonesia. Women were responsible for planting the seeds in holes in dry-rice plots, and in raising and transplanting the seedlings in wet rice fields. Weeding was similarly considered to be a female task. When the rice ripened, they were the principal harvesters; the separation of padi from the husk was likewise women's work. Furthermore, women were prominent in the fertility rituals associated with rice production because the spirit of rice is believed to be female. In addition to rice, women grew other food crops such as vegetables which were either consumed by the family or else exchanged in the market.

In a number of areas, notably eastern Indonesia, wild sago remained the most important food item. As with rice, legends frequently link women and sago together. In western Indonesia, on the island of Siberut, off West Sumatra, the original sago tree was believed to be the reincarnation of a young girl. The harvesting of sago was carried out by men but the conversion of the pith into food demanded particular skills which were the preserve of women. In eastern Indonesia these skills were intimately involved with commercial life because baked biscuits made of sago were a major exchange item.

By the end of the 18th century the beginnings of a plantation economy under Dutch auspices was apparent in Java, Sumatra, and Kalimantan. Previously, Indonesian villagers had grown cash crops for the market in

A woman market trader, by C.W. Mieling after van Pers, Nederlandsch Oost-Indie Typen (The Hague 1853-62)

A woman doing business with an Indian trader. From J. Nieuhof's Remarkable Voyages and Travels to the East Indies 1653-1670, compiled by A. Churchill (1732).

FEMALE ATTENDANTS

In several courts female attendants, sometimes carrying arms, were responsible for performing duties within the palace. Some gained a privileged position in relation to the ruler, which allowed them to demand gifts in return for favours and thus amass considerable wealth.

de Bry, 1598

Women weavers in Java. From The Illustrated London News, *1875.*

small plots or gardens, where women, children and other family members performed essential duties. But larger plantations, developed during the late 18th century, tended to accord a more dominant role to male labour. Pepper and gambier production, for example, was increasingly the preserve of Chinese males or Indonesian men who often moved to other districts to work seasonally as hired labour.

Women as Traders

Indonesian women are expected to be shrewd traders and thrifty housewives, and when Europeans first arrived in the region they commented that it was the women who were most obvious in small scale trading. Indonesian men generally entrusted the management of the household economy to their wives, and women usually had their own income because they sold poultry, food or garden products in the market as well as medicines they had made from native plants.

Because of the commercial importance of women, it was common for a foreign trader, particularly a Chinese, to negotiate a local marriage. His wife could then assist him in his business matters. Should he decide to leave the country, the relationship could be ended without animosity. Indeed, marriage relationships were traditionally easily dissolved, primarily because women had access to independent sources of income. When a merchant died his business could be continued by his wife; widows could also assume their husband's commercial position, and are occasionally mentioned as holding the position of syahbandar, responsible for overseeing port commerce and collecting duties. Although long distance and high capital trade was generally dominated by men, high ranking females could participate, often using male agents. In a number of courts, queens and noble ladies were heavily involved in commercial activities, often sending their own vessels overseas to trade. The

royal women in Javanese courts, for instance, frequently accumulated large fortunes because of generous court stipends and gifts from those seeking their favour.

Women and the Textile Trade

An important female activity was the production of a range of items which could be used by the family but also sold to augment the household income. Of these activities, probably the most significant was weaving. Cloth played a vital role in many rituals, and in most communities specific textile designs and weaving techniques helped confirm a sense of group identity. In some areas women made barkcloth for everyday wear by beating the bast of certain trees. Some groups decorated their cloth with elaborate beadwork and embroidery. Despite the imports of cheap Indian cloth, trade in local textiles expanded during the 17th and 18th centuries.

Women were also largely responsible for the expansion of Javanese batik making that occurred during this period. Most of this work was cottage industry production, but some entrepreneurs may have been developing small workshops. In Banten around 1600, for example, women slaves were weaving for the market. The royal palaces were also sponsors of female activities; in the early 18th century it was said that there were 4,000 females involved in spinning, weaving, batik manufacture and embroidery in the central Javanese court of Mataram.

One of the most important female tasks was the husking of rice. This illustration shows a Javanese woman standing beside her lesung (pounding log), with the alu or pestle nearby.

A woman trader selling toys, by C.W. Mieling after Auguste van Pers, Nederlandsch Oost-Indie Typen (The Hague, 1853-62).

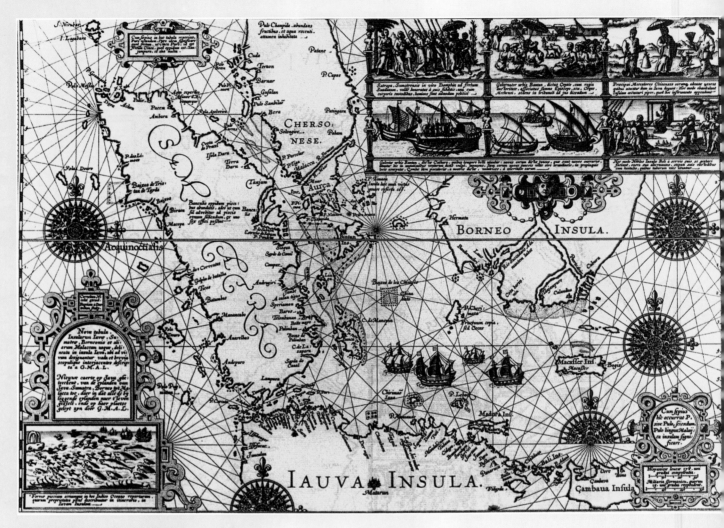

THE FIRST EUROPEAN IMAGES OF INDONESIA

Maps and visual images of the Indonesian Archipelago were both scarce and fantastic until the Dutch voyages of around 1600. Scarcely any graphic images (though plenty of statues and bas-reliefs) have survived from Indonesia itself before the 19th century, while the images appearing in early European and Chinese sources are almost entirely fantastic. The Portuguese were anxious to keep their discoveries as secret as possible, and therefore gave Europe as little in the 16th century by way of maps or engravings of Asia.

The Netherlands, by contrast, was at once the most literate and the most scientifically curious society in Europe, and publishers were quick to circulate accounts of the first Dutch voyages, well-illustrated with lavish engravings. Three different narratives of the first Dutch voyage to Java appeared within two years of its return in 1596. The most influential was the account of Banten and Bali by Lodewycksz, first published in 1598, and republished several times thereafter. The second voyage, which visited Tuban (in Java) and Maluku, was also quickly published. In particular it was the engravings which accompanied these texts which were copied and adapted in a whole series of subsequent publications. The most active publishers in this first phase were the de Bry brothers in Frankfurt, who brought out numerous volumes in Latin, French and German in the first decade of the 17th century. They redid the same limited set of images in a variety of ways, often reversing the original image from left to right.

These images gave Europe then, and modern readers today, a glimpse of the Islamic port-states at their peak — particularly the pepper-port of Banten, the more traditional port of Tuban, and the spice centre of Banda. The map above has grouped six of the images from Willem Lodewycksz's original publication in the top right corner. The coloured versions of these same images that appear on the right, are later copies made the de Bry brothers, and in some cases they are reversals of the originals.

❶ A 'Sumatran chief' who greeted the Dutch at their first landfall in the Bay of Lampung in southernmost Sumatra. He showed them their first pepper-vine (visible at right) and provided information on Banten.

❷ The 'Governor of Banten city, named Chepati (Kiai Patih)', in discussions with the Muslim 'Bishop or Sheikh' who had come to Banten from Mecca. This correctly reflects the unusual situation in Banten at the time, where the powerful merchant-princes governed in the name of the boy-king.

❸ A Chinese merchant and a pepper-buyer are illustrated here. The woman in the centre is the Javanese wife of the Chinese merchant.

❹ A warship belonging to one of the principal men of Banten, said by Lodewycksz to have been constructed in Lasem, a ship-building centre near the teak supplies of Java, on the instructions of a Banten-based Turkish builder.

❺ Four different types of vessel encountered by the Dutch at Banten: a Chinese junk, a large Javanese junk, a Javanese coastal prahu, and a small fishing boat or lighter.

❻ A Balinese noble being carried by his slaves at Gelgel.

ISLAM AND THE PORT-SULTANS

Indonesian states were at their most powerful in the period 1570-1650, just before their fall. The states which arose with the trade boom of the 'long 16th century' and reached their peak in the early 17th century, had common sources of strength. Their capitals were large cities deriving unprecedented wealth through trade; they had new firearms and ships which enabled them to dominate their hinterlands; and a new Islamic concept of the state overcame the sacred sanctions of local spirits.

These trade based states began as cosmopolitan Muslim ports, initially paying tribute to Majapahit or other powers providing a congenial basis for the rising trade. Chinese diplomatic activity of the Yongle emperor (1402-24) brought a lively system of East Asian trade and tribute into being, in which Archipelago based Chinese, often Muslim, played a leading role. Pasai, Pidië, Barus and Palembang in Sumatra, Gresik, Tuban, Jepara, Demak and Sunda Kelapa in Java, and Ternate and Banda in Maluku all became vigorous trade centres of very mixed ethnic origin in the 15th century. These populations gradually became Indonesianised as the dynamic commercial and political elite of the new period. Gradually the Islamic port states such as Demak, Aceh, Banten and Gowa obtained the upper hand against the older Hindu-Buddhist polities. During the period 1500-1650 it was these maritime city-states which dominated the affairs of the Archipelago.

The high point of most of these states was in the second half of that period, when a huge influx of Japanese and American silver fuelled the world's demand for Indonesian pepper and spices. Large populous cities such as Aceh, Banten and Makasar became the scene of an opulent and creative urban culture, in which foreign ideas, technologies and fashions were eagerly seized upon, translated, adapted or discarded. Islamic ideas were particularly influential, and appear to have reached their most brilliant local expression in this period in literature, theology, architecture and law.

The power of these states was brittle, however, because there was no institutional resolution to the differing interests of the mercantile urban elite (*orang kaya*) and the king. Powerful kings briefly held the system together, usually endangering commerce by concentrating it too much in their own hands. Meanwhile the VOC sought relentlessly to monopolise the life-giving trade by exploiting any moment of internal weakness or division in the Muslim port–states.

Samudra Pasai

*I*n the 13th century Samudra Pasai and Pidië, which lie on the north coast of Sumatra along the Straits of Melaka, became centres of international trade first by exporting silk and later pepper. It is believed that much of the northern Sumatran coast, including Barus on the west coast and Ramni on the northern tip of the island, must have been included in Samudra Pasai's subordinate commercial realm. Though known as Pasai in Malay texts and Portuguese reports, the port was known as Samudra (ocean) by traders from India, and eventually gave its name to the whole island.

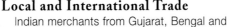

Queen Nahrasiyah, as imagined by a modern Indonesian artist.

Calligraphy of Surat Yasin from the Holy Qur'an on the gravestone of Queen Nahrasiyah, in Samudra Pasai, North Sumatra.

Local and International Trade

Indian merchants from Gujarat, Bengal and South India and traders from Pegu, Siam and Burma mingled in the Melaka Straits ports with merchants from China, Arabia, Persia and Java. Pasai was the dominant port in the 14th century, though challenged by Pidië, while Melaka became dominant in the 15th century.

Trade relationships between Pasai and Java developed extensively. Javanese traders brought rice to Pasai, and from this harbour city they transported pepper to Java. In Samudra Pasai Javanese merchants were privileged by being exempted from export and import duties.

The Portuguese factor, Tome Pires, believed that Pasai exported about 8,000 to 10,000 *bahar* of pepper every year, or 15,000 *bahar* if there was a large harvest. Apart from pepper Pasai also exported silk, camphor and gold from the hinterlands. It is believed that the method of processing silk was introduced to Pasai by Chinese.

Samudra Pasai envoys had been bringing tribute to China since the 13th century. From Chinese sources of the Yuan dynasty (1280-1367) it appears that the King of Samudra sent his envoys to Quilon in West India, in 1282, ten years before Marco Polo arrived in Perlak. Responding to suggestions made by Chinese envoys, Samudra Pasai sent two envoys (named Hassan and Sulaiman) to China. The emperor of China also sent his envoy, Zheng He, to Samudra Pasai in the years 1403, 1414/5 and 1430. In 1405 Zheng He met Tsai-nu-li-a-pi-ting-ki; who was probably Samudra-Pasai's Sultan Zain al-Abidin Malik al Zahir (1383-1405).

Pasai as a Centre of Islam

Between 1290 and 1520 the Pasai Sultanate became not only an important trade city in the Straits of Melaka, but also the centre of the development of Islam and of Malay as a literary language. Besides trading, the Gujarat, Persian and Arabian merchants spread Islam. As described by oral tradition and by the *Hikayat Raja-Raja Pasai*, the Pasai Chronicle, the first king of Samudra Pasai who adhered to Islam was Meurah Silau, who adopted the Islamic title Malik al–Saleh, and died in 1297 AD. A poem in Arabic was chiseled on his tombstone. A free translation is as follows:

1. *Verily the world is perishable*
2. *The world is not eternal*
3. *Verily the world is like a web*
4. *Woven by spiders*
5. *Verily what you achieve in this world will suffice*
6. *People who seek strength*
7. *Life is just a short moment*
8. *All must die*

Through the influence of Pasai a similar poem was carved on the grave of Sultan Mansyur Syah of Melaka, who died in 1477 and also on the grave of Sultan Abdul Jamil of Pahang, who died either in 1511 or 1512.

Islamic Tombstones at Pasai

The most beautiful grave in Samudra Pasai, made of marble, belongs to Queen Nahrasiyah, who died in

GOLD COINS
Samudra Pasai, as an advanced trade harbour, released its own coins made of gold which were called *dirham*. As the trade relationship between Pasai and Melaka thrived after 1400, the Pasai merchants took the opportunity to introduce their gold coinage to Melaka. Morever, the first king of Melaka, Parameswara, established an alliance with Pasai in 1414, adhered to Islam and married the princess of Pasai.

As early as the reign of Sultan Muhammad (1297–1326) Samudra Pasai issued gold coins which were inscribed with features similar to those in the box (right).

OBVERSE	Muhammad Malik al–Zahir
REVERSE	al–sultan al–'adil
DIAMETER	10mm
WEIGHT	0.60 gram
QUALITY	18–20 carats

Source: *J. Hulshoff Pol*, The Gouden Munten van Noord Sumatra, *1929:7.*

All Sultans of Samudra Pasai considered it necessary to carve the phrase al–sultan al–'adil on their *dirhams*. *'Adil*, which means justice, is always hoped for by mankind in the past or at present. The Sultans of Pasai took the phrase from the *Holy Quran*, XVI: 90; 'God commands justice, the doing of good, and liberality to kith and kin, and He forbids all shameful deeds, and injustice …'.

SAMUDRA PASAI AND ISLAMIC INFLUENCE

Pasai's influence as an early Islamic centre spread to all the parts of northern Sumatra, and was eventually absorbed not only into Aceh, but also to the Malayan Peninsula and Java. A sheikh from Pasai is recorded as having converted the ruler of Patani, while Melaka regarded Pasai as its mentor in religion. Tombstones in Melaka and Pahang often bear quotes copied from those in Pasai. One of the greatest sons of Pasai was Sunan Gunung Jati, the founder of Islam in Cirebon, Banten and Jakarta.

1428. Her tombstone is similar to that of Umar ibn Ahmad al–Kazaruni in Cambay, Gujarat, in India, and who died in 1333. It also has some similarities to the grave of Sunan Gresik, Maulana Malik Ibrahim, in east Java. Two other Pasai graves are bedecked with beautiful calligraphy and ornamentation, the first belonging to Prince Abdullah of the dynasty of Abbasiyah, Baghdad, who died in Pasai in 1407, and the second to an Iranian descendant, Na'ina Husam al-Din, who died in 1420.

At the grave of Na'ina Husam al-Din one can find a poem by the famous Persian poet Syaikh Muslih al-Din Sa'di (1193-1292), author of the well known *Gullistan and Bustan*. Written in the Persian language with Arabic characters, this is the only such poem found in Southeast Asia. Besides the carving of a beautiful tree, there is also an inscription from the Qur'an II: 256, known as *Ayat Kursi*, the same as that found on the tombstone of Queen Nahrasiyah.

Sa'di's poem on the tombstone of Na'ina Husam al-Din omits three *baits*, namely the sixth, the seventh and the ninth, which is also the last.

A translation of Muslih al-Din Sa'di's full text is as follows:

1. *Countless years pass over our earth (or: grave), while the water of the spring passes and the zephyr blows.*
2. *This life (five days' period) is (but) a span of human days, why then do others pass over the earth with pride?*
3. *Oh friend! when thou passest by the funeral of a foe, do not rejoice, since even such an event will happen to thee!*
4. *Dust will penetrate into thy bones, oh thou of the impudent eye (i.e. proud one), like a surma-box (a cosmetic box) into which penetrates tutiya (a kind of ungent).*
5. *Whosoever goes over the earth today, (proudly) drawing up his skirt. Tomorrow the dust of his body will evaporate.*
6. *The world is a mean rival and a faithless beloved; when he passes along, at all events leave him alone till he is gone.*
7. *This is the condition of the body that thou seest beneath the earth; whoever comes forth to precious life, whither does he go?*
8. *There is not confidence in the canopy (i.e. protection) of good deeds, Sa'di but goes under the shadow (i.e. protection) of God's grace.*
9. *Oh Lord! do not seize (i.e. punish) a wretched and helpless slave, since from thee groweth generosity and from us emanate errors.*

Pasai's End

Pasai lost its commercial dominance of the Melaka Straits area in the mid-15th century, and was disrupted by the Portuguese in the period 1511-20. Finally it was absorbed into the rising Aceh sultanate in the 1520s. Its heritage of cosmopolitan Islamic civilisation was however continued and developed in Aceh.

Muslih al-Din Sa'di's poem in 12 vignettes on the tombstone of Na'ina Husam al-Din, Samudra Pasai, North Sumatra.

« *The tomb of Malik Ibrahim in Gresik, East Java is dated 1419. The tombstone is believed to have been imported from Cambay, Gujarat, in Northwest India.*

Some of the calligraphy of Surat Yasin and Ayat Kursi carved on the tombstone of Queen Nahrasiyah, in Samudra Pasai, North Sumatra.

Banten: From Pepper Port to Emporium

*T*he western, or Sundanese speaking third of Java has always been distinct from the Javanese speaking remainder. Wet rice agriculture and urban life were both slower to develop there. With the foundation of Islamic Banten by Javanese conquerors, however, west Java became divided between an urban cosmopolitan coast and a lightly-populated and relatively isolated Sundanese interior.

Characters of Banten sketched by the Danish merchant Cortemunde in 1673. An Indian Muslim merchant (left), a Javanese noble, and a Chinese merchant.

The minaret (foreground) and Great Mosque of Banten, first built in the 16th century but often restored.

The New Muslim Dynasty

When the Portuguese arrived, the Sundanese area was loosely held together by the Hindu–Buddhist kingdom of Pajajaran which was centred near modern Bogor. The Portuguese visited only its two ports, Sunda Kelapa (modern Jakarta) and Banten which lies 100 kilometres further west. They made a treaty with these ports in 1522, but when they returned in 1527 they found that Muslim forces from Demak had just taken control and wanted nothing to do with the crusading Christians. A new ruling elite took hold in Banten which was Javanese in language and culture, Sunni Muslim in religion, but cosmopolitan in its ethnic origin and commercial orientation. The founder of this new Muslim dynasty was a Sumatran from Pasai,

who is today revered as the *wali* Sunan Gunung Jati. He placed his son Hasanuddin in charge of Banten, initially as a tributary of Demak, and instructed him to build a new capital at Surosawan, adjacent to the increasingly busy anchorage. Hasanuddin further encouraged pepper growing in west Java and in south Sumatra, and made Banten the leading supplier of pepper to China by about 1550. Information becomes abundant about the town of Banten in 1596, the same year in which its young king Muhammad was killed trying to capture Palembang, and was replaced by another boy king, Abdul Kadir.

Early European Accounts of Banten

The first Dutch expedition under Cornelis de Houtman reached the city in 1596, and several of its members provided accounts of the city's life. Jan Hans Kaerel reported that foreign ships anchoring at Banten needed the permission of the syahbandar, and that to enter the city from the port one had to pass through the toll gate. Banten had a circular wall of brick, and the large mosque (often restored) which still stands, had been constructed near the market. A more detailed map of Banten drawn by the Dutch in the 1630s showed further development.

The fullest account of the life of Banten in 1596 was that of Willem Lodewijcks. He described three markets; the biggest to the east of the town (Karang Antu) where each morning were found 'merchants of all manner of nations, such as Portuguese, Arabs, Chinese, Turks, Kelings, Pegus, Malays, Bengalis, Gujaratis, Malabaris and Abbyssinians, and from all quarters of India'. Lodewijcks described a free wheeling city governed in the interest of commerce in the name of a boy king, Abdul Kadir. In 1609, however, one of the nobility, Prince Ranamanggala, came to power and tried to return to the pattern of state control of commerce familiar in other Indonesian states. In part this shift was a reaction against the excessive liberties taken by the Dutch and English in

the port, and the VOC in particular objected to the controls imposed by the regent. In 1619 Governor General Coen seized the Banten dependency of Jayakarta and made it the VOC headquarters under the name Batavia. A virtual state of war ensued as the Dutch blockaded Banten in an attempt to monopolise pepper supplies. Only with the overthrow of Ranamanggala in favour of King Abdul Kadir in 1624 did relations gradually improve, especially as the VOC and Banten faced a common threat in the rising power of Mataram.

Banten's Prosperity

In 1628 Banten's fortunes looked up when the English decided to establish their major Southeast Asian base in the city, guaranteeing both an outlet for pepper and some security against continuing attempts at blockade by the VOC. Peace with Batavia was agreed in 1639, and the following 40 years marked the high point of Banten's fortunes. In particular, in the years 1660 to 1680, under Sultan Abulfatah Ageng and guided by the capable Chinese syahbandar Kaytsu, Banten surpassed Makasar and Aceh as the greatest non-Dutch port in the Archipelago. English style royal ships were equipped each year for Manila (to obtain the valuable Mexican silver), India, Jeddah, Vietnam, China and Japan.

In 1677, however, war with Batavia broke out again over control of Cirebon. When Sultan Ageng was forced to retreat on that issue, he yielded power to his son, Sultan Haji (1680), who pursued a more peaceful policy with Batavia. The unpopularity and incompetence of his son quickly gave rise to a strong movement to bring the old sultan back, however, and in 1682 Sultan Ageng rode back to the city at the head of a large crowd. In desperation Sultan Haji took refuge in his fortress and sent an appeal for help to the Dutch.

This was the ideal opportunity for the Dutch to take control of their old rival's trading activities. A fleet was quickly sent which rescued Sultan Haji and gradually gained the upper hand for him in the bitter civil war which ensued. Sultan Ageng was forced to capitulate after a year, and died in captivity in Batavia in 1692. A rearguard guerrilla action, in which the famous *ulama* Syeh Yusuf played a prominent part, continued the struggle for several years. But Batavia had won the essential battle for the port, from which they immediately demanded that all foreigners be expelled. Henceforth, they insisted, the VOC would monopolise the pepper trade of Banten, maintaining a garrison in the palace to ensure it was enforced. As a security measure the Dutch tore down the existing fortifications and built their own Fort Speelwijk, which still stands, at the entrance to the harbour.

The Banten kingdom survived for 150 years, but only by following all instructions from the Dutch in Batavia. The city was only a shadow of its former cosmopolitan glory.

The 17th century royal cemetery, at Kenari, the resting place of two of Banten's Sultans; Abulaali (d. 1650), and Abulmafakir (d. 1651).

☞ *Banten, with the palace in the centre, the square before it flanked by the great mosque to the west, and city market to the north.*

THE KI AMUK CANNON
According to legend, this cannon in the square at Banten and whose name means the raging fury, is the male half of a pair of cannon. Its female counterpart, Si Jagur, stands in Fatahila Square, Jakarta. The two cannons were said to have been united during the constant battles between Banten and Batavia during the 17th century, and the prosperity and power of the kingdom of Banten would again be assured the day the two are re-united. There are inscriptions on the cannon. The one illustrated here reads 'There is none victorious but Ali, there is no sword but Dhul-Fakhar (Ali's sword)'.

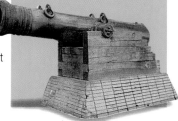

Aceh, between Port and Palace

In the 16th and 17th century Aceh was the leading Southeast Asian base for Muslim traders. But the attempts of its strongest rulers to unite a traditionally divided area, and resist aggressive foreigners conflicted with the needs of trade for security of life and property. After oscillating between tyranny and anarchy, Aceh found a solution to this dilemma in female rule.

An orang kaya, or wealthy merchant, of Aceh. This image was sketched in the 1640s by Peter Mundy.

The royal procession of Sultan Iskandar Thani to the Aceh mosque, for the feast of Idul Adh in 1637, after a sketch by Peter Mundy.

Aceh; the Unification of North Sumatra

Divided by geography and history into a number of rival trading centres, each with its own language according to Marco Polo (1292), the northern (now Acehnese) coast of Sumatra was only united in 1520-24 by the first Aceh Sultan, Ali Mughayat Syah. Clumsy Portuguese intervention in the old pepper exporting entrepots of Pidië and Pasai during the previous decade had so compromised their rulers that even a conqueror from the hitherto small rival port of Lamri (Banda Aceh) was a welcome alternative.

Ala'ad-din Ri'ayat Syah al-Kahar

Aceh quickly became the major base for all those Muslim traders who had to abandon Melaka when it fell to the Portuguese, and who sought to continue the struggle against the infidel intruders. Under the crusading Sultan Ala'ad-din Ri'ayat Syah al-Kahar ('the conqueror', 1539-71) Aceh became the Southeast Asian base for a revived Muslim trading route, which carried Malukan spices and Sumatran pepper to the Red Sea, and thence by caravans to the Mediterranean and Venice. This role brought al-Kahar into contact with the Turkish rulers of Egypt and the holy places, from whom he received cannons, gunsmiths and soldiers for his wars against Portuguese Melaka and its non-Muslim Batak allies in Sumatra. Through these crusades al-Kahar probably retained the support of the wealthy Muslim traders of

THE MERITS OF QUEENS

Although Islamic political doctrine strongly discourages female rule, it was when Muslim states were at their peak that the Archipelago made its most interesting experiments with queens. Pasai, which preceded Aceh as a commercial and Islamic centre in Sumatra, had already put two successive queens on its throne at its most commercially flourishing period (1405-34). Women also presided over the most flourishing periods of Japara, Jambi, Sukadana and Solor, while the Sultanate of Patani on the Peninsula had more than a century of female rule. The first Aceh queen, Taj al-Alam (1641-75), was uniquely qualified as Iskandar Muda's only surviving child and Iskandar Thani's widow. Although foreigners later reported that Aceh had switched to queens in reaction against the tyranny of Iskandar Muda, it is more likely that it was the success of Taj al-Alam's reign which made the *orang kaya* reluctant to go back to the dangerous unpredictablility of male rule. Even the orthodox theologian Raniri conceded that Aceh 'was extremely prosperous at that time, foodstuffs were very cheap, and everybody lived in peace'. Three further queens were raised to the throne after her death, in a deliberate attempt to preserve a regime sympathetic to trade and property. This was an experiment in developing a monarchy which could be both predictable and consensual. The later queens increasingly lacked Taj al-Alam's prestige, however, and encountered growing opposition from forces outside the port-capital and unsympathetic to its needs. In 1699 they secured a letter from Mecca condemning female rule, and succeeded in ending the system.

diverse origins who had made Aceh their home. After his death and that of his son Ali Ri'ayat Syah in 1579, however, there followed a period in which the commercial magnates held the upper hand. Five rulers were dethroned in the space of ten years, often with the approval of 'all the rajas and *ulubalangs*' according to the *Hikayat Aceh*. As the French Admiral Beaulieu described this period in Aceh's memory, 'The *orang kaya* (merchant aristocrats) had beautiful, large, solid houses, with cannons at their doors, and a large number of slaves, both as guards and

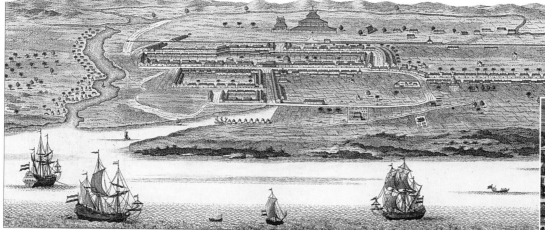

Aceh, from an early 18th century copper engraving by Jacob van der Schley (Haye, 1746–70).

servants.... Such great power very much diminished royal authority, and even safety'.

Sayyid al-Mukammil

This period was ended by another military figure, the *laksamana* or admiral who used his position as guardian of a boy king to seize power himself, and rule as Sultan Ala'ad-din Ri'ayat Syah Sayyid al-Mukammil (1589-1604). He managed to have killed not only his young ward, but most of his potential rivals. As an English visitor reported, 'he ended the lives of more than a thousand Noblemen and Gentlemen, and of the rascall people made new lords'. Al-Mukammil was all the more ready to welcome the English and Dutch who arrived in pursuit of pepper during this reign, because he had so alienated the Asian traders of Aceh.

Iskandar Muda

A similar policy of ruthless centralisation was carried out by his grandson, Sultan Iskandar Muda (1607-36), the strongest of Aceh's rulers. He personally controlled a large proportion of Aceh's pepper trade. But his relentless policy of conquest and monopolisation exhausted the country and alienated even the English and Dutch companies whom he had tried to use against the Gujaratis. He was broken by the defeat of his massive expedition against Portuguese Melaka in 1629.

Iskandar Thani

Having killed potential male heirs, Iskandar Muda was succeeded by his son-in-law, a pious prince of Pahang known as Iskandar Thani (1637-41). Under him and his widow Taj al-Alam Aceh appears to have been at its most peaceful and prosperous, ruled by law rather than royal caprice. Iskandar Thani is renowned especially as the patron of the great orthodox *ulama* Nurud-din ar-Raniri, who encouraged him to impose a *shari'a* system of law, and to execute Muslims he regarded as heretics as well as Portuguese captives who declined to accept Islam. On the other hand the royal garden (Taman Ghairah) built by Iskandar Thani, of which the surviving artificial mountain (*gunungan*) was a feature, embodied elements not only of Islamic mysticism but of Hindu symbolism.

After his patron's death, Raniri was chased from Aceh by a mob seeking revenge for his harsh legalism. Relentless Dutch pressure had succeeded by 1670 in detaching from Acehnese authority both the pepper producing west coast of Sumatra (Padang, Pariaman and Tiku), and the tin producing areas Iskandar Muda had conquered on the Malayan Peninsula. Under the later queens, pressures rose for a style of kingship both more Acehnese and more Islamic. The restoration of male rule in 1699 inaugurated a painful time for Aceh, with the port in decline and civil war endemic.

A Dutch engraver's image of the funeral of Iskandar Thani in 1641.

At the front of the procession (below) are elephants with 'sithes' attached to their tusks, and bearing soldiers with pikes. Behind, elephants carry soldiers with cannon, and others carry archers. These are followed by more elephants, and a squad of soldiers with guns, several men on horseback, and a guard of eunuchs on horses. These flank horsemen carrying pikes from which flags flutter. The sultan, who is leaving his palace, seated in a litter, borne by an elephant and is preceded by fan and umbrella bearers.

Sultan Agung – Epitome of Javanese Kingship

*M*ataram had a brief moment of splendour in the first half of the 17th century, when Sultan Agung (1613-1646) united the Javanese cultural areas of central and east Java on a Javanese-Islamic syncretic base. He lives on in Javanese memory as the greatest source of royal wisdom as well as the model of kingship. But the kingdom he built was both fragile and short-lived.

The Brantas River was a major trade artery up until the 18th century. Long, narrow vessels with oars and sails took rice and cotton down to the port cities, bringing back salt and trade goods. The number of boats plying this waterway was large. In 1709 a prince of Mataram sent 70 vessels to Gresik for trade.

☞ *The layout of the Mataram court at its height around 1650, as observed by Rijklof van Goens, a frequent Dutch envoy to the court.*

Emergence of Mataram

Mataram re-emerged into the historical scene in the second half of the 16th century. According to Javanese chronicles, the region around modern Yogyakarta, which in its heyday had witnessed the foundation of the great stupa Borobudur and the magnificent temple of Prambanan, was desolate when a certain village elder called Pamanahan settled there in the 1570s as a vassal of the King of Pajang (near modern Solo). This signalled the beginning of Mataram's supremacy. After Pamanahan's death his son refused to pay homage to the King of Pajang, and in the confrontation that ensued he finally defeated Pajang in 1587 leading the way to supremacy in the region. He embarked on an expansion of his power, first to the north coast (capturing Demak and the surrounding districts), then to the east, challenging Surabaya's supremacy in east Java with his conquest of Madiun and Kediri.

After only a short reign (he died in 1601) he had transformed Mataram from an insignificant vassal into a major power, equal to, if not surpassing, the more established ones, Surabaya in eastern and Banten in western Java. He was known to later generations by the name of Senapati 'The Commander of the Army'— an apt epitome of his legendary power and prowess on the battlefield.

Sultan Agung

It was under Senapati's grandson, known as Sultan Agung ('The Great Sultan'), that Surabaya was finally subdued. This was achieved in 1625 after the city

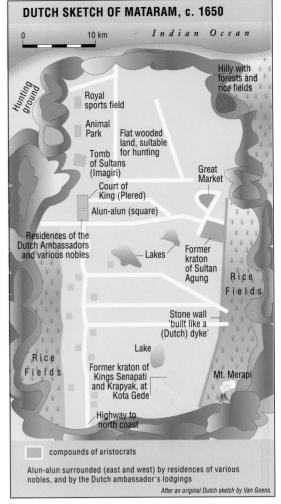

DUTCH SKETCH OF MATARAM, c. 1650

0   10 km

Indian Ocean

Hunting ground

Hilly with forests and rice fields

Royal sports field

Animal Park

Flat wooded land, suitable for hunting

Tomb of Sultans (Imigiri)

Court of King (Plered)

Alun-alun (square)

Residences of the Dutch Ambassadors and various nobles

Lakes

Great Market

Former kraton of Sultan Agung

R i c e   F i e l d s

Stone wall 'built like a (Dutch) dyke'

Lake

R i c e   F i e l d s

Former kraton of Kings Senapati and Krapyak, at Kota Gede

Mt. Merapi

Highway to north coast

☐ compounds of aristocrats

Alun-alun surrounded (east and west) by residences of various nobles, and by the Dutch ambassador's lodgings

After an original Dutch sketch by Van Goens.

had been besieged for years. To isolate Surabaya from the likely sources of supply, Agung conquered Surabaya's allies one by one — the Brantas River was even dammed to cut off the city's water supply, which eventually brought Surabaya to its knees.

Agung now directed his enormous drive for the conquest of Banten. However, by then a new element had entered into the political landscape of west Java. On the route between Mataram and Banten was the small harbour-city of Jayakarta, and there in 1619 the VOC had built a fortified trading post they later called Batavia. Agung made two attempts to dislodge the Dutch from their strategic position in 1628 and 1629, but both failed disastrously in inhospitable surroundings. Some 500 kilometres away from their base, without sufficient logistics to support them, his army suffered greatly from disease and starvation. Undeterred by the debacle in Batavia, he resumed his campaign in eastern Java, with Balambangan as the main target. With support from the Hindu ruler of Gelgel in Bali, Balambangan valiantly withstood the onslaught, but after years of relentless attacks it was finally subjugated in 1640 and most of its population was deported.

MATARAM IN JAVA BY 1645

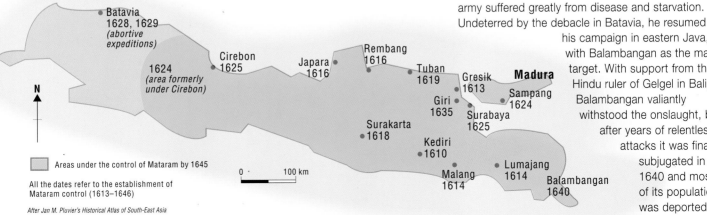

Batavia 1628, 1629 *(abortive expeditions)*

Cirebon 1625

1624 *(area formerly under Cirebon)*

Japara 1616

Rembang 1616

Tuban 1619

Gresik 1613

Madura

Giri 1635

Sampang 1624

Surakarta 1618

Surabaya 1625

Kediri 1610

Lumajang 1614

Malang 1614

Balambangan 1640

N

☐ Areas under the control of Mataram by 1645

All the dates refer to the establishment of Mataram control (1613–1646)

0   100 km

After Jan M. Pluvier's Historical Atlas of South-East Asia

THE HERITAGE OF SULTAN AGUNG

The early parts of the Javanese chronicles, usually called by the generic name *Babad Tanah Jawi* ('History of the Land of Java'), were probably written during the last years of Agung's reign, not long after he assumed the title Sultan in 1641. The *Babad* is a motley collection of legendary and historical narratives, the main function of which is to legitimise the rise of the kingdom, and to glorify the reigning king. The legitimation is achieved mainly by creating a connection with the past: Pamanahan, the founder of the dynasty, is said to have been a great-great-grandson of the last king of Majapahit; at the same time, a link with Islam is maintained by claiming that Senapati received blessings and guidance from the Muslim saint (*wali*) Kalijaga. How strong the Islamic elements in early Mataram were, however, is far from certain. Apart from his reliance upon Kalijaga, there are hardly any particularly Islamic traits in the chronicle accounts of Senapati–his power is attributed to his rigorous conduct of the pre-Islamic practice of meditation (*tapa*), his exploits to his mystical marriage to the goddess of the Southern Ocean (Nyai Lara Kidul).

It was during Sultan Agung's reign that Islam apparently became an important factor in the conduct of state affairs. In 1624, the year before the final assault on Surabaya, Agung assumed the title *Susuhunan* ('honoured lord')–hitherto used mostly by venerated religious teachers, especially the legendary nine saints (*wali songo*), and in 1639, the year before the subjugation of the last Hindu kingdom of Java, Balambangan, he sent an envoy to Mecca to obtain the title Sultan. It was also under his reign that the new Javanese calendrical system based on the Islamic system was introduced (in AD 1633). Remarkably, Agung did not simply adopt the Hijrah year (1043), but continued to use the Saka year (1555) as the beginning of the new era, clearly indicating his strong desire to retain much of the pre-Islamic tradition despite his complete acceptance of the new faith.

was populous; it is said that when signals were sounded, in a matter of hours 200,000 people would gather at the court. But the devastation of the coastal areas must have been detrimental to inter-island trade, the neglect of agriculture in the hinterland, as men were recruited to fight the endless wars, and conquered populations were deported, must have led to starvation and epidemics in many parts of the country.

In the end Agung's achievement proved ephemeral. Built by conquest, the empire depended solely on the virtues of one person, the king. It was so inherently fragile that it could only be maintained by a large military force. Almost from its inception it was beset with rebellions by former allies who felt they were treated unfairly, by disgruntled members of the royal family, by vassals whenever they saw the slightest chance of regaining their independence, or by devoted followers of influential religious teachers unhappy with the erosion of their secular power. Not surprisingly, barely 30 years after Agung's death the state he had built was in ruins.

It was the end of a long campaign, begun by Senapati more than half a century earlier. Throughout this period of expansion hardly a year passed without witnessing the troops marching out from Mataram on their way either to conquer new territories or to quell rebellions. However long a campaign took they always returned victorious, apart from the ignominious defeats they suffered in Batavia. Sultan Agung was undoubtedly the most successful Javanese conqueror in modern history, if not of all time, and by the time of his death in 1646 Mataram's suzerainty was acknowledged not only by almost all the rulers in Java, but also by some from the other islands such as Sukadana in Kalimantan and Palembang in Sumatra. He was appropriately buried in the graveyard he built on top of a hill called Imagiri (the Great Mountain), situated some 15 kilometres to the south of Yogyakarta, from which one has an expansive view over the very centre of the empire he created.

The Fragility of the Empire

Such an empire, however, could only be established at a high price. The capital city may have looked prosperous, and indeed it

«« Parang Kusomo: south coast of Java. This location is where Senapati is supposed to have re-emerged from the sea after his marriage to Nyai Lara Kidul, goddess of the South Sea. Regular ceremonies by the Yogya court are still conducted here.

« Gateway to the grave of Senapati at Kuta Gede, Yogyakarta. The roof of this gateway betrays a pre-Islamic legacy, as can be seen in temple reliefs from the Classic period. Evidence suggests that Senapati was a convert to Islam who sought to ally himself with the wealthy and militarily advanced Islamic element of the pesisir.

Decorative carving, on the grave of Senapati. Early Islamic graves often used fanciful animals as decoration.

Model of the sultan's tomb on the peak of Imagiri. The terraced form can be traced to pre-Islamic Indonesian sites.

Ternate, 'Ruler of Maluku'

*I*n a tradition recorded by Europeans in Ternate in the early decades of the 16th century, Ternate is known as 'Ternate, Kolano ma-luku' (Ternate, Ruler of Maluku). The title proclaimed Ternate's cosmological and political centrality in the region of the spice islands of northern Maluku. But its dominance was a relatively recent phenomenon since older traditions speak of the pre-eminence of Bacan, another island to the south.

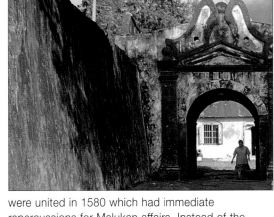

⚓ Fort Oranje in Ternate was built by the Dutch in the 17th century. The Dutch took several steps to control Ternate and its spices realising very well their value in Europe.

The Centre of the Spice Trade

By the early 16th century Ternate had begun its transformation from simply one of a number of volcanic islands blessed (or cursed) by a canopy of clove and nutmeg trees, to the dominant force in the spice trade. It accomplished this in a familiar process of consolidation contained in myths shared by other islands. The original village was said to have been located on the mountain top, and then slowly moved downward toward the sea in response to international trade. With the coming of Islam in the late 15th and the Portuguese in the early 16th centuries, Ternate became the leading centre of the spice trade in the region. The revenues of the clove trade strengthened the ruler, the court, and the entire kingdom, and helped to make Ternate the dominant power in the region.

TERNATE IN THE 17th CENTURY

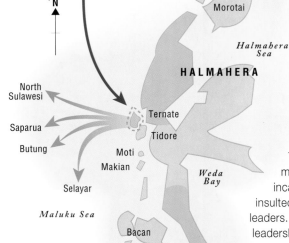

Areas under the influence of Ternate
→ Ternate's expansion into other areas
→ Spanish attack on Ternate in 1606
- - - Establishment of effective control by the Dutch in Ternate in 1606

Sultan Babullah and the Apogee of Ternate

Early relations between Ternate and the Portuguese were amicable because each saw the mutual benefits of cooperation. In time the Portuguese desire to establish a monopoly in the spice trade brought it into conflict with the ruler. Through a series of arbitrary measures, the Portuguese incarcerated Ternate's rulers and insulted its nobles and religious leaders. Finally in 1575 under the leadership of Sultan Babullah (1570-83), the Ternatens succeeded in seizing the Portuguese fortress and removing the Portuguese from the island.

Babullah's success against the Europeans was aided by Muslim teachers, and his reign was characterised by a stronger influence of Islam in the court than ever before. It was also a time of Ternate's rapid expansion abroad into areas as far afield as north Sulawesi, Salayar, Butung, and Saparua. Although the Portuguese attempted to reclaim their former position with the help of Tidore, a neighbouring island with a dualist relationship with Ternate, they were unsuccessful. Meanwhile, in Europe the Portuguese and the Spanish Crowns

were united in 1580 which had immediate repercussions for Malukan affairs. Instead of the centre of Portuguese Asian power being located in faraway Goa on the west coast of India, it was now situated in Spanish Manila. It was from Manila that a strong Spanish expedition arrived in Ternate in 1606, conquering the kingdom and carrying off its king, crown prince, and many high nobles to the Philippines. The Spanish left sufficient forces behind, where they remained as the furthest outpost of the Spanish empire in Asia until their total withdrawal from Ternate in 1663.

The Dutch Gain Control

The Dutch first came to Ternate in 1599, but it was only in 1607 that they established a permanent presence on the eastern side of Ternate. Neither the Dutch nor the Spaniards were sufficiently powerful to overwhelm the other, and an uneasy *modus vivendi* resulted. As the years went on, the Dutch East India Company became increasingly dominant in the Archipelago after the founding in 1619 of Batavia, the VOC headquarters in Asia. By the time of their withdrawal, the Spaniards were no longer attempting to compete for cloves and survived on the good graces of the Dutch governors.

Relations between Ternate and the VOC were amicable at first because both saw the value of maintaining their friendship against mutual enemies, the Spanish and their allies, the Tidorese. But as with the Portuguese in the 16th century, the Dutch began to interfere excessively in the affairs of Ternate, especially with regard to the spice trade. The Dutch, like the Portuguese, attempted to introduce a monopoly over the spice trade. When it was clear that patrolling the waters was insufficient to prevent 'smuggling', the VOC took the unprecedented step of attempting to control production by uprooting all spice trees except those grown on Ambon and the Banda islands. This *extirpatie* (eradication) policy introduced in 1652 included the provision of compensation to the ruler and his chief officials for the right to destroy all spice trees in the land.

Repercussions of the *Extirpatie* Policy

The *extirpatie* policy had important repercussions in Ternate. The ruler and his court gained considerable wealth and power as a result of the compensation, which was redistributed to gain and maintain

followers. Conversely, the minor lords and officials lost their most important source of revenue, and thereby became more dependent on royal largesse. With the VOC as the major dispenser of wealth, court politics became increasingly a story of intrigue with the aim of winning the favour of the Dutch. The situation bred resentment and division in the kingdom, and even the rulers who owed their positions to the VOC came to deplore their status.

In 1679-81 Sultan Amsterdam led his people in a war against the Dutch but was defeated. In a treaty signed in Batavia in 1683 Ternate was made a 'vassal' (leen) of the VOC, and the Dutch no longer guaranteed that the Crown would remain in the current ruler's family. Rulers of Ternate retained the right to govern their lands, but only on behalf of the Dutch Company. The latter also declared that Ternate should maintain order in all of its lands, including areas which had never been securely under Ternate's jurisdiction. In this arrangement Ternate was made lord to a far more extensive kingdom than had ever been the case in the past. This requirement that Ternate maintain order in its extensive lands led to increasing Ternaten involvement in its periphery, leading to more frequent conflicts, and eventual Dutch armed intervention. For the remainder of the 17th and much of the 18th century, the VOC came to exercise a stronger influence in the Ternate court. The 1683 treaty had given it the right to transfer the royal line to another family, thereby making each ruler eager to demonstrate his loyalty to the Dutch. Moreover, as the Company demanded evidence of

(Above) 'The Execution of the King of Ternate', depicted here by Valentyn. The picture depicts King Hairun being beheaded in front of his people in 1570. His son, Sultan Babullah was embittered against the Portuguese because of this.

(Top left) A view of the town and fort of Ternate, by Heydt (1744), showing the fort defences, the high court, part of the town and church, and the ships of the Company in the harbour. 'According to what the elders say, when the Europeans arrived, there was a king living on this island who ruled over all the islands which lie around it. Goods from all these islands were traded here, and the merchants of Ternate resold them to the others who came, and made a great profit ...'.

success in the spice eradication campaign in the periphery, the Ternate court was forced to rely on Dutch help. Malukan perception of Ternate's growing submission to Dutch authority led to support of Prince Nuku of Tidore who led a successful war against the Dutch beginning in 1780. Throughout this long war Nuku was able to gain support not only among his own Tidore folk, but also from many Ternatens who abandoned their own ruler. By the end of the 18th century the VOC had gone out of existence, Nuku had become the pre-eminent ruler in Maluku with the help of the English, and Ternate was temporarily subservient to Tidore. But Ternate once again regained its favoured position in Maluku with the return of the Dutch in 1802 and the death of Nuku in 1805.

The royal tiger with a scorpion on its back to symbolise close relations between the ruler of Ternate and his Tobaru warriors.

Types of vessels used by the Bandanese, from de Bry vol.V, An Account of the Dutch Voyages to the Moluccan Islands of Bantam, Banda and Ternate in 1598–1600. The rulers' strength at sea lay in large and fast armed galleys (korakora). The king's vessel is described as having a structure extending from each side of it, almost touching the water, to seat the bondsmen or slaves who, linked pair by pair, work the oars.

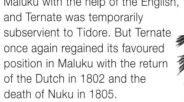

Makasar's Moment of Glory

In the early 16th century a Portuguese visitor commented that 'the region which particularly bears the name Makasar is very small'. But by the end of the century, the Makasar region was transformed by the spectacular economic and political success of the twin kingdoms of Gowa and Tallo. Through major restructuring these two kingdoms, which to outsiders came to be known simply as Makasar, became the most powerful state in the eastern half of the Indonesian Archipelago for the remainder of the 16th and much of the 17th centuries.

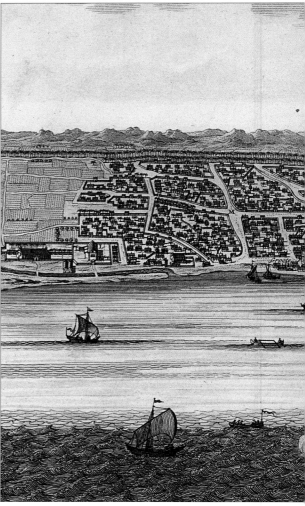

Origins of Makasar

The Makasar kingdom of Gowa began as a typical small community in South Sulawesi. It had its *tumanurung* ('being who descended [from the heavens]') which became the basis of the royal family; *gaukang* (sacred objects), which formed part of the royal regalia; and *Bate Salapang* (the Nine Banners (denoting the original villages), which was the core of the Council of State. Sometime in the first half of the 16th century the kingdom underwent a major reorganisation under its ninth ruler, Tumapa'risi' Kallonna. He arranged the union between the two Makasar kingdoms of Gowa and Tallo, instituted a new code of laws, and systematised the collection of taxes under a new office, the *syahbandar*. These measures were reinforced by his successor Tunipalangga (1546-1565), who not only continued the reorganisation of the government but also revolutionised traditional warfare. He was the first to introduce cannon to local forts, the production of bullets, and the use of

THE STATES WHICH SIGNED THE TREATY OF BUNGAYA IN 1667

smaller shields and shorter spear staffs for greater manoeuvrability in battle. These innovations, coupled with his brilliance as a war strategist, resulted in Gowa's successful conquests on Sulawesi, Banggai, Butung, Sula and Sumbawa.

A Growing Port City

Gowa's trading ships began plying the waters of Maluku and captured a sizeable part of the trade in cloves, nutmeg, and mace. The port of Makasar became a major international entrepot, attracting traders from China, India, Europe, mainland Southeast Asia, and other kingdoms in the Malay-Indonesian Archipelago. Through the wealth from this trade and the contacts with foreign merchants and other visitors, the Gowa court exhibited a sophistication and cosmopolitanism which attracted the admiration of European observers. A French Jesuit described one 17th century Makasar lord, Karaeng Pattingalloang, as having 'read with curiosity all the chronicles of our European kings... had books of ours in hand, especially those treating with mathematics... (and) had such a passion for all branches of this science that he worked at it day and night'.

Gowa's Decline

As Gowa's fortunes rose on the strength of the spice trade, the Dutch East India Company (VOC) began to view this development with alarm. To protect its

» The Makasarese were very skilled boatbuilders, and the speed and elegance of their galleys (sketched here about 1636) drew the admiration of Europeans.

View of the Gowa (Jeneberang) river near Makasar, Temminck (1839-44).

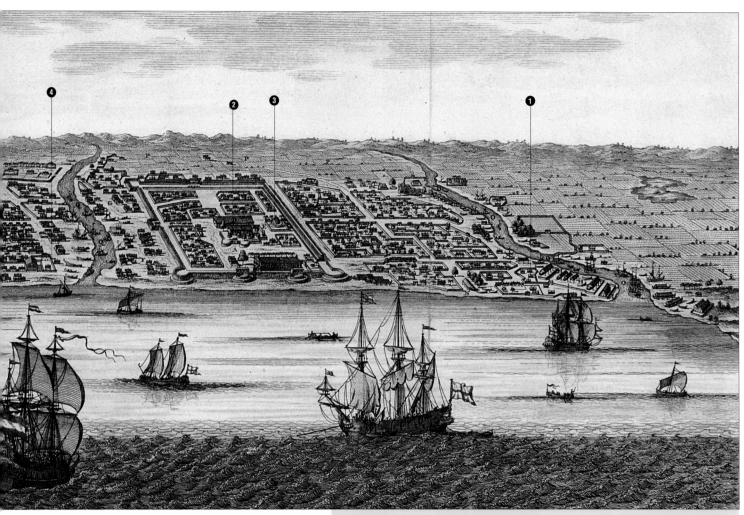

spice monopoly, the company enlisted the aid of the Bugis of Bone, embittered by their subjection to Makasar, to launch a successful attack on Gowa in 1666. Sultan Hasanuddin (1653-69) and his warriors fought gallantly, but were eventually overwhelmed and forced to sign the treaty of capitulation at Bungaya on 18 November 1667.

Gowa never regained the dominance in the region that it had enjoyed in its heyday in the 16th and 17th centuries. The port of Makasar, however, continued to play an important role as an international entrepot for its new masters, the Dutch East India Company.

PORT–CITY OF MAKASAR, c. 1638

Makasar gave rise to three major citadels, of which the most important, Sombaopu, contained only the dwellings of the royal family and their retainers. On the right of the port-city of Makasar around Fort Sombaopu is the mouth of the Jeneberang river, with the royal galleys pulled up on its banks. Moving to the left is a space indicating the main southern market ❶, and the fort of Sombaopu ❷, with the wooden palace at the front elevated on mighty pillars. The round building at centre right of the fort is the royal mosque ❸. To the left of the fort are the quarters inhabited by Gujaratis and Portuguese, and then a small river artificially cut shortly before. The position of the great northern market is further left again ❹, surrounded by suburbs of mixed population.

From Valentyn 'Oud en nieuw Oost Indien' (published by Dordrecht, 1724–26).

Fort Rotterdam was built at Makasar by the Dutch in the 1670s. This lithograph was produced by Temminck (1839-44).

Language and Power: The Minangkabau Kingdom

*T*he Minangkabau kingdom in Central Sumatra has long been regarded as a paradox. Early travellers to the region have described the reverence in which Minangkabau kings were held by many of the Malay inhabitants of the Archipelago. Yet despite their renown, outsiders have found it difficult to understand and explain the basis of Minangkabau royal authority.

» *The royal seal of the Minangkabau kingdom. The Minang had three kings: Raja Adat for custom, Raja Ibadat for religion, and Raja Alam for daily administration.*

MINANGKABAU CULTURE AREA

SUMATRA

Minangkabau
culture area

Pagarruyung

Kuantan River

Batang Hari River

Longsat River

Rejang

Bengkulen

Sriwijaya
(Palembang)

N

Musi River

0   200 km

The sacred royal aura inherited from Sriwijaya appears to have moved up the Batang Hari river to the capital of Adityavarman, and finally to Pagarruyung, closer to the source of the gold which gave all these kingdoms their wealth.

The Minangkabau Rulers

Residing deep in the mountains of central Sumatra, Minangkabau rulers were rarely seen by their coastal subjects and only one 17th century European traveller dared to visit a Minangkabau king before the core of the dynasty was destroyed by Muslim reformers in the early 19th century.

The aura of mystery surrounding these rulers in the mountains irritated European commentators who thought they lacked 'real' power and described them in derogatory terms as 'popes' and 'priest kings'. Minangkabau rulers were, according to one European writer, 'Kings without soldiers: the poorest pretence of monarchs the world has known'. Yet the very real influence which these same rulers held over the hearts and minds of their subjects was also evident.

William Marsden noticed at the end of the 18th century that 'The country of Minangkabau is regarded as the supreme seat of civil and religious authority in this part of the East, and next to a voyage to Mecca, to have visited its metropolis, stamps a man learned, and confers the character of superior sanctity'. Minangkabau rulers claimed descent from *nabi* Adam via Iskandar Zulkarnain or Alexander the Great. The formation of their home in the island of Sumatra was coeval, they stated, with the creation of the world.

Adityavarman

While precise details about the origins of Minangkabau kingship are lost in time, the most famous Minangkabau ruler was probably one of the progenitors of the royal dynasty. This was Adityavarman, a forceful and energetic ruler, who presided over central Sumatra between 1347 and 1374 AD, and who left behind him numerous inscriptions extolling the power and glory of his rule.

Many of these inscriptions, written in a combination of Sanskrit and Old Malay, remain to be deciphered. What is clear, however, is that Adityavarman emphasised the role of his spiritual power, derived through tantric rituals, as a crucial element of his authority. Adityavarman seems to have been a devotee of Kalacakra, a syncretic form of Siva-Buddhism which involved sacrifices and the ritual partnership of a Bhairawa (an emanation of Siva) and his *sakti* who aim at achieving the highest truth and non-duality through the body union. The inscriptions refer to these rites in a manner which presents the king as both fearsome and benevolent. He was Maharaja di Raja, a 'great lord of Kings' whose dominion was 'absolute', yet he also distributed divine bounty to his subjects whose 'welfare (he had) continually in mind'.

The Land of Gold

The Minangkabau kingdom was rich in gold adding to its allure for merchants and sailors who visited the Archipelago. In inscriptions Adityavarman referred to his realm as Swarnadwipa (Land of Gold) and to himself as 'Sovereign of the Land of Gold'. Later Minangkabau kings also emphasised the importance of gold, the collection of which was said to be a preserve of the royal dynasty. In their letters the Sanskrit name for the region, Swarnadwipa, is expressed in Malay as *Pulau Emas,* and numerous sacred golden objects are said to be kept by the rulers. Gold, and also pepper, attracted European merchants, especially the Portuguese and the Dutch who, in the 16th and 17th centuries, attempted to make contact with the rulers of the gold lands in the interior of Sumatra.

ADITYAVARMAN
The huge Bhairawa figure is probably a representation of Adityavarman. It was found at Sungai Langsat on the headwaters of the Batang Hari, and now stands overlooking the courtyard of the Museum Nasional in Jakarta. The figure, which has much in common with the art of Singosari, stands upon a pedestal of skulls. It holds a sacrificial knife and cup, and a miniature Bodhisattva figure sits in the headdress.

The Relationship between the Dutch and the Minangkabau Kings

In the 1660s the Dutch East India Company (VOC) established itself on the west coast of Sumatra and entered into an unusual relationship with the Minangkabau court. This relationship was one whereby the VOC undertook to govern the coastal regions on behalf of the inland rulers in return for recognising their royal authority and making regular payments to the court.

While the Dutch aimed to use the prestige and royal name of the Minangkabau kings as a means of negotiating with the local population, the indications are that the Minangkabau rulers, on their part, saw this approach in terms of a traditional relationship between ruler and vassal, and accepted gifts from the VOC as tribute. The Dutch presence in west Sumatra did nothing to expunge links between the coastal population and the inland court. On the contrary these were probably strengthened. As the VOC's monopolistic trading practices became more and more onerous, delegates from the west coast travelled inland to seek help and leadership from the Minangkabau court. Between the late 17th and early 18th centuries Minangkabau princes and delegates from the court led widespread resistance to the VOC in Sumatra, and further afield in Melaka, Ambon and Java. The attribute which made these envoys so effective in focussing anti-Dutch feeling was their identification with the spiritual powers of the Minangkabau court.

The Role of Royal Letters

Minangkabau royal letters help us to understand the nature of this connection. In the absence of personal contact between the ruler and his subjects royal letters and delegates functioned as a means of linking the inland court with the *rantau*, the far flung periphery of the Minangkabau world. Dutch and other European commentators mocked the 'pompous' rhetorical language of the Minangkabau letters, but they failed to appreciate how royal language, like Adityavarman's inscriptions, served to transmit blessings to the ruler's subjects and to include those subjects within the divinely sanctioned sphere of Minangkabau authority.

Divine Power

After conversion to Islam Minangkabau kings explained their authority as being derived from Allah by means of the dynasty's direct descent from Adam and Iskandar Zulkarnain. In the early 18th century one Minangkabau ruler described himself to the VOC as 'the lustre of God, the all powerful, and a descendant of Iskandar, who is like divine radiance and who possesses the crown of the world's two parts, who is worshipped through the power of God and his Prophet'.

More explicitly than most other rulers in the Archipelago, Minangkabau kings claimed a direct and unmediated relationship with God. Indeed these claims probably account for the Padri's decision to remove the rulers when Islamic reform spread to Sumatra. As a 19th century Minangkabau letter attests, 'Much greater than the lustre of the sun and moon is the Sultan who possesses Pagarruyung, the abode of peace, who alone receives the bounty of the most exalted God'.

Like Adityavarman, who was a Maharaja di Raja and combined 'dominion' and 'welfare', later Minangkabau kings articulated their authority in terms which emphasised the impact of divine power in this world. As Inderma Shah of Suruaso told the Dutch in the 18th century, 'I am Sultan over the earth and the sea, possessed of a power and force which comes from God. Verily I can make war and peace and I also exercise continual welfare. The mightiest Sultan in this world, I am the seat of all kings and the crown of the whole world'.

Not only did Minangkabau royal language convey a consistent message of authority from Hindu-Buddhist to Islamic times, it also had the very real effect of providing a local discourse of power and resistance when the inhabitants of the Archipelago were faced with the challenge of the 'kafir' Dutch in the 17th century. The paradox of Minangkabau kingship disappears if we examine the power of language in its own terms, and appreciate the substance which lay within this kingdom of words.

A traditional rumah gadang in central Sumatra. Although the origins of these houses are unknown, they were formerly homes to extended matrilineal families. The system of matriliny is pre-Islamic and may have been extant during Adityavarman's reign. The larger dwellings could house over 100 people. The points of the soaring roof line are compared by the Minangkabau with the horns of the legendary victorious buffalo.

SACRED REGALIA

Swords, like this one from Pagarruyung, were symbols of ancient Minangkabau kingship. This example probably dates to the time of the 14th century ruler, Adityavarman. The two sides of the blade are decorated with incised figures of a Buddhist Bhairawa and Bhairawi outlined in gold.

Contests and Entertainments

In Indonesian the word 'play' (main) has even more meanings than in English—from sacred ritual through elephant-fights, theatre and music to love-making. The activities covered in this broad category must certainly have occupied a large proportion of people's time in early modern Indonesia.

The youth of Sultan Iskandar Muda is described in the court chronicle as full of miraculous feats with elephants and horses. Once on the throne Iskandar Muda may no longer have ridden his elephants but he certainly enjoyed putting them on show. This drawing is based on an original in Peter Mundy's 'Travels in Europe and Asia, 1608-1667'.

Games and Festivals

The Malay and Javanese writings of the period give a great deal of attention to ceremony, courtship, music and dance, while European visitors complained that they could not sleep for the constant nocturnal 'racket of gongs and instruments'. For a royal wedding in Banjarmasin, its chronicle tells us, the city feasted for 40 days and 40 nights, while the celebrations for a royal circumcision in Banten lasted for more than a month. Because the climate was mild and the basic diet more dependably available than in other parts of the world, Indonesians indeed appear to have had more time to devote to such activities than their counterparts in Europe or China.

Such games and festivals did not need to be centred around a king, as we know from later times when cock fights, wayang, and elaborate weddings and funerals were staged by anybody who wished to demonstrate their status. As John Crawfurd noted of the early 1800s, 'The Indian Islanders... are passionately fond of play... On a market day, in every part of the country where open gaming is not absolutely prohibited, men and women, old and young, form themselves into groups in the streets of the market, for the purposes of play... their grave, orderly and calm manners are changed into impatience, eagerness and boisterous noise'. Because powerful rulers dominated the 16th and 17th centuries, however, they were at the centre of the most spectacular festivities in this period. The state drew much of its essential power 'from its imaginative energies, its semiotic capacity to make inequality enchant', as Clifford Geertz has argued for his 'theatre state' concept. By their capacity to mobilise thousands of people in processions, performances and contests, these rulers placed themselves at the centre of their societies to an even greater extent than theatrical contemporaries like James I of England or the Mughal rulers Akbar and Jehangir.

One example was the circumcision of the boy King of Banten in 1605, as described by the resident English merchant. Every prominent person or social group had to bring presents of rice, cloth and coins

to the king, carried in procession by beautifully attired women who followed armed men, musicians and performers, 'with the greatest show they are able to make'. Each day for over a month a different group presented its performance before the court in the royal square (*alun-alun*). Some staged battle scenes with forts erected on the square; some brought in procession floats resembling ships, miraculous gardens or trees, others presented jugglers, acrobats, fireworks, dances, dramas or 'significations of historical matters of former times'. The English themselves contrived an artificial tree hung with birds and 'strange beasts', but since they had no access to the hundreds of women who graced other processions, they borrowed 'thirty of the prettiest boys we could get' to carry their presents.

Main Features — Contests

In most of the celebrations for every royal or religious occasion, the key features were processions, dances and contests. In Kalimantan and eastern Indonesia the processions and contests often involved elaborately equipped boats designed to resemble *naga* (dragons), but in Java and Sumatra elephants and other large animals took centre stage as symbols of kingship. Aceh had the readiest supply of

elephants, and was able to dress 260 of them in rich silks and gilt tusks for a royal funeral in 1641, along with rhinoceros, horses, and thousands of armed men. The biggest annual procession in Aceh at this time was at Idul-Adh, the Muslim feast of sacrifice when 500 buffaloes were slaughtered before the great mosque. Both Acehnese and foreign witnesses describe the hundreds of animals and tens of thousands of men who then accompanied the sultan in procession to the mosque.

Contests were so regular a feature of royal events that they must have had more than simple entertainment value. Some pre-Muslim idea may have survived, that the shedding of blood, first of humans and later of animals, propitiated the presiding deities. Early Chinese and Portuguese sources report that Javanese tournaments were very bloody affairs, with warriors frequently being killed in contests

both on horseback and on foot. One Acehnese ruler in the 1570s was also notorious for making men fight to the death before him. By the 17th century the tournaments or human contests in Java, Aceh and Maluku were no longer bloody affairs. Javanese courts held a weekly *senenan* (so called because they were usually held on a Monday, *Senen*), when the young braves would process on horseback, then engage in a series of charges and manoeuvres aimed at knocking the rival off his horse with a blunt spear.

Animal Fights

Animal fights followed these contests, and by the mid-17th century they were the main attraction. In Aceh under Iskandar Muda the contests were usually between rival male elephants, or less frequently buffaloes or rams, though sometimes an elephant might be pitted against a tiger. In Java, where elephants were rare imported luxuries, the favourite battle was between a strong buffalo and a tiger. In the 18th century this tended to be replaced by the *rampogan*, where hundreds of pikemen surrounded and killed a tiger. Common to these contests was the need for the royal side — elephant, buffalo or pikemen — to prevail against the tiger, which represented savagery and disorder. Even in cockfights, of which Sultan Iskandar Muda was particularly fond, the ferocity with which the king punished any noble unlucky enough to beat him suggests that more was believed to be at stake than money or pride. As Geertz explained of the Balinese cock fight, these contests involved status relationships, which were 'matters of life and death'.

Games of Skill

There were many other games of skill, like chess, draughts, backgammon, cards (introduced by Chinese), top-spinning and kite-flying. All such games played by adults were opportunities for gambling, save one. The type of football known as *sepak raga*, in which a hollow wicker ball was kept in the air as long as possible by kicking with the foot or knee, was played to promote and demonstrate dexterity, but not to win. The Malay Annals already describe a Malukan prince with exceptional skills in this game in the 15th century, and it was from Maluku that we have the first European account of the game in 1600.

The royal tournament (senenan) of Tuban in 1599, as observed by Dutch traders.

Sepak raga observed by Dutch traders in Maluku in 1599.

Javanese cock fighting. In these contests more was believed to be at stake than money or pride.

The circumcision of the King of Banten, 1605, which involved the whole city, including the foreign merchants. This is a fanciful European portrayal based on verbal descriptions.

Islamic Literature and the Fostering of a Culture

*T*he consolidation of Islam in the Malay world in the late 13th century led to a body of Islamic literature being grafted on to the literary expression of the existing society. In the process, stories were adapted, adopted and extensively recast — all reprocessed to fit an Islamic mould.

HIKAYAT NUR MUHAMMAD

The *Hikayat Nur Muhammad* or the Story of the Mystic Light of Muhammad, 17th century. It was said that those who owned or read the *Hikayat Nur Muhammad*, would be guarded by four archangels, and would have acquired the merit of the pilgrimage to Mecca, and of one who had circled the Kabah seven times.

The commemorative inscription at the tomb of Syech Bachrin.

Imported Islamic Works

Hindu–Buddhist literature, which had existed in the Malay world long before the arrival of Islam, was subjected to new demands to adapt to the changing times. A number of pre-Islamic Hindu stories were reprocessed to fit an Islamic mould. This was supplemented by the importation to the Malay world of a significant number of Islamic stories deriving from the Arab world and Persia.

The imported stories were of various types. Some of them concerned the Prophet Muhammad and were often embellished with details derived from folklore or mystical belief. Such a story, for example, was the *Hikayat Nur Muhammad* (The Story of the Mystic Light of Muhammad), the Malay translation of which dates from no later than the middle of the 17th century, and which was attuned to the mystical inclinations of Indonesian Muslims of that time. Other stories were also often devoted to the prophets of Islam and were based on the traditional *Qisas al-Anbiya* (Stories of the Prophets) which had gained great currency in the Arab world. These stories were characteristically graphic in their imagery, highly entertaining in their narrative qualities, and quite captivating in their appeal to Malay societies brought up on a diet of colourful epic narratives.

Another type of story which had immense appeal for the Malay audiences, dealt with significant non-prophetic figures from the period of the Companions of the Prophet or the following generation; an example is the 'Story of Muhammad Hanafiah' dealing with the military campaigns of a half brother of Hasan and Husein, the sons of the assassinated Caliph Ali, which was translated into Malay around the 15th century and within a short space of time assumed a significant position within the Malay literary tradition. Another such story is the *Hikayat Amir Hamzah*, a narrative romance of legendary proportions based on the figure of Hamza ibn Abd al-Mutallib, the uncle of the Prophet Muhammad. All the above types of stories were guaranteed a highly receptive audience among Malays of the early Islamic period who had a centuries-old tradition of drawing on colourful and lengthy Hindu epics for didactic and entertainment purposes.

Works on theological subjects, including commentaries upon the Qur'an, were also adopted from the corpus of Arabic Islamic literature and translated into Malay for the benefit of the increasingly numerous Malay Muslim audience 'below the winds' (Southeast Asia). Unlike the lengthy anonymous stories referred to above, the principal works of Malay theological scholarship can generally be attributed to a particular author. An important work in this respect was the first commentary upon the entire Qur'an in Malay, *Tarjuman al-Mustafid*, written around 1675 by the great Acehnese scholar Abdurrauf as-Singkili and based principally upon the famous Arabic commentary *al-Jalalayn*.

Early Malay Theologians

Such cross fertilisation between cultures and literatures could not have been possible without regular travel between the different parts of the Muslim world. Malay scholars frequently journeyed to various parts of the Muslim world, especially to the Arabian peninsula and to Cairo, in order to enhance their knowledge of the Islamic sciences and Islamic literature. The earliest evidence of such educational wanderings is found in the writings of the Acehnese mystic Hamzah Fansuri, who travelled to the Arab world to study Islamic mysticism with a number of leading Arab scholars. Hamzah's greatest contribution to the development of Islamic literature in the Malay world is in his mystical poetry, though he also wrote a number of influential prose works. In his writings, Hamzah embraced an extreme, pantheistic form of Islamic mysticism derived from the writings of the medieval Arab scholar Ibn Arabi focussing upon perceiving God as immanent within all things, including the individual, and seeking to unite one's self with the indwelling spirit of God.

Hamzah's mystical teachings were enlarged upon by Shamsuddin as-Sumatrani, who was chief advisor to Sultan Iskandar Muda of Aceh during the first three decades of the 17th century, and who wrote a number of works elaborating on his mystical system based on seven grades of being, his chief writing being *Mir'at al-Mu'minin* (Mirror of the Faithful). The lengthy period of prominence of Shamsuddin during Aceh's golden age meant that heterodox mystical teachings dominated both the religious life of much of the Malay world, as well as its literature, for the formative period of Malay Islam. However, the star was to set on heterodox Islamic mysticism shortly after Shamsuddin's fall from grace in the early 1630s as Sultan Iskandar Thani, who assumed the throne in Aceh in 1636, invested Nuruddin ar-Raniri, who arrived shortly afterwards from India, as his chief advisor in Islamic matters.

By the time of Nuruddin ar-Raniri's departure

PESANTREN

Pesantren Purba Baru, North Sumatra. A large Islamic boarding school where the students live in small handmade dwellings much like their predecessors probably did in early Islamic times and perhaps even earlier when Buddhism and other literature was studied.

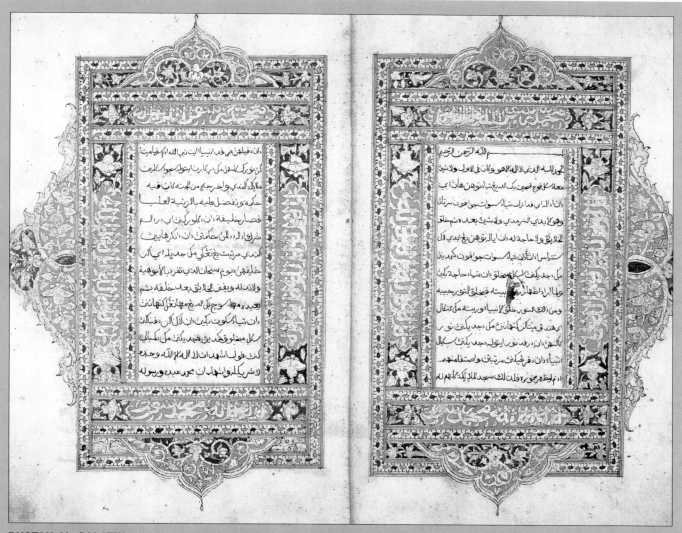

BUSTAN AL–SALATIN

Nurruddin ar-Raniri's prolific writing and vitriolic attacks upon his mystical predecessors were to lead to a dramatic upheaval in the religious life of the leading Islamic state in Southeast Asia. His principal work was the multi-volume Bustan al-Salatin (Garden of Kings), of which an early 19th century copy from Pontianak is illustrated here (and now part of the collection of the Royal Asiatic Society, London). It dealt with core Islamic doctrines such as creation, the prophets, kings and heroes, as well as the various sciences. This manuscript belonged to J. Hunt, the British Resident in Pontianak in 1812. His name is pencilled in the top corner of the right hand page of the illustration.

from Aceh for India in 1644, the Malay world had been presented with a menu of great theological variety. These comprised heterodox mysticism on the one hand to a more orthodox view regarding God as transcendent, on the other.

Upon Abdurrauf's return to Aceh in 1661, after having spent 19 years studying in Arabia, he was commissioned by the female sultan of the time, Taj al-Alam Safiyat al-Din, to write *Mir'at al-Tullab* (Mirror of Students), a thesis on jurisprudence. During the remaining 32 years of his life Abdurrauf wrote prolifically about a extensive range of Islamic subjects, reflecting the diverse nature of his earlier training in Arabia. His highly successful commentary upon the Qur'an was supplemented by works on theology, mysticism, and various other Islamic subjects. Abdurrauf's personal comportment, as the leading theologian of his period, served to re-establish a considerable degree of social stability which had suffered during the earlier disputes between the followers of Nuruddin ar-Raniri and of his mystical predecessors.

The Continuing Heritage

Despite these polemics, mysticism survived and flourished in the writings of the various Malay Islamic litterateurs over succeeding centuries. The inclination of Indonesian Muslims towards mystical practice is, in part, reflective of their earlier Hindu-Buddhist roots. Not only have the literary works of great mystical scholars survived and contributed to the fostering of the Islamic culture in the Malay world, but the tombs of Sufi saints have come to represent focuses of pilgrimage for their followers. The tomb of Abdurrauf in Aceh is surrounded by a complex which houses a mosque, school, dormitories and various facilities. Some mystics who did not attain the prominent literary profile of Abdurrauf nevertheless came to represent guideposts for the faithful over a period of time. Such is the case with Syech Bachrin, whose tomb in north Sumatra identifies him as an immigrant from the Arab world. His legend has grown to the point where, it is believed, he is supposed to have died at the age of 200 in 1716.

Pages of a manuscript copy of 'Tarjuman al-Mustafid' belonging to the library of the religious school at Tanoh Abee.

The Charisma of Kings

*T*he royal courts of the Indonesian Archipelago often impressed foreign travellers with their wealth and grandeur. Yet while riches and magnificence were a desirable expression of royal power in the eyes of local rulers, these were not, alone, a sufficient basis for kingship. It is one of the cliches of European writing on the Archipelago that visitors were often surprised by what seemed to them to be exaggerated respect and reverence in which commoners held even relatively impoverished chiefs and princes who were considered to possess royal descent.

Charisma

Neither fitness to rule, nor the wise and benevolent exercise of power were considered necessary equivalents of sovereignty. Good government is often described, in local chronicles, as a manifestation of royalty, but only in exceptional circumstances did abuses of royal power lead to the unseating of a king.

Kings and kingdoms were central to the social and political organisations of the Archipelago in pre-modern times, yet the essence of their role lay as much in their divine as their political powers. The quality of sovereignty, encapsulated in the Malay word *daulat,* derived from a variety of seemingly intangible sources. Chronicles usually emphasise an illustrious genealogy connecting the ruler with a semi-divine ancestor. At the same time royal status might also be announced unexpectedly and by miraculous means. One prince emerges from a bamboo shoot while another is discovered to possess white blood. What distinguished rulers from their subjects was their link with spiritual power, a divine gift, or charisma. This quality was often equated with a special radiance, known as *cahaya* or *wahyu*, which emanated from the ruler and illuminated his domain.

A 19th century photograph of the Balinese ruler of Buleleng with his scribe.

MANUSCRIPT FROM MINANGKABAU

Section of a manuscript from Minangkabau in central Sumatra depicting a royal structure, probably a *balai* or *istana*. Around the decorative pillars and spiked roofs segments of text are used to identify and place items in the Minangkabau royal regalia. These include a royal parasol, a flag, a crown, items made of gold and other precious and sacred objects held in the keeping of the ruler.

King as the Mediator

By encapsulating sacred power on earth rulers were able to mediate between the natural and

STATE CROWN

The name of this crown, the state crown of Bima (East Sumbawa, 1790 or earlier), is Songko Masa Sangajikai (king's golden crown). Symbolising the precept of *dou la-o dana na* (the raja upholds society and the state), it is one of the three *pusaka* legitimising the installation of the ruler as Sangaji, or Sultan. The others are the state kris and the ceremonial umbrella.

The form of the crown shows Bugis influence, but it was made in Bima, either copying an earlier one dating from the 16th century (made by the 12th Raja of the pre-Islamic dynasty known as Dewa Maja Paruwa) or restoring it. The first ruler to be consecrated with it was Syafiuddin (1791-95), Sultan IX of the Dewa Dalam Bawa dynasty of the colonial era.

The red stain is characteristic of the work of Bimanese goldsmiths, who were influenced by Balinese craftsmen in the use of the Chinese-derived foliate motifs like those of the crown's á-jour and embossed body. The former wealth of Bima – a kingdom ideally situated to profit from the maritime trading patterns between the spice islands of Maluku and the large polities of Java and Sumatra, and which dominated Flores and Sumba for four centuries until the mid–19th century – can be deduced from the impressive total of more than 700 fine diamonds that contribute to its weight of nearly three and a half pounds.

Source: Jessup. H. Court Arts of Indonesia, pp. 260–261

supernatural worlds and, it was believed, to assist their subjects in propitiating the forces of nature and harnessing divine bounty. This association is evident in the way rulers were frequently associated with mountains, the homes of the Gods, and with the seas and waters which influenced the harvests.

Royal temples were built to imitate the sacred mountains and palaces, lagoons and pleasure gardens were planned on cosmic principles to reproduce the celestial spheres. In the literature of

powerful mythological impression reminiscent of the chariots of the gods in the friezes at Prambanan.

The Singhabarwang carriage is claimed to belong originally to the old Pakungwati kraton. When the court was split into the Kasepuhan (elder) and Kanoman (younger) palaces in 1677, the Kasepuhan received this carriage.

The Singhabarwang carriage from Cirebon, West Java, said to date

from 1549, was pulled by four white buffaloes and used by the sultan, its elephant head, eagle wings and lion body giving a

the royal courts natural events, such as thunder and earthquakes, were associated with events in the lives of kings.

The Possession of Pusaka

The divine status of rulers was marked by ceremony and the possession of *pusaka* (or heirlooms) and other objects which encapsulated the sacred qualities of kingship. Since rulers were regarded as a channel for divine power on earth it follows that these signs of authority were not simply tools of political legitimation, but were seen as actual

ROYAL JACKET

Sultan Hamengkubuwono VII of Yogyakarta, pictured in the late 19th century wearing a royal jacket, named Kyai Antakusuma, which was made of patchwork materials and was believed to possess magical powers. The sultan is also wearing a hat and ear ornaments, or *sumping*, which betoken his royal status.

Traditions relate that the first Antakusuma jacket was made by an early Islamic saint, Sunan Kalijaga, and was worn in battle. Sacred royal jackets, inscribed with verses from the Koran were worn by Ottoman sultans. A British colonial official, Frank Swettenham, recorded having seen such a jacket worn by a ruler on the Malay Peninsula. It was believed that inscribed amulets and sacred garments were able to embody divine power and protect the wearer (Jean Demmeni, large format folio photograph, published 1911).

embodiments of spiritual power. Hence, the great significance attached to royal regalia and court ceremonial throughout the Archipelago. Among the objects which served to signify and encapsulate royal charisma were weapons, particularly spears and swords, musical instruments, items of costume and ceremonial jewellery such as crowns, rings, bracelets and anklets, parasols, woven textiles and manuscripts.

Royal Chronicles and Genealogies

Writing was a particularly potent means of expressing the essence of kingship, not only was the written word regarded as having sacred properties, particularly for Muslims, but the composition of a manuscript extolling the glory of the realm and the qualities and possessions of the ruler was another means of realising and preserving these attributes. In this sense both writing and reading were ritual acts. Thus royal chronicles and genealogies themselves became part of the royal *pusaka* and could serve as a sign of the ruler's role as an earthly intercessor with the Gods.

« *The ritual fan (jongan) of 19th century Riau-Lingga, East Sumatra is now part of the collection of the Museum Nasional, Jakarta.*

RITUAL FAN

This ritual fan *(jongan)*, said to have formed part of the regalia of the Sultans of Riau-Lingga, is made of gold and inscribed in Malay *(Jawi)* in Arabic script. The text praises God and announces that the fan belongs to a ruler who came down from Bukit Seguntang (the Sumatran origin of all Malay rulers) and was descended from Iskandar Zulkarnain (Alexander the Great). The king is said to have been just and his sovereignty *(berdaulat)* encompassed the throne of kingship and the insignia and dignities of greatness in those settlements *(negeri)* which lay within the area of Tanah Melayu. The shape of the fan resembles the *gunungan*, or mountain symbol, used as the centre piece in *wayang* performances.

Symbols of office such as the umbrellas were essential accompaniment to a ceremonial appearance of the ruler. The most important were gold, had elaborate finials and were reserved for the sovereign. Other ranks were allowed to be sheltered by specific colours and forms, and golden umbrellas are still used to cover pusaka objects when they are moved from one place to another. This exquisitely embossed and chased piece is decorated with *motifs that cannot be precisely identified. Birds with clearly marked wings are found on the upper portion of the peak, whose nine-tiered tip is set into a lotus flower cupping, while small anthropomorphic figures are depicted on the lower section, which has a stupa-like form. The umbrella finial (8th–9th century) is from Cirebon, West Java and now is part of the collection of Museum Nasional, Jakarta.*

A Seventeenth Century Enlightenment

The influx of new money, goods and technologies during the age of commerce was not an unmixed blessing. Warfare was endemic in most of the Archipelago, and even the most flourishing cities tended to be lawless places where each wealthy citizen maintained his own armed guard. Nevertheless, Indonesia's maritime cities managed to combine an exceptionally dynamic cultural life with considerable feuding and disorder.

Colophon of an 1824 manuscript of the Taj-us-Salatin, a manual of statecraft written by Bukhari in Aceh in 1603 (British Library, Or. Ms 13295).

The Hikayat Muhammad Hanafiah, a source of inspiration to warriors and courtiers (British Library, Malay B.6, f 1v-2r).

Experimentation in Styles

In the port states of which we have excellent descriptions in the early 17th century, foreign and local notables competed in the magnificence of their dress, the glamour and skill of their performances, the exoticism and ingenuity of their gifts. Each ethnic group celebrated its own festivals with public displays of its theatre and dance; while the major royal celebrations required each group to participate in its own way. Hence, the large urban populations of these cities became familiar with a great diversity of cultural styles.

Entertainments

Though written in relatively out-of-the-way Sumbawa, the *Hikayat Dewa Mandu* could refer familiarly to 'all kinds of entertainments like Indian dances, Siamese theatre, Chinese opera, Javanese puppet theatre and music of the violin, lute, kettledrum, flute, bamboo pipe, flageolet, *kufak* and castanets'. European factors wrote home from ports such as Banten and Makasar to request novelties and 'rarities that others have not'. Even dress styles became extremely diverse as each wealthy notable attempted to outdress his rivals. The *Hikayat Banjar* had good reason to protest that Banjarese should not 'dress according to the style of the Dutch, or of the Siamese, or of the Acehnese, or of the Makasarese, or of the Bugis'.

Literature and Drama

This marketplace of national styles also applied to literature and drama, with each of the national groups presenting their own epics at their feasts. The Malay language was the primary medium by which literature in Persian, Arabic, Chinese, Javanese, Portuguese and Spanish became known to other groups in the cosmopolitan port cities. Since poetic forms such as the *sya'ir* and *hikayat* were always intended to be recited aloud, it is easy to imagine that translations first took place orally into Malay verse forms, and these were only written out in response to some particular crisis or need. When, according to a later story of the *Hikayat Hang Tuah*, the King of Melaka had the *Hikayat Muhammad Hanafiah* read to boost and inspire his warriors preparing to fight the Portuguese in 1511, the text referred to may have been still in the original Persian but the poetry recited was already in Malay.

Few texts written prior to the 17th century have survived, and thus the burst of creative activity in Malay in the period 1590-1670 may have had predecessors now lost. Nevertheless, it is astonishing how quickly the fullest flower of Malay literature was reached, after Hamzah Fansuri declared around 1590 that he was going to write a mystical treatise in Malay (Bahasa Jawi), 'in order that all servants of God who do not understand the Arabic and Persian languages may discourse upon it'. Within a generation splendid Malay poetry as well as sophisticated mystical theology and Malay versions of a variety of Persian and Arabic classics were being written in Aceh by Hamzah (a Sumatran born in Siam), Syamsud-din and Abdul Rauf (both Sumatrans), Bukhari (of Johor) and Nurud-din ar-Raniri (of Gujarat), while in Makasar Syeikh Yusuf and Ence' Amin have also left us enduring works. The creative effort of adapting and translating the Islamic religious system and its rich associated culture into an idiom that could be appreciated 'below the winds' proved extremely fruitful.

Historical Writing

This interaction with foreign models also introduced the first historical writing to record events by date in a systematic fashion. As the Makasar chronicle of Gowa put it, 'there are two dangers of ignorance; either that we think ourselves all great lords, or that others may take us for people of no consequence'. Makasar was particularly advanced in the introduction of a system of court diaries (using both Muslim and Christian dating) which provided the

basis for its court histories. These in turn have a surprisingly modern sense of progress, recording for each king which set of technical or cultural innovations were attributed to his reign. Elsewhere, Raniri (c. 1640) wrote a factual history of Aceh and Melaka, while the dated chronicle (*Babad Sangkala, 1738*) brought new precision to Javanese writing.

Karaeng Pattingalloang in Makasar

Much of the exceptional cultural innovation in Makasar was probably the work of Karaeng Pattingalloang (1600-54), chancellor of the kingdom from 1634. Learning Portuguese, Spanish and Malay from childhood from the communities resident in Makasar, he became insatiably curious about the new discoveries of geography, mathematics and physics. He accumulated a large library of European and Malay books, and seized any chance to learn more from such visiting scholars as the great French Jesuit Alexandre de Rhodes, who arrived in 1646. Rhodes has left an engaging portrait of a man 'exceedingly wise and sensible', speaking Portuguese like a native, constantly reading European books and especially knowledgeable in mathematics and in European history.

Karaeng Pattingalloang also ordered maps from the Dutch and telescopes from the English. He commissioned a fine Malay history of Ambon from the refugee Rijali, and must have been behind the translations into Makasarese of Spanish and Turkish texts on military technology, and the beginnings of map-making and diary-keeping in Sulawesi. In his day Makasar was a Renaissance city.

A copy of the Hikayat Banjar, *a royal chronicle which protested against the adoption of foreign styles of dress by the Banjarese (British Library, Add. 12392, f 67v-68r).*

⟪⟪ *A Javanese courtier reading, as depicted in a late 18th century manuscript of the Damar Wulan story (British Library, Jav.89, No.59 J).*

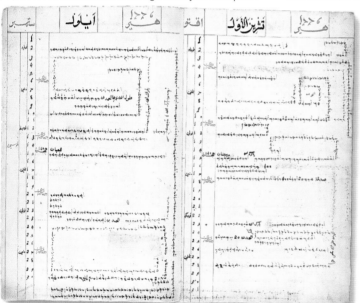

The Bugis-language Diary of the King of Bone, for September and October 1776 (British Library, Crawfurd collection, Add. 12354, f 17v-18r).

A Bugis compendium of firearms, including material originally translated at Pattingalloang's initiative (British Library, Crawfurd collection, Add. 12358, f 35v-36r).

LITERACY

There are conflicting reports on the extent of literacy at this time, but paradoxically the most positive evaluations concern pre–Muslim writing systems. Thus Rijklof van Goens, the most experienced Dutch envoy to Mataram, claimed that the majority of Javanese could read and write, in contrast to only four in a hundred coastal Malay speakers. Others give the same picture of Balinese, and of Batak, Rejang and other Sumatrans writing on bamboo or palm-leaf in their old *ka–ga–nga* alphabet, which was closely related to the Filipino writing systems the Spanish reported to be almost universally understood there. The explanation appears to be that the old scripts were used for ephemeral purposes such as reminders and love letters, and knowledge of them was passed on in the home, particularly by women. The new Arabic (and later Romanised) script carried much more status as the bearer of sacred truth and the instrument of the state, but it remained somewhat alien to all but a minority of elite males who had been to religious schools.

DUTCH ATTACK ON MAKASAR IN 1660

The struggle between the VOC and Makasar was crucial to the watershed of the mid-17th century. Makasar represented freedom of trade in Indonesian waters, and had the military strength by sea and land to defend that freedom against Dutch attempts at monopoly. Hence, as the Dutch noose tightened around the clove and nutmeg producing areas in Maluku, Portuguese, English, Spanish and Muslim traders all made Makasar their base for buying what spices could be smuggled there. The VOC could not contemplate attacking Makasar while it was united under its highly competent rulers of the first half-century, but when Sultan Hasanuddin came to the throne in 1653 internal enemies began to multiply and to give the VOC hope of success.

In June 1660 the VOC struck the first telling blow against Makasar, depicted in this drawing by Frederick Woldemar. Each of the 33 Dutch ships in the attacking fleet is shown. At centre left some Portuguese ships are shown stricken by Dutch fire and burning. A 'Moorish' (Golconda) ship (G) and a Chinese junk (H) are left unmolested.

At right Dutch troops are shown landing at Fort Pankkukang, the southern bastion of the city, which they successfully occupied and held for some months until Makasar agreed to a humiliating treaty including the expulsion of the Portuguese residents. The kampungs surrounding the fort were set on fire, and Makasar troops are depicted fleeing (S). The remainder of the city facing the bay is set out schematically by the artist. At the left extremity is Fort Bontokeke (A), the northern bastion of the city. Proceeding to the right along the coast is the Portuguese quarter (C), the Dutch lodge (D), the English lodge (E), the Moorish (Indian) quarter (H), the royal citadel of Sombaopu (K), the Ternate quarter (L), and the Makasar shipyards adjacent to the Jeneberang rivermouth (O).

(Above) Dutch attack on Makasar in 1660, by Frederick Woldemar.

Cross-section of a Dutch trading vessel as depicted by Homann Heirs, published in Nuremberg (1712).

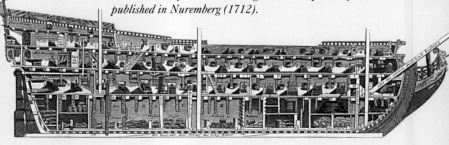

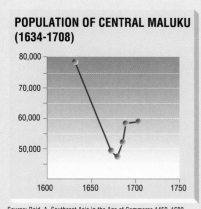
Climate may have been a contributing factor in the crisis which affected the Archipelgo in the middle of the 17th century. It is well known in the Northern Hemisphere that the period 1650–1700 was a 'little ice age', when temperatures were at their lowest at any time in the last thousand years. In Indonesia a weather crisis also appears in tree-rings from teak trees cut in Rembang (Central Java) in the 1920s, which indicate through the thickness of annual rings the extent of rainfall in that season. The graph above shows how far rainfall varied within a 150 year period (1570–1720). The period 1643 to 1671 experienced the lowest rainfall of any period in the four centuries, with not a single year reaching the long-term average.

There appears also to have been a decline in the population in Java and some other areas in the same period, as an effect of both climatic difficulty and an increase in mortality from wars. The graph above shows population in the best-documented part of Indonesia, the Dutch-controlled areas of Central Maluku (Ambon and Lease), which dropped 17 per cent between 1634 and 1674, most of the loss probably occurring in the turbulent 1650s.

A CRISIS AND CHANGE OF DIRECTION

In the economically expansive 15th and 16th centuries, the Indonesian Archipelago was drawn more fully into a worldwide system of commerce in goods and ideas. The rapid urbanisation, commercialisation, monetisation, state centralisation and religious change were similar to those taking place in Europe and other parts of the world at the same time. The increased demand from China after 1567, followed by the arrival of the Dutch, English, Japanese, French and Danish ships after 1596, created fierce competition for Indonesian spices and pepper. While initially intensifying the above trends, this influx of heavily armed ships brought dangers which became manifest by the 1620s. While the Dutch and English began by attacking and replacing the earlier established Portuguese and Spanish, they found it increasingly attractive to use their superior naval power to try to enforce monopolistic contracts with Indonesian suppliers. The Dutch East India Company, the most heavily capitalised institution of the 17th century, was a particularly formidable force as it targeted one vulnerable centre of production and trade after another. The Verenigde Oost-Indische Compagnie (VOC) managed to drive the Portuguese out and establish local spice monopolies in several islands. It also struck many other commercial centres enforcing its monopoly.

Its victories were the more crippling because they established Dutch dominance over a declining market. The influx of American and Japanese silver which had fuelled the trade boom went into decline after 1630, and the prices paid for Indonesian pepper and spices fell in the 1650s. The era in which Indonesian products dominated the world's trade was over by the middle of the century, as European tastes shifted to other products. Moreover, the 1650s and 60s witnessed a succession of droughts, famines and epidemics, at their worst in 1664-5, when population fell in many areas.

A crucial turning point for Indonesian states came in 1629, when Sultan Iskandar Muda of Aceh mounted a massive expedition and siege of Portuguese Melaka, while Sultan Agung of Mataram tried to oust the Dutch from Batavia. The dismal failure of both attempts appears to have convinced Indonesian rulers that they could not beat the Europeans at their own game. The European sea-power was dominant. Increasingly thereafter there was a shift to smaller scale defensive and guerrilla strategies. The surviving Indonesian states sought to limit their reliance on the world market, while new and foreign ideas lost much of their attraction.

The World Trade System of the VOC

With a monopoly of cloves and nutmegs and a string of forts from Melaka to Ambon, the VOC was, by the mid-17th century, the dominant commercial and naval power of Southeast Asia. The Dutch East India Company established astonishingly regular and intensive shipping networks to take a large share of the region's export produce.

An 18th century Japanese print of a Dutch East Indiaman, in the collection of the Koninklijk Instituut voor Taal-, Land- en Volkenkunde. Images of the Dutch in Asia became popular themes in Japanese print art during the VOC period.

VOC Directors in Council, by J. de Baen (1682). The VOC was governed by 17 directors, known as the 'Heren Zeventien', or Gentlemen Seventeen.

The First Multinational Company

As a business conglomerate the VOC (Verenigde Oost-Indische Compagnie) set new standards in the organisation and management of overseas trade between early modern Europe and Asia. First of all it was a genuine joint-stock company based on long term investment, a great advance on the traditional kind of shipping company which settled accounts with the investors after the return of every ship's voyage. Yet because huge sums were needed to fit out the India-bound fleets, the contracting of short-term loans at the Amsterdam financial market became a regular feature of the Company's operations.

Some economic historians have characterised the VOC as the world's first multinational because of its personnel from many countries and its widely dispersed trading network in Asia. The Company was not only a trading venture, it was also designed to play a role in the national struggle against the Spanish crown. The States General of the Dutch Republic provided the Company's ships with part of the guns and ammunition needed to attack the Spanish and Portuguese colonies in Asia. The VOC made a vital contribution by successfully bringing to an end the war of independence (1568-1648) against the Spanish crown.

The Company progressively strung together a vast chain of trade factories and territorial possessions. After the Napoleonic wars what came to be known as the colonial empire of the Netherlands East Indies, arose out of the ashes of the Company's former possessions in the Indonesian Archipelago. It is so imprinted in Indonesian memory, that in colloquial speech colonial times are often referred to as *jaman kompeni*, the age of the Company.

Company Monopolies

Since the Europeans originally had little to offer Asia's burgeoning marketplaces in terms of home produced commodities (apart from bullion such as silver and gold), they tried to gain access to the Asian trade. They began either by building strategic strongholds overlooking the emporia along the shipping routes so that they could police and tax the traffic passing by, or by gaining the monopoly on the purchase and sale of specific local crops, notably cloves, nutmeg, mace and cinnamon. From the beginning, the Dutch made a relentless effort to control spice producing Maluku, and then to force

TONNAGE AND NUMBER OF VOC SHIPS (1602–1795)				
Years	**Outward bound**		**Homeward bound**	
	ships	tonnage	ships	tonnage
1602–10	76	34,970	49	22,580
1610–20	117	56,280	50	29,130
1620–30	141	54,720	71	37,380
1630–40	157	63,970	75	40,300
1640–50	164	100,950	93	74,240
1650–60	206	123,990	103	84,560
1660–70	238	129,349	127	89,240
1670–80	232	147,647	133	99,132
1680–90	204	130,849	141	105,322
1690–00	235	143,295	156	108,123
1700–10	280	186,364	193	135,407
1710–20	311	228,066	245	185,274
1720–30	382	289,233	319	251,662
1730–40	375	280,035	311	236,640
1740–50	314	252,715	234	185,605
1750–60	291	278,845	244	237,760
1760–70	292	291,605	233	231,720
1770–80	290	290,340	244	245,500
1780–90	297	243,424	228	170,923
1790–95	118	80,717	113	92,520

'The number of ships sailing from patria (Holland) was far greater than those departing from the Asian ports for the homeward voyage in the 17th and 18th centuries. Only to a small degree this can be explained by the fact that some ships had not completed their voyage to Asia or were, upon their arrival in Asia, in such a bad state that they had lost their sea–going capacity. In fact, outward voyages rarely ended in disaster; during the two centuries of the company's existence only 105 vessels were lost due to the hazards of the sea, while 36 VOC ships fell into hostile hands. So, only two to three per cent of the 5,000 outward voyages were not completed. Hence, the difference between the amount of outward and return voyages has to be ascribed to another factor: the Dutch Company used many of its ships in the intra–Asian trade. It can be concluded that in the 17th century a quarter to half of the ships remained in Asia'.

Source: Bruijn and Femmes S. Gaastra Ships, Sailors and Spices: East India Companies and their Shipping in the 16th, 17th and 18th century. p.179

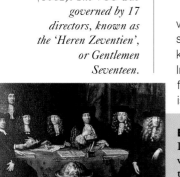

BIRTH OF THE DUTCH EAST INDIA COMPANY

Dutch expansion to Asia started out as a series of long distance expeditions financed by several trading companies which were especially set up in various ports in the Dutch Republic with the goal of trading for pepper and spices at their Asian source. In between 1595 and 1601 65 ships sailed for ten different companies from the coastal provinces of Holland and Zeeland to the East. Their intense rivalry brought about a steep fall in the price of spices when these were auctioned off in Holland in great quantities without any form of coordination.

In 1601 the *raadspensionaris* (advocate) of the Dutch States General, Johan van Oldebarnevelt, launched the revolutionary idea of merging all existing companies into one United East India Company (*Verenigde Oost-Indische Compagnie*), best known then and now under its logo VOC. On March 20, 1602 this enterprise was inaugurated as a joint-stock company with a founding capital of 6.5 million Dutch guilders which was granted by the States-General the monopoly on the trade 'East of the Cape of Good Hope'.

To unify this conglomerate against the Portuguese and Spanish in the East, it was governed by 17 directors, the so-called *Heren Zeventien*, who represented the sixty-odd directors of the participating chambers of Amsterdam (8), Hoorn, Enkhuizen, Rotterdam, Delft and Zeeland (4 each). The States-General authorised the Company to make treaties with Asian princes in its name, establish forts and garrisons, appoint governors and preserve law and order in the overseas territories. It was the young Jan Pieterszoon Coen above all who provided both the planning and execution of strategies that shaped the trading network of the VOC, spelled out in his *Discourse to the Honourable Directors Touching the State of the Netherlands Indies* (January 1614).

VOC SETTLEMENTS IN THE 18th CENTURY

Surat • Hughli • BENGAL
BURMA
Malabar Coast
Coromandel Coast
Cochin ① ② Negapatnam
SIAM • Ayutthaya
Colombo ③
CEYLON
INDIAN OCEAN
SUMATRA
Melaka
Padang
Palembang
Batavia
Banten
Cirebon
JAVA
Semarang
Kupang
Canton •
Macao •
FORMOSA
VIETNAM
South China Sea
PHILIPPINES
JAPAN
④ Deshima
BORNEO
Pontianak
Banjarmasin
SULAWESI
Makasar
Manado • • Ternate
Ambon • Banda
Timor

0   400 km

N

⚑ Areas under Dutch sovereignty
● Other Dutch Posts

the Spaniards and Portuguese out of key positions elsewhere in Asia.

A monopoly of nutmeg was more or less achieved with the conquest of Banda in 1621, and of cloves with the Ambon wars of the 1650s, though 'leaks' were not fully stopped up until the subjugation of Makasar in 1667. This was the end of the last Asian-controlled emporium east of Java. Like Melaka before it and Banten after it, Makasar was reduced to a VOC outstation of purely local importance. The English, Portuguese, and Muslim long-distance traders had to fall back to Banten, Cambodia, or Ayutthaya. The VOC's attempt to replace the Portuguese and Spaniards in the extremely profitable trade with the Far East was less successful. Because the Dutch were rebuffed by the Chinese, they were forced to set up their Far Eastern regional headquarters on the island of Formosa in 1624. However, 38 years later, in 1662, they were chased away from their first large territorial possession in Asia by the Ming loyalist warlord Cheng Ch'eng-kung (Koxinga). From then on the Company came to rely on the junk trade to Batavia for its Chinese products. In 1727 a trading factory was established by the Dutch in Canton. In Japan the Dutch were more successful. After having established a trade factory at Hirado in 1609, they were moved by the Tokugawa government to Deshima in the bay of Nagasaki. They continued to trade even after the country was closed to all other western shipping in 1640.

Dutch Hegemony

When the key Portuguese position in Southeast Asia, Melaka, fell to the Dutch after a long siege in 1641, the VOC continued its vigorous offensive against Portuguese strongholds elsewhere in Asia. The island of Ceylon (Colombo, 1656) and a string of harbours along the Malabar coasts (Cochin, 1663) on the southwestern coast of the Indian peninsula were conquered in the 20 years that followed. By 1690 the VOC was at the peak of its power in Asia. On an average 80 to 90 Company owned ships served the huge intra-Asian trading network connecting 22 factories from Persia in the West to Japan in the East. The payroll counted 11,500 employees, which would mushroom to 24,879 European employees by 1753. Company servants were by no means all Dutchmen. It has been calculated that around 1770 no less than 80 per cent of all soldiers and 50 per cent of all sailors originated from outside the Dutch Republic which, at that time, had a population of less than two million people. Half of all personnel were stationed on the VOC's prize possessions, the islands of Java and Ceylon. During the course of the 18th century Dutch hegemony at sea in Asia was successfully challenged by the English East India Company which, unlike the monopolistic VOC, left room in its Asian operations for private entrepreneurs, the so-called country traders.

The Fall of the VOC

Corruption and lax management have generally been held responsible for the ruin of the Dutch East India Company at the end of the 18th century. Virtually bankrupt, the VOC was nationalised in 1795. When its charter was revoked in 1799 its debt amounted to 219 million guilders. Recent research has suggested, however, that the decline of the Company owed more to the losses suffered during the fourth Anglo-Dutch War (1780-1784). Because almost all home bound shipping was seized by the English navy, the Gentlemen Seventeen who ruled the VOC were no longer able to repay the costs of fitting out the outward bound fleets. A venerable institution, which had annually contributed some ten per cent of the total Dutch national income, now overburdened by debts, came to an ignominious end.

❶ *The Dutch General enters Cochin (Malabar Coast), Churchill (1702).*
❷ *View of the VOC settlement of Negapatnam (Coromandel Coast), Schouten (1780).*
❸ *The splendid audience given by the King of Kandy (Ceylon) to Gerard Hulst, Director–General of the Indies, Churchill (1702).*
❹ *View on Deshima, the VOC settlement in the Bay of Nagasaki, Japan, a copper engraving from* Grant-schappen aen de Kaisaren van Iapon *(Amsterdam, 1669).*

Chinese porcelain for the VOC market, depicting a Dutch ship.

Coen and the Founding of Batavia

*J*an Pieterszoon Coen of Hoorn (1587–1629), Governor-General of Netherlands India for two periods: 1619–23 and 1627–9, was instrumental in the planning and execution of the major strategies that not only shaped the trading network of the Dutch East India Company in Asia but also led to the founding of Batavia in Indonesia.

⤳ The city of Jayakarta was conquered by the Dutch under the command of Jan Pieterszoon Coen on May 1619, as depicted by Valentyn (1724).

The Founding of Batavia

The ideal state of trade in Asia had to be achieved in an insecure environment of feigned friends and declared enemies. Therefore, Coen attached great importance to the foundation of Dutch colonial settlements on strategic spots throughout the Indonesian Archipelago. This visionary project turned out to be very difficult to put into practice at Banten, and after suffering set-backs in the pepper trade and countless harassments from the local ruler, Coen decided in 1618 to move the factory to nearby

Jayakarta where he quickly fortified the Company warehouses. This aggressive step provoked local attacks, but in 1619 the Dutch garrison was relieved by troops rushed in from Maluku. Coen, now Governor-General, ordered the fortress of Jayakarta to be razed to the ground, annexed Jayakarta's territory for the VOC and rebaptised it Batavia, after the valiant tribe of the Rhine delta that a millenium and a half earlier had flung off the Roman yoke.

The city of Batavia went on to reveal both the possibilities and impossibilities of European settlement in the tropics. It turned out to be very hard to transform company servants into self reliant citizens — there was no shortage of tavernkeepers or

BATAVIA

Batavia, the city that Coen founded in 1619, was built on the site of Sundakelapa, an important port of the kingdom of Sunda Pajajaran (13th-16th centuries). In 1522, the Portuguese gained permission to erect a fortress nearby, which became an obstacle to the dissemination of Islam. Five years later, Sundakelapa was attacked by combined Muslim forces from the Sultanates of Demak and Banten, and was defeated, confirming its conversion to Islam. To mark this great event, the city was renamed Jayakarta (jaya=victory). Batavia grew into a wealthy metropolis with, around 1730, some 20,000 townsmen of different nationalities within the walls and another 100,000 people living in the direct surroundings, the *Ommelanden*. Visited by ships all over Asia, the brick built town with its many treelined canals became known as the 'Queen of the East'. That romantic picture did not last very long however. A combination of social and economic friction between town and countryside contributed to a revolt by Chinese plantation workers against Dutch authority in town, which in turn set off the massacre of the Chinese of Batavia in October, 1740. The reckless deforestation of the hinterland for sugar cultivation and the outlay of stagnant fishing pools in the direct vicinity of the city walls turned Batavia during the course of the 18th century into an ecological nightmare. By the 1790s most of the inhabitants had moved out of the malaria infested city to the higher lying area of *Weltevreden*, a few kilometres away from the coast, the centre of today's Jakarta.

Stadhuis/City Hall

Old graveyard

New Church

Chinese quarters

Bugis quarters

Gallows

Soldier's quarters

Governor-General's Residence

Bugis coastal sailing crafts

Dutch ships arriving

pimps yet it was almost impossible to find a single able carpenter, bricklayer or blacksmith willing to set up store. When Coen sent for Dutch maidens to marry his settlers, he is said to have been provided with ladies of questionable background whose uncouth behaviour made the Dutch the laughing stock of the local population. Convinced that he would only be able to push through his colonisation projects if enough room were given to free enterprise by Dutch colonists, Coen left in 1623 for the Netherlands where he also married, hoping that other senior company officials would follow suit. Initially Coen's proposal for the liberalisation of trade received a willing ear from the directors of the company but not so from the shareholders in Holland. When Coen returned to Batavia for his third term (1627–29) he did not succeed in establishing the virtuous and enterprising Dutch community he had projected.

When Coen died in 1629 of an epidemic disease, the Dutch lost a stubborn and often pugnacious leader who had understood the limitations but left as his motto 'Never give up (*ende desespereert niet*)'.

COEN'S APPRENTICESHIP

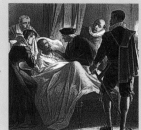

Born in 1587 of a burgher family in the prosperous West Frisian seaport of Hoorn, Jan Pieterszoon Coen spent his teenage years between 1600 and 1606 in Rome learning Italian bookkeeping. At the age of 20 he signed up with the VOC as a junior merchant for his first trip to the East. The fleet of 13 ships under the command of Pieter Willemszoon Verhoeff, heavily armed to inflict as much damage as possible on the Iberian enemies, was not particularly successful. Verhoeff was murdered during negotiations with Bandanese headmen almost under Coen's eyes, which may have contributed to the later brutality of his conquest of Banda in 1621. When Coen returned home in 1610 , the directorate of the Company had appointed a Governor-General who was to rule the overseas possessions from a central point in Asia, with the assistance of a Council of the Indies. It had also agreed to centralise the system of bookkeeping. It was in the execution of this reorganisation that Coen was to distinguish himself during his second tour to the Indies (1612-1623), putting his Italian experience into practice as bookkeeper-general of the VOC in Asia. In 1613 he was appointed to the presidency of the important VOC trade factory at Banten near the Sunda Strait, the first and last port call for all Dutch ships sailing to and from the Archipelago. There he received his appointment in April 1618 as Governor-General, at the age of only 31.

Portrait of Jan Pieterszoon Coen, Governor-General of Dutch East Indies, Valentyn (1724).
Coen on his death bed, 1629. From Het Land Van Jan Pieterszoon Coen *by Dr W.A. Terwogt, published Hoorn (c.1880).*

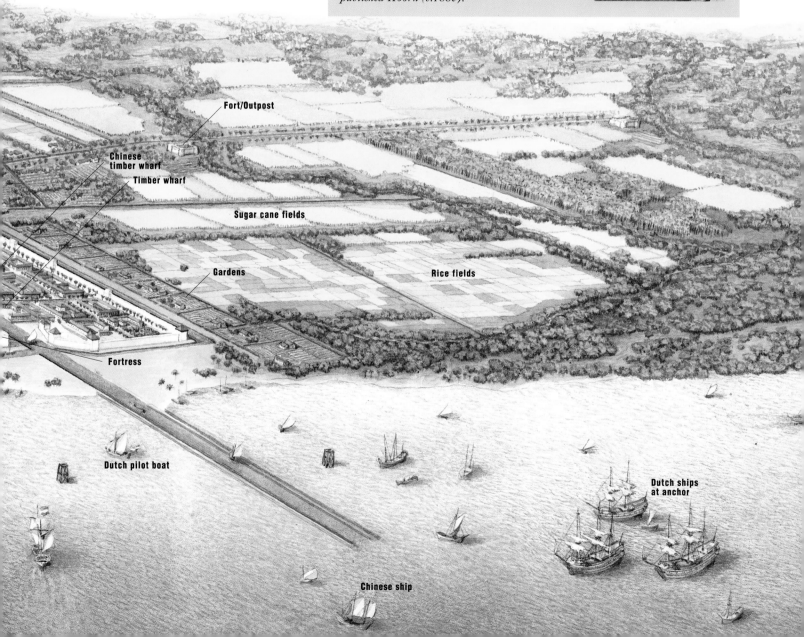

A Retreat from Commercialism

The 17th century witnessed a turning away by many Indonesian societies from dependency on the world market for their goods. Cash-cropping gave way to subsistence crops and the trading cities lost much of their influence over the hinterlands.

The passage to the gunpowder magazine, at Fort Speelwijk, Banten, built in 1685.

» The Dutch Fort on the Island of Banda as depicted in Prévost's (1746–1780) Histoire Generale du Voyages.

The Habit of a Malayan and his wife at Batavia, published by Churchill (1660). The Malay speaking coastal Javanese were described as being 'not so much addicted to trading as the Chinese ... they live for the most part on fishing'.

VOC Monopolies

The precious crops which had drawn the attention of the world to Indonesia began to seem a very mixed blessing in the 17th century. The Portuguese had already tried to use their naval power to enforce monopolistic contracts, but the power that the VOC was able to mobilise in Indonesian waters was many times greater.

The vulnerable Banda islands suffered the worst fate, as the VOC virtually depopulated them in 1621 and then introduced a new slave population to tend the valuable nutmeg trees. In northern Maluku ritualised forms of warfare had been endemic between the different federations associated with Ternate and Tidore respectively. But when the Dutch and Spanish raised the stakes after 1600 by backing different sides in pursuit of a clove monopoly, the inhabitants were again the chief sufferers. The Dutch Commander Reael explained how the Malukans abandoned their practice of selling cloves and buying rice in favour of a more self-sufficient pattern once the Dutch monopolised both the cloves and the rice. The Company concentrated all clove production in Ambon in the 1650s against a fixed payment of 56 rijksdaalders per *bahar*, about one seventeenth of what it earned on the Amsterdam market.

Forsaking Pepper

Although pepper was too widely grown to be monopolised, it also began to attract unwelcome pressures from the Dutch. Banten, the largest pepper port in the early 1600s, was particularly vulnerable to blockade from nearby Batavia in pursuit of Dutch commercial goals. In the 1620s and 30s when these blockades were virtually constant, Banten had to try to turn its pepper gardens into rice fields, however unpromising the terrain. Considerably lower world prices for pepper after 1650 further discouraged growers. Rulers such as the Sultan of Palembang, whose economy rested on buying from highland growers and selling to the Dutch (once they gained the upper hand), were forced by these lower prices to squeeze suppliers even harder.

By the end of the 17th century most Indonesian pepper was being grown as an obligation under fixed contracts between rulers and the Dutch and English Companies, not for a free market. It was not surprising that the *Hikayat Banjar* warned, 'Let no-one in this country plant pepper, as is done in Jambi and Palembang. Perhaps those countries grow pepper for the sake of money.... There is no doubt that in the end they will go to ruin'.

Decline of Javanese Trade

The Javanese (meaning predominately people of the coastal *pesisir*) were known as a commercial people in the 16th century. Javanese ships traded throughout Southeast Asia, Javanese commercial minorities dominated distant ports like Melaka, Patani and Banda, and merchants in Banten and Gresik

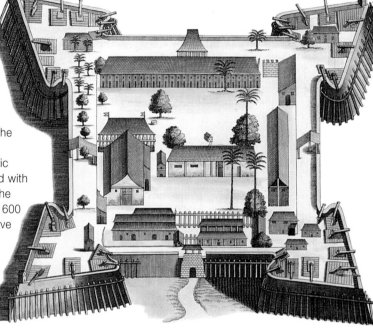

kept their accounts in Javanese or Malay. One early Dutch factor complained that a Javanese would sell his own grandmother for a profit. From 1615 onwards, however, the shippers and traders of the *pesisir* came under dual attack. The VOC did its utmost to destroy their shipping, especially the rice trade to Portuguese Melaka and to spice exporting Maluku. In consequence Makasar took Java's place supplying food to Maluku during the 1620s. Meanwhile Sultan Agung of Mataram (1613-46) took advantage of the *pesisir's* troubles to launch a sustained assault upon it. He progressively conquered Lasem, Pasuruan, Tuban, Madura and finally Surabaya and Gresik in the period 1616-25.

Sultan Agung subordinated the commercial interests of the ports to his own imperial ambitions, including monopolising the rice supply to Batavia and staging some external naval adventures as far as Sukadana in Kalimantan. His successor, Amangkurat I (1646-77), obsessed with the danger of internal opposition, went to great lengths to destroy any commercial autonomy in the *pesisir*. He forbade Javanese to sail abroad, and in 1655 ordered that all

(Left) 'Sketch of Traders from China who do Business on Banten', from *The Second Part of the Voyage taken by the Dutchman Johan Hugo Linschoten*, published by de Bry (1598). They were described as travelling from village to village collecting pepper from the countryside at fixed prices. In order to avoid being tricked, they carried their own scales and placed the pepper in a bag hung from it.

(Right) Foreign traders in Banten. The figure on the left (D) represents a trader from Melaka who makes his profit by lending money at a 200 per cent profit. The figure on the right (E) is from Quilon in the Deccan, who does business by buying up wholesale goods imported by the Chinese, and then revalues and sells them at a profit when the Chinese have gone. The figure in the middle is the wife of a trader.

Javanese vessels be destroyed, even those intended for fishing. No doubt Javanese vessels and traders did escape to other places, but at home it was reported in 1677 that they 'were now completely lacking in vessels of their own', and had become dependent on others for all external trade. In the following reign the *pesisir* became contested ground between royal troops, Trunajaya's rebel Madurese, Bugis adventurers and the VOC, and it must have been a relief to merchants when the Dutch took effective control in 1680.

Ethnic Categories

Ethnic labels can be fluid, and depend at times not only on language and dress but on occupational niches. After the crisis of the mid-17th century, those who remained active in archipelago trade tended to be classified as 'Malay', 'Chinese' or 'Bugis', while the stereotype took hold that 'Javanese' were not a commercial people. No doubt many sailors whose origins lay in Java, Bali or Maluku were reclassified as 'Malay', since there were advantages in being recognised as merchants outside the constraints of state hierarchies. In Makasar, and Bima in Sumbawa, the privileged autonomy of the Malay community was recognised by contract, though its origins were certainly diverse, while Dutch port administrations also acknowledged through their *Kapitan Cina* and *Kapitan Melayu* the autonomy of commercial minorities distinct from the local society.

Although immigrant merchants appear previously to have assimilated readily into the upper class of the port states, this became less common in the 17th century and subsequently. The Dutch presence in Batavia and other ports certainly encouraged separate identities and removed the incentive to assimilate into a ruling aristocracy. A separate Peranakan or Mestizo identity had become established, even before local born Chinese had abandoned the Hokkien of their fathers for the Javanese or Malay of their mothers, and who would earlier have simply been assimilated into local society.

The increasingly agrarian and hierarchic caste, particularly in Javanese society, created strong disincentives for those engaged in trade to identify with it. Progressively, therefore, a trend took hold to identify commerce and the culture associated with it as the business of foreigners.

Large Cities

Cities have been central to the advance not only of commerce, but of the whole modern world–view; its disenchantment with nature; its spirit of competition and contestation; and its accumulation of productive capital. The age of commerce was a period of relatively large cities which dominated their hinterlands in cultural as well as political and economic terms. Around 1650 cities such as Makasar, Banten and Aceh had populations close to 100,000, which must have been between 10 and 20 per cent of the population of the whole regions which they dominated. Mataram was even larger. This degree of urbanisation was not again attained until the 20th century.

All Indonesia's major cities, except Aceh and Dutch Batavia, were destroyed by war at some time in the 17th century, and the decline of their commerce ensured that they did not quickly re-establish themselves. The bulk of international commerce became concentrated in Dutch ruled ports, which deliberately distanced themselves from a potentially hostile interior and peopled themselves with outsiders. They had much less cultural impact on the increasingly rural people of the Archipelago than their predecessors.

The siege and capture of Ambon by the Dutch in 1605. The Dutch were to centre their clove monopoly in Ambon, and the Kasteel Victoria became their stronghold there.

The Kingdoms of Bali

*B*ali, with its Hinduised religion and rich cultural and ceremonial life, occupies a unique position in the Indonesian world. Although Bali's past is closely linked with that of pre-Islamic Java, the Balinese did not embrace Islam as it swept through the Indonesian Archipelago in the 15th century. Instead, Bali retained its unique Hindu religion and culture. Moreover, Bali remained relatively unencumbered by Dutch colonial interference until the middle of the 19th century.

᭢᭢ One of the Balinese customs that shocked European observers, was the self immolation of wives on their husband's funeral pyre. (After de Bry, 1598).

The Balinese nobles are described in de Bry's Voyages... *as either being carried by slaves, or riding in carriages. The example illustrated here was 'drawn by a pair of magnificent buffalo, themselves strewn with decorations and valuable tapestries. Behind the king in the carriage sat a bondsman to carry the king's sunshade. In front of and to the rear of the carriage marched the king's retinue of public officials, armed with long spears ending in flame-shaped top and other projectiles'.*

The Babad Dalem illustrated (right) is now part of the collection of the Leiden University Library in the Netherlands (L. Or. 5054). It is made from strips of lontar palm leaf, bound together.

The Majapahit Legacy

From at least the 11th century Bali had been incorporated into the cultural, social and, intermittently, also the political world of Java. According to Balinese historical traditions, Bali was conquered in 1334 by Javanese expeditionary forces sent by the famous Majapahit Prime Minister, Gajah Mada. A Javanese noble, Kresna Kapakisan was sent to rule over the newly subdued island with the help of a number of other Javanese nobles. The first capital was established at Samprangan. On the death of Kresna Kapakisan, his son and successor, Dalem Samprangan, proved to be an ineffectual leader. He was soon deposed by his younger brother, Dalem Ketut Ngulesir who moved the capital to Gelgel. The Balinese court was modelled on that of Majapahit in Java, and the Balinese came to see their own political and cultural world as directly linked to that of pre-Islamic Java. The majority of present day Balinese noble families trace their origins back to these founding ancestors from Majapahit Java.

The Gelgel Dynasty

Details of the early Gelgel rulers are sketchy, but in the mid–16th century, one of Bali's most famous rulers, the legendary Baturenggong, came to the throne. With his accession, Bali entered its golden age. Together with his court priest Nirartha, who came as a refugee from Javanese Islam and who is considered to be both the progenitor of all brahmana descent groups and instigator of the caste system in Bali, Baturenggong ruled over a land of peace and prosperity in which literary and cultural activity flourished. Balinese chronicles record that during his reign Bali's hegemony extended westward to incorporate the eastern part of Java as far as Pasuruan, and eastwards to include the adjacent islands of Lombok and Sumbawa.

The 17th century, by contrast, saw a weakening of the centralised power base in Gelgel. Disputed succession and internal dissension reached a crisis point and during the reign of Baturenggong's grandson, Di Made, the Gelgel dynasty came to an end when the rebel Prime Minister, Maruti, seized power. In 1686, Di Made's son, Dewa Agung Jambe, succeeded in overthrowing the usurper, Maruti, and re-established the core line at Klungkung, about three kilometres to the north of the old capital at Gelgel.

Balinese Kingdoms of the 18th Century

By the end of the 17th century, the central Balinese state of Gelgel had fragmented into a number of independent kingdoms. Although the Dewa Agung of Klungkung, as direct heir to the Gelgel dynasty, continued to be recognised as paramount ruler, a number of other powerful, independent kingdoms, the most important of which were Karangasem,

BABAD DALEM

The history of the Balinese Gelgel dynasty is related in the *Babad Dalem* (*'Chronicle of Kings'*) or *Pamancangah*. The *babad* begins with the tale of the mythical origins of Bali, and details the Majapahit conquest and the rule of each of the Gelgel rulers from Kresna Kapakisan to Di Made. The fortunes of the various ministers and officials who accompanied Kresna Kapakisan to Bali are also detailed in the *babad*. The *Babad Dalem* genealogy is incorporated into many later *babad* through which the Balinese ruling families traced their descent.

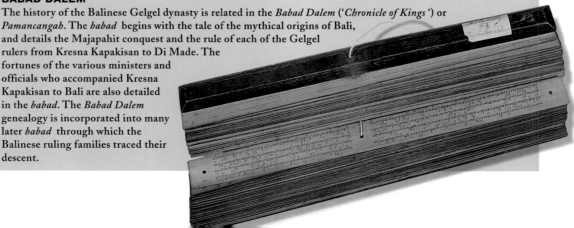

Mengwi, Badung and Buleleng, co-existed throughout the 18th and 19th centuries. Rivalries and tension between these kingdoms meant that an almost constant state of warfare existed in Bali during this period.

Balinese–Dutch Interactions of the 19th century

After the failure of the Dutch to form an alliance with the Balinese against the Islamic rulers of Java and Sulawesi, at the beginning of the 17th century, the Balinese and Dutch paid little attention to each other for the next 200 years. In the early 19th century, however, political and economic imperatives, particularly the lucrative slave trade, the question of salvage rights to vessels shipwrecked on the Balinese coast and the increasing English presence in the region, brought Bali once again under Dutch scrutiny. Although at the time of the first Dutch contact in 1597 Bali had been a powerful realm united under the rule of a single king, by the 19th century the Balinese political structure had altered markedly. Bali now comprised a number of fiercely independent kingdoms and the Dutch were forced to negotiate individually with each one.

Initially, the Dutch established a presence in the port-based kingdom of Badung in South Bali. However, Dutch interests soon began to assume a more political character. Between 1841–3, treaties were negotiated with Klungkung, Badung, Karangasem, Tabanan and Buleleng, as well as with the Balinese kingdom of Mataram on the neighbouring island of Lombok. Under the terms of the treaties these treaties were to play a pivotal role in the defeat of the Balinese kingdoms.

Within a few years, alleged breaches of the clause dealing with salvage rights resulted in direct Dutch military intervention. Between 1846 and 1849, the Dutch launched three military expeditions to enforce the treaties. The first expedition against the northern kingdom of Buleleng in 1846 was successful, but when the ruler of Buleleng refused to pay the compensation demanded, a second military expedition was sent in 1848 to exact it by force. On this occasion the Dutch were defeated, and they swiftly launched a third retaliatory campaign. In 1849, they bombarded Buleleng into submission and succeeded in ousting the rulers of the easternmost kingdom of Karangasem. When they marched on the Dewa Agung in Klungkung, however, they met such strong resistance that peace was eventually negotiated, and in July 1849 new treaties were signed.

The Dutch Conquest

It was to take another 60 years and require two further major military engagements before the last of the Balinese kingdoms fell to the Dutch. Not all kingdoms chose armed resistance. The entry of the Dutch into Balinese political affairs served the interests of a number of Balinese rulers, particularly those of Mataram on Lombok and the smaller kingdoms of Bangli and Gianyar. They seized the

BALINESE ILLUSTRATION OF A SCENE FROM THE BHARATAYUDDHA
In Bali, the literary and cultural heritage shared with pre-Islamic Java continued to flourish through literature and the performing and visual arts. Balinese poets continued to write epic *kakawin* poetry and the Javanese classics were revered. The illustration shows a 19th century Balinese painting of the famous love scene related in the 12th century Javanese *kakawin* Bharatayuddha ('The War of the Bharatas'), when Salya takes leave of his wife Satyawati to lead the Kurawas into battle against the Pandawas (Or. 3390–172, Leiden University Library).

opportunity to further their own political and economic ambitions by siding with the Dutch. Throughout the second half of the 19th century, the fragile unities between the remaining independent Balinese rulers were placed under increasing stress. Rival kingdoms were in an almost permanent state of war. To this was added a succession of natural disasters and epidemics that heightened the political instability.

With the establishment of the Residency of Bali and Lombok in 1882, north Bali came under direct Dutch colonial rule. From then on events moved swiftly as the Dutch sought to bring an end to Bali's independence. Through military superiority, but assisted also by internecine wars and rivalries that ensured the Balinese were never able to present a united front against them, the last of the kingdoms fell to Dutch hands; Mataram and Karangasem in 1894, Gianyar in 1900, Badung and Tabanan in the *puputan* of 1906 and finally in 1908, Bangli and the traditional centre of Balinese power, Klungkung.

The Balinese state of Gelgel fragmented into several independent kingdoms by the 18th century (see map below). There were constant tensions and rivalries between these kingdoms up to the early 19th century when the Dutch began to negotiate treaties.

BALINESE KINGDOMS

- - - Frontiers of Balinese kingdoms

N

0   25 km

Source: J.A. Boon, The Anthropological Romance of Bali. (Cambridge, 1977)

The Javanese Kingdom in Crisis

Sultan Agung, the great and terrible architect of Mataram's glory, was succeeded by a son of lesser gifts. Susuhunan (Emperor) Amangkurat I (1646–77) is depicted in Javanese sources as the quintessential tyrant. Contemporary VOC reports support this view of the king. His reign marked the beginning of a crisis which lasted from 1646 to 1755.

Captain Tack and Surapati as mythology; Tack as a wayang kulit ogre ; Surapati as a heroic figure in both wayang kulit (right) and wayang golek (bottom).

Amangkurat I

Amangkurat I sought to centralise the governance and revenues of his empire which, however, lacked the administrative institutions, communications or military resources to make this possible. So he turned to arbitrary commands, general brutality and, in particular, the murder of recalcitrant lords to achieve his ends. In a kingdom in which control of resources was dispersed because of both geographic circumstances and political traditions, Amangkurat I's tyranny had little chance of success. He killed those very lords whose support he needed and thereby ensured the fear and enmity of their successors. The king became isolated in his court. As resistance grew on the fringes of this kingdom, he dared neither leave the court to command an army nor give command to any of his lords.

By the 1760s even the Crown Prince was prepared to conspire to overthrow his father. A prince of Madura named Trunajaya entered into a secret compact with the Crown Prince around 1670, and shortly thereafter launched a full–scale rebellion. Madurese and Makasarese played a major role in the first stages of the war, but soon Javanese joined. In 1677 the court fell to the rebels. Amangkurat I fled his conquered court and headed for the north coast of Java, where he hoped to win the military support of the VOC. He died before reaching his destination.

Amangkurat II and the VOC

The Crown Prince succeeded as Amangkurat II (1677–1703). He had lost any influence over Trunajaya, so Amangkurat II, too, had nowhere to turn for support but to the VOC. The defeated dynasty's decision to seek the aid of the VOC, and the Company's eventual decision to offer it, had momentous consequences for both sides. Amangkurat II was restored to his throne in 1679 and Trunajaya was killed early in 1680. The king then built a grand new court at Kartasura, near present day Surakarta. The Susuhunan now found that the VOC expected him to make good his promises of extensive commercial concessions and repayment of the VOC's military costs. This he was reluctant to do. As the VOC became more demanding and overbearing in its manner, the king resolved to rid himself of his irritating European allies. In 1686 the VOC sent a special ambassador, Captain François

Tack, to Kartasura to renegotiate its treaty with the court. The king employed a fugitive from the VOC's service, a flamboyant Balinese adventurer named Surapati who was already responsible for the deaths of several Europeans, to deal with this ambassador. An elaborate trap was contrived and Tack obligingly and foolishly rode into it. In February 1686 he and 74 other Europeans were killed at Kartasura by Surapati and his band, supported by the king's own forces. The VOC withdrew its survivors from Kartasura. The Javanese court and the Europeans eyed each other warily, both expecting war but neither being prepared to start it.

Pakubuwana I

In 1703 Amangkurat II died and was succeeded by his son Amangkurat III (1703–8). Within months of this accession the dead king's brother rebelled, won the support of the VOC and was installed by the Europeans as Susuhunan Pakubuwana I (1704–19). The Dutch East India Company could now pursue revenge for the killings of 1686. With the help of Pakubuwana I's supporters, the Company fought a series of campaigns in east Java, which took a dreadful toll, more because of disease than battle. Surapati was killed in action in 1706.

The VOC in Javanese Disputes

The VOC was now firmly established as a force in Javanese political life. This perhaps gave the ruling dynasty a degree of physical security but at the same time it questioned the dynasty's very legitimacy. The intimate involvement of the Christian Company in the affairs of the state was found to be unacceptable. The VOC also sought to redirect the Javanese economy to its own advantage. It expected repayment of its past military costs, and

needed Java's rice and timber for its growing headquarters at Batavia.

By the end of Pakubuwana I's reign, Java was again at war and the VOC was again involved on the side of the dynasty. A rebellion began at Surabaya in 1717. On the king's death in 1719 a succession war among his sons broke out in central Java. The rebel princes soon withdrew eastwards and joined the Surabayans and their Balinese allies. Heavy fighting and epidemic disease devastated large parts of east Java. In 1723 the rebellion finally collapsed with the surrender of the surviving leaders.

Neither the VOC nor the Javanese court could regard their half century of alliance as a great success. The Company was owed a great deal of money for its military expenses by the court, money which it had little prospect of ever recovering, and its attempts to exploit Java's agricultural resources were of limited success. Susuhunan Amangkurat IV (1719–26) meanwhile tottered forward as a monarch with only moderate influence over his kingdom and even less affection from his subjects.

Pakubuwana II

The nadir of this cycle of disunity, violence and intervention came in the reign of Susuhunan Pakubuwana II (1726–49). At the start, a circle of influential courtiers sought to create a better realm by making the king a model mystic (*Sufi*) monarch. He responded to this positively and the style of the court became more self–consciously pious and Islamic. Because for 14 years there were no wars requiring VOC intervention, the court elite had more room for initiative than its predecessors since the 1670s. When the Chinese War broke out in 1740, the king decided to join the anti–European cause. His forces captured the Company's fortress at Kartasura

and killed several of its officers. But when the tide of war turned in the Europeans' favour, the king changed sides to ally again with the VOC. The rebels consequently turned upon him and in 1742 captured Kartasura. The wretched Pakubuwana II took flight into the wilderness and was only restored to his throne in 1743 through the support of the VOC. In 1746 he moved to his new court of Surakarta. On his deathbed in 1749, Pakubuwana II signed a treaty surrendering his entire kingdom to the Company.

Division of Java

The treaty of 1749 marked the low point of the dynasty's fortunes. The crisis of the previous seven decades may be attributed principally to two interconnected causes; unsuccessful leadership within the Javanese royal elite and VOC intervention. The VOC was by now in such difficult financial circumstances that its willingness and ability to intervene was nearing an end. And the royal elite was at last producing leaders of stature, notably Mas Said (Prince Mangkunagara I) and Prince Mangkubumi. The former rebelled during the Chinese War, the latter launched a major rebellion in 1746. In 1749 Mangkubumi was crowned king by his followers. By 1755 the VOC was fought to a stalemate, but he realised that VOC defence of Pakubuwana III ruled out total victory. So a compromise was reached in the Treaty of Giyanti (February 1755) between Mangkubumi and the VOC, by which Mangkubumi was given half the kingdom. He established his new court at Yogyakarta and took the title Sultan Hamengkubuwana I (1749–92). The stage was set for a last flowering of the pre–colonial Javanese state.

Susuhunan Pakubuwana II conferring with Adipati Natakusuma, Arya Pringgalaya and Tumenggung Tirtawiguna.

↙ *Death of François Tack by Balinese soldiers of Untung Surapati in the kraton of Kartasura near Solo (1686). Tack was buried in the Dutch Church under the tombstone of van Hoorn (No. HK 26). Popular drawing from Yogyakarta.*

An old Dutch grave on the hill Danareja at Japara, locally identified as the grave of Captain Tack.

Remnants of the Sri Menganti (which separated the inner precinct of the kraton from the outer areas to the north) in the ruins of Kartasura.

«« *Babad Mangkunagara, a Javanese history dated 1800 chronicling the exploits of Mas Said, the first Mangkunagaran ruler (British Library, Add. 12280, f 2v–3r).*

Trade, Industry and Agriculture in Java

The economy of Java has always been unique within the Indonesian Archipelago. Its industries were relatively developed, and the use of money was widespread. A variety of economic activities were pursued by a society that became increasingly multi-ethnic.

CENTRES OF TRADE AND INDUSTRY IN JAVA

An old photograph of a coffee plantation in the 19th century. Coffee became one of Indonesia's most successful export crops.

An old 19th century photograph of a tobacco plantation. Tobacco smoking in the form of cheroots had begun to be popular among men, women and young children in Indonesia by the end of the 17th century. Tobacco also became an important export crop.

A coffee plantation in the present day, Blawan Bondowoso, Java.

Trade

In the 17th century and earlier, Java's soils were extremely fertile, its population was denser than elsewhere, and its economy was extremely dynamic. Whereas in most other parts of Indonesia swidden agriculture was still common, in Java there was intensive cultivation of wet rice. Java's economy remained dynamic even after the end of the 18th century, despite the efforts of the Dutch East India Company to gain absolute control of it.

At the start of the 17th century Java was an important centre of trade in Southeast Asia too. Javanese merchants provided Melaka with most of its food, and ports like Surabaya, Gresik and Banten were important entrepots for such items as cloves, pepper and Indian textiles. This trade did not disappear, although it was drastically curbed by the

COFFEE
Coffee was introduced to Java by the VOC at the beginning of the 18th century. It did not take the chiefs and peasants of the Priangan area of West Java long to realise the possibilities of this new crop. Within 20 years, the Priangan was producing as much as Yemen, the homeland of commercial coffee production. The VOC did not allow the Javanese to sell coffee to anyone but the Company. For commercial reasons it destroyed all coffee plants in the central areas of the island. Nevertheless, at the end of the 18th century Java was one of the largest coffee producers in the world, and ships came from America and elsewhere in search of this 'black gold'.

VOC. As the 17th century progressed, two ports emerged as the leading entrepots in Java, Banten and Batavia. They struggled fiercely for total domination of the inter-island trade, a struggle that was eventually won by Batavia after Dutch military intervention in Banten in 1682.

Even after that date, however, trade remained important for Java. Admittedly, by the end of the 18th century an important part of this trade had fallen into the hands of the Dutch and Chinese. The VOC forbade Javanese prahu to sail to eastern Indonesia, and it prohibited all trade in the commodities that were most lucrative, such as spices, opium and Indian textiles. Nevertheless, Javanese prahu carried large quantities of rice, salt, batik cloth, tobacco, and many other items to places as far away as Patani and Perak. Even at the end of the 18th century about one fifth of the captains who sailed were Javanese, and about the same proportion were natives of other islands in Indonesia.

Trade within Java
The overseas trade was closely connected with a trade network in Java itself. Transport was mainly by water, because the rugged terrain made overland transport difficult. Consequently, commodities that were traded from central Java to west Java went first by river to the coast, and from there by sea. The main rivers used for trade were the Solo and the Brantas. The Javanese had developed a special type of prahu for river transport, the so-called *belukan*, which had a shallow draught. Although land transport was more difficult, it was important too. A road ran between Semarang and Mataram, which was frequently used by caravans. The villagers along the road made a living by carrying goods. They carried these on their backs, though horses were also used. A large part of the trade was conducted on behalf of the Javanese elite. Both courtiers and Regents employed professional merchants, Javanese as well

On the island of Onrust, near Batavia, the VOC established the largest shipyard in Asia, where mostly Indonesian labourers worked under Dutch supervision. Elsewhere in Java, in places like Semarang, Rembang and Tuban, Javanese shipwrights continued to produce large numbers of prahu each year. Copper engraving by Mattheus Sallieth after Johannes Rach from Petrus Conradi's Batavia, De Hoofdstad van Neerlands O. Indien *(Amsterdam, 1782–83).*

as Chinese. At the beginning of the 18th century, for instance, the village of Solo was inhabited by merchants who carried on trade along the river and who were financed by the crown prince of Mataram. Later in that century the son of this former crown prince built his palace in Solo. In port towns like Semarang the local Regents owned a weighhouse and warehouses, which they rented to foreign merchants. Besides trade financed by the elite, there was much trade conducted as a sideline by people mostly engaged in fishing and farming. On the local level especially, these were women. Thus, women from Madura crossed the strait everyday to sell fruit at the market of Gresik.

Industry

At the beginning of the 17th century Java had a thriving ship building industry, and even large junks were produced here. The ship building industry remained important, although it came to be partly controlled by the Dutch. For this industry, as well as for house construction, vast quantities of teak were needed. In Demak, Japara, and especially Rembang, timber cutting became a major industry, in which the Kalang people in particular were engaged. After the logs were cut, they were dragged by buffaloes to a nearby river and allowed to float to the coast. The VOC carried much of the timber direct to Batavia in its ships. In Juwana, Japara and Semarang, Chinese and Javanese processed timber in numerous sawmills. From here planks, barrels, furniture and oars were exported to Batavia and other places in Indonesia.

The production of batik cloth was centred on the kratons of central Java and near the towns of Banten, Semarang, and Kudus. In the kratons the cloth was produced and dyed in large workplaces by the many wives of the rulers, and by other women. In and around the towns on the north coast the batik was made by peasant women in their houses, in cooperation with Chinese merchants. Javanese batik, being of superb quality and moderately priced, was in great demand in the other principal islands of Indonesia.

Export Crops

In the 17th and 18th centuries various new export crops were successfully introduced in Java. The most important were coffee, tobacco and cane sugar. Around 1650 traditional sugar producing centres like south China and Taiwan were torn by civil war. Javanese Chinese filled the gap arising as a result by setting up sugar mills in the areas around Batavia and Japara. At the beginning of the 18th century Java had approximately 140 mills, making it the largest producer of cane sugar in Asia. Its sugar was sold in Japan, Persia, India and Holland. Thousands of Javanese men from central Java migrated each year to the area surrounding Batavia to work in the fields and mills. Other areas in Java specialised in breeding the buffaloes that were needed to turn the mills.

SALT
Of old, the north coast of Java has been a major producer of salt. The salt was exported to most other islands of the Archipelago. For the Dayak people in the interior of Borneo, Javanese salt was so important, in fact, that they treated it like money. The salt was produced in numerous salt-pans along the seashore, in which seawater was allowed to evaporate. The main production areas were Sumenep on Madura, Gresik and Rembang. On the south coast, salt was made by boiling seawater in cauldrons.

« A peasant woman making batik in her house. These peasant women were largely from the northern coast of Java. Javanese batik was in great demand throughout Indonesia.

Envoys and Letters

*R*elations between rulers of the eastern Asia world appear to have developed first through mechanisms of tribute, and only evolved with much difficulty into relations between formal equals. The language with which rulers were addressed always implied inequality; indeed it was difficult to imagine terms of greeting which did not suggest either superiority or inferiority.

A European image of ambassadors at the larger courts. This illustration shows the procession with which the ruler of Tuban, in Java, received the Dutch who had arrived in his port in 1600, sitting on a huge elephant and accompanied by his nobles and attendants. Published in Frankfurt by de Bry, between 1590 and 1608.

Status Disputes

The trade relations between upriver communities and port-kings at the river mouths were usually couched in terms of tribute and fealty. Even between port kings trading with one another by sea, the only stable and harmonious relations were those of inequality, the lesser port and power accepting the supremacy of the greater.

The Melaka chronicle (*Sejarah Melayu*) provides two 15th century examples of the tensions surrounding relations of equality, both involving the North Sumatran sultanate of Pasai. In one the ruler of the Karo Batak or Malay kingdom of Aru, near modern Medan, sent a letter to the ruler of Pasai expressing his greetings (*salam*). But the Pasai letter-reader rendered this word as obeisance (*sembah*), so enraging the Aru envoy bringing the letter that he ran amuk, much blood flowed and a prolonged war ensued. Subsequently the ruler of Melaka decided he would get around this Pasai arrogance (justified by Pasai's greater antiquity as an Islamic state, but no

longer by its power), by sending no letter but an envoy who had memorised the message which carefully addressed Pasai as a younger rather than an older brother of Melaka.

Letters

This strategy was the more striking because it was normally the king's letter, not his ambassador, which was seen as the extension of his authority to another place. Every *nakhoda* (captain or supercargo) of a large ship crossing the Indian Ocean would attempt to equip himself with a royal letter from his home port. This would usually ensure an extravagant reception. In Aceh the letter would be placed in a

silver dish and carried in state to the palace on an 'elephant caparisoned in red cloth, with people in front of it playing on tamborines, trumpets and flutes'.

The envoys would follow only slightly less magnificently, carrying their gifts of cloth, arms, clever manufactures or exotic rarities. At the palace they would be dressed in royal gifts of local cloth and a kris, before being ushered in to the sultan's presence. If all went well, the formal exchanges of greetings would be followed by feasting, dancing, and perhaps such entertainments as a play or animal-fight.

The earliest letters extant, from the 17th and 18th centuries, usually began with a magical placing of the king from whom it came in relation to the presumed cosmic sources of power. Minangkabau letters for example began with three seals purporting to be from the rulers of Rum (Rome-Constantinople-Turkey), China and Minangkabau, and described its author as 'Sultan of Minangkabau whose residence is at Pagarruyung, who is king of kings; a descendent of Raja Iskandar Zu'lkarnain; possessed of a crown brought to heaven by the prophet Adam' and so forth. These letters served to project the charisma of rulers far beyond the reach of their arms, as much as to communicate specific information.

Diplomatic Relations

As communications multiplied and European powers joined the diplomatic game, pressures grew for a system which could better acknowledge the nominal equality of sovereign states — the cornerstone of modern diplomatic arrangements. The earliest period on which there is much data, the 15th century, shows an east Asian pattern of diplomacy conducted in Chinese and Arabic, in which all players recognised the superior status of the Chinese emperor in return for gifts of great value and even more valuable access to the Chinese market during the period of the tribute mission. Majapahit or its successors sent 50 tribute missions to China in that century, Pasai 22, and Melaka 29, including three missions led by its ruler. In turn each of these states received tribute from lesser ports seeking indirect access to Chinese goods. In the 15th century the small kingdom of Ryukyu (modern Okinawa) became a major player in these exchanges between Southeast Asia and China as China itself progressively lost interest, and exchanged many letters with Java and Palembang. In the 16th century Ottoman Turkey and Portugal-Spain joined China in

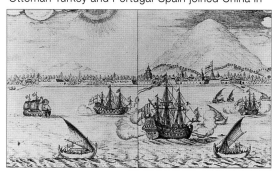

the category of semi-legendary distant powers, while by the 17th century it became clear that Indonesian rulers inhabited a very plural world which could no longer be conceptualised in the old tributary terms.

Aceh, Banten, Mataram and Makasar all had extensive diplomatic relations in the 17th century, with each other and other powers such as Siam, Golconda (South India), Spanish Manila, Portuguese Goa, the Dutch, English, French and Danes. These were beginning to be seen as relations of equality, yet problems of language, precedence and marriage always threatened to upset them. Most rulers welcomed the daughters of other kings into their harems as a way of consolidating a tributary relationship, but were extremely reluctant to part with their own daughters to foreign kings. The relationship between Aceh and Siam, which endured intermittently through the century, for example, was twice ruptured when Sultan Iskandar Muda requested a Thai princess to wed. He also requested the English to send him a couple of young women for his harem whose children could act as mediators between the two countries. Relations between Mataram and Makasar were not helped in the 1650s when Amangkurat I requested one or two daughters of Sultan Hasanuddin.

Ambassadors to Europe

Part of the royal function of royal emissaries was to observe foreign lands and report back about their strength and achievements. No doubt this was more salient in the case of distant and mysterious destinations such as the missions Aceh sent to Istanbul in the 1560s, and also in the representatives of Banten and Aceh which Dutch expe–ditions carried back to the Netherlands in 1598 and 1601 respectively. The latter was received by Prince Maurits in some state, but the Indonesian rulers probably thought Holland too distant and unpredictable to send people of high status in a normal embassy. It was otherwise in 1681, when Banten was very anxious to establish whether it could rely on English support in a showdown with the Dutch. A formal embassy of two experienced aristocrats and 29 retainers spent three months in London the following year. The envoys were lionised by English society and knighted by King Charles II as Sir Abdul and Sir Ahmad. None of this was much help to Banten, however, which was already in Dutch hands by the time they returned.

The two Banten envoys, who were both of equal status despite the hierarchic positioning here, from a broadsheet popular in London at the time.

A Danish ship and envoys being greeted in the roads of Banten in 1673. The two vessels flanking the Danish ship are carrying important Bantenese officials, as indicated by the umbrellas. From the journal of Cortemunde J.P..

A LETTER FROM ISKANDAR MUDA

A letter from Iskandar Muda of Aceh to King James I of England, dated 1024 Hijra (1615). This magnificent letter is nearly a metre high, and three quarters of it is devoted to spelling out the glory of the Acehnese Sultan. It is now held in the Bodleian Library, Oxford.

Karo Batak, an old photograph.

Minangkabau, by H.D.T. Willink (1883).

Timor, by C.J. Temminck (1839-47).

Indonesians both economically and politically adjusted to the new period of Dutch trading influence by developing a smaller scale of operation from the 17th century onwards. Rather than contesting the large-scale international routes with large ships, Indonesian traders now linked hundreds of small ports with a network of prahus of less than 20 tons. The Bugis of Wajo' were remarkable examples of this type of networking, but there were even more small boats criss-crossing the Archipelago under captains who bore the fluid ethnic labels 'Malay' and 'Chinese'. In 1780, for example, there called at Dutch Melaka 178 Malay vessels, 106 Chinese and 66 Bugis, almost all of them bringing cargoes from Sumatra and Riau. These networks gave rise to polities at the junction of river ocean which were usually too small and fluid to be bothered by VOC guns.

LIVING WITHOUT STRONG STATES

Kora-kora from Gebe, North Maluku, 1818, Alphonse Pellion (1796-1869). Watercolour over pencil. Inscribed in pencil : ... Pellion and Pirogues de Guébé devant Pissang.

After the fall of Banten in 1684, Indonesian societies had to adapt to VOC domination of the long-distance trade in the most profitable items. The defeat or decline of strong states which had used the revenues of trade to dominate their hinterlands necessitated a return to local forms of decentralised decision-making. In south Sulawesi the numerous Bugis and Makasar states resumed their rivalries after the short-lived centralisation under Makasar. In Bali the somewhat shadowy unity imposed by the Gelgel kingdom gave way to a confusing variety of states and subdivisions. In Java Sultan Agung's military conquests proved short-lived, as succession conflicts, external Dutch pressures and the divisive political traditions of Java reduced the power of Kartasura to order Javanese life. In Sumatra the hegemony of Aceh, Palembang and Banten was eroded, and a multiplicity of small river ports proved better able to evade Dutch monopolies than the large city-states.

The VOC had played a part in the passing of the strong states, but it should not be imagined that it had taken their place as the dominant power. While the Company was by far the strongest commercial force in the Archipelago by 1650, it had neither the capacity nor the desire to set the cultural and political agenda for Indonesians. At its peak as a world commercial power around 1680 the VOC ruled less than ten per cent of Indonesians. Even these, located chiefly along the north coast of Java and in Maluku, were much more likely to embrace Islam to stress their difference from the Dutch than to imitate the fashions of the Hollanders.

Politically a pattern of personal and kinship networks became re-established after the brief period of semi-bureaucratic absolute states. In Bali a sophisticated literary culture was able to flourish which was held together by complex patterns of ritual and family relationships rather than a state in the modern sense. Similar networks allowed Minangkabau, Toba Batak and Malukan societies to develop strong common cultures, and minimise warfare. Even Acehnese, Palembangers and Javanese were effectively ruled by a variety of local chiefs within the ideological framework set by the mighty rulers of the past. This period of weak state authority allowed experiments with collegial, pluralistic institutions which came close to democracy. The Bugis of Wajo', in particular, developed a powerful ideology which required each new ruler to acknowledge the established freedoms (*am-maradeka-ngenna*) of Wajo' — freedom to express opinions and to move within and beyond the state.

Opium: The Fuel of Empire

In the 18th century the Dutch empire in Indonesia, like those of the other colonial powers in Asia, became closely linked to the expansion of the international opium trade. Indeed, opium may be called the fuel of empire.

Lanrick, the only ship built on the Mersey (Britain) specifically for the opium trade, by lithographer T.G. Dutton.

➹ *One of the first examples of European industrial technology to appear in the Dutch East Indies by the beginning of the 20th century was the factory built to refine (top) and package (bottom) opium for Indonesian consumers.*

➹➹ *Accessories often associated with opium-smoking, from Hugo V. Pedersen's* Doorden Oost-Indischen Archipel *(1908).*

Chinese opium shops such as these formed part of a growing commercial network in the rural areas of Java. A wood engraving after Thiriat from L'Illustration *(Paris).*

Uses of Opium

Control of the opium trade in the Indies gave the Dutch rulers of Batavia many powerful advantages. First, trade in the drug supplied them with a ready source of cash. Secondly, the trade was a means by which the Dutch could secure a dominant role in the trade with China. Thirdly, the opium monopoly pioneered the organisation of the colonial administration. Drug profits underpinned the costs of VOC trade and warfare in the 18th century and later financed the establishment of the colonial administration throughout Java and the other islands. From the very beginning of European imperialism in Southeast Asia, opium had been seen as a source of profit for traders coming to the region from the west. Arab and Indian merchants had introduced the drug to eastern Asia as early as the 8th century. It was widely used as a pain killer, cough suppressant and a cure for diarrhoea. The plant had long been a part of the traditional *materia medica* of the civilised world. In India and among the Malays, there are reports that it was used as a stimulant by soldiers before going into battle. Alfonso d'Albuquerque recommended that the King of Portugal should plant his fields with opium to reap the wealth of the Indies. There is no evidence that he tried, but it is certain that Portuguese traders found the trade in opium a ready source of profit.

Dutch Opium Trade

The Dutch however, must take the credit, or blame, for perfecting the opium trade of Asia. In the 1650s the Dutch began to buy opium in Bengal, the region of India which soon became the most abundant supplier of opium to Southeast Asia and China. Dutch traders of the VOC shipped elephants from Sumatra as well as Sri

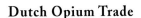

Lanka and the Malay Peninsula to Bengal in exchange for opium. Java, the Malay states, Sumatra and other parts of Southeast Asia were markets for this opium. The first reports of opium smoking are also from Java. Engelbert Kaempfer, the German pharmacist, inspected primitive opium dens and described Javanese smoking a mixture of opium and tobacco. 'In Java, I saw flimsy sheds (made of reeds) in which this kind of tobacco was set out (for sale to passers-by). No commodity throughout the Indies is retailed with greater return by the Batavians than opium, which (its) users cannot do without, nor can they come by it except it be brought by the ships of the Batavians from Bengal and Coromandel'.

Thus, the Dutch taught Asia a new vice, whereas before, opium had only been ingested, now people learned to inhale it. It was not long before the Chinese learned to smoke pure opium. Opium had been transformed from a medicine which was occasionally abused to something quite different, 'a recreational drug'. By the 1660s the habit appears to have spread to the Dutch outpost on Taiwan and from there to Fujian and the Chinese mainland.

Alexander Hamilton, the country trader, described how the Dutch began to trade Indian cloth and opium for gold dust with Bengkalis in Sumatra. A VOC factor named Lucas from Melaka pioneered the trade in the 1680s but kept it to himself, and in ten years' time was said to have made a profit of ten tonnes of gold. After retiring with his earnings, he revealed the secret to the Company who then took the trade into their own hands.

Thomas Stamford Raffles, who later founded Singapore, took control of Java from the Dutch in 1812 during the Napoleonic Wars. He also took over the Dutch monopoly of selling opium to the peoples of Java. His observation on the usefulness of drug sales is succinct and enlightening; 'opium has the effect of

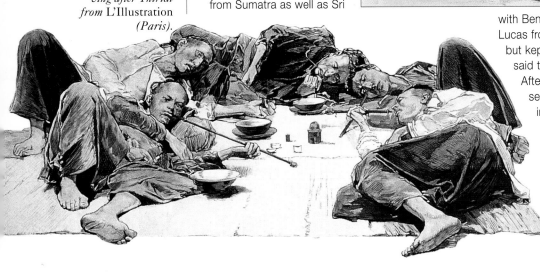

bringing into circulation the specie that might have 'wasted' away in the treasuries of native Javanese princes'.

During the pre-industrial era, Europeans had little to offer Asians in the way of trade goods. Outside of firearms, there were few European products that Asians coveted. The Dutch, and before them the Spanish and Portuguese, had come to Indonesia in search of spices and other tropical goods which Europe lacked. The same was true for European trade with China. The Dutch also found that opium was an easy way to obtain trade commodities in Southeast Asia which had a market in China or the west. Much of Sumatra's tin, pepper and gold; much of Java's sugar, coffee and indigo were sold, not for silver or cloth, but for opium. If Europeans wished to trade in Asia, they had to pay cash, which for them was an unsatisfactory alternative. They found, however, as have the drug dealers of the 20th century, that an addictive drug was a substitute for cash.

British Trade

At the beginning of the 19th century, the Dutch lost control of Java, first to the French under Daendels and then to the British under Raffles. Long before this, however, they had lost control of the opium trade at its source in India, to the British. Opium thus provided leverage for British trade to dominate Asia in the 19th century. It was not just an expeditious way to pay for their tea purchases, but it also gave them a measure of control over all the commerce of Asia. During the 19th century the Netherlands Indies expanded to what is now Indonesia. The Dutch still depended on the British, however, for opium, and it was from opium, which the Dutch sold to their own subjects in the Indies, that the colonial government reaped its greatest profits.

JOHN CRAWFURD'S REMARKS ON THE OPIUM TRADE IN EARLY 19th CENTURY JAVA

Opium, in all ages of the European intercourse with the Indian Islands, has been a considerable article of importation, and is at present a very great one. Throughout the islands, it is made with more justice than under the government of the country of which it is the produce, a subject of heavy duty. The native princes usually monopolise the sale, and the European government of Java farms the privilege of vending the drug in a medicated or prepared form. When the supplies were regular, the cost to the consumer was about 3,500 Spanish dollars per chest, or £787,10 sterling. Under this form of levying an excise on opium, the duties, if judiciously managed, would realise to the government, exclusive charges of collection, about a million of Spanish dollars a year, or £225,000 sterling.

The quantity exported from Bengal to the Indian Islands, one year with another, when the whole supply was from that country, was about 900 chests, of which Java alone consumed 550 chests. The quantity consumed depends, however, as in every other commodity, upon the price. The effects of this principle were illustrated in a most striking manner in all the sales in Java, of which I had personally a remarkable example in those under my own authority, within the territories of the sultan. When the retail price was about 5,000 Spanish dollars per chest, as it was on the British first taking possession of the island, the whole consumption was only 30 chests a year. When the price fell to about 4,000 dollars, the sales rose to about 50 chests, and when the price finally sunk to 3,500, the consumption advanced to near 100 chests. When the price was moderate, many had recourse to the drug who never used it before. When it was extravagantly high, many who had before used it moderately, desisted altogether, and those whose habits were more confirmed, had recourse as substitutes to native narcotic drugs, less agreeable and more pernicious.

Crawfurd, J. History of the Indian Archipelago (Frank Cass, London, 1967 reprint of the 1820, Edinburgh original) Volume III, pp 518–521

A Chinese opium smoker, by C.W. Allers (1898).

Javanese opium smokers, by C.W. Mieling (1853-62). The most important customers for opium from the Dutch monopolies were the ordinary Javanese peasants.

Papaver Somniferum, the opium poppy, from Kohler's Medizinal Pflanzen (1887). Its use as the source of the narcotic has been known since prehistoric times. The green seed pod of the plant is cut and the sap which exudes from the incision is collected as raw opium. From this substance smokable opium or chandu is made, as well as the more refined opiates, heroin, morphine and codeine.

Farming System

This was accomplished first through the farming system, in which wealthy Chinese privately purchased the right to retail opium to the population, while later an official government monopoly took over the processing and sale of opium. These systems lasted until the 1940s, and functioned mainly to free the Chinese labourer and the Javanese peasant of his spare cash. Throughout this period, Dutch officials expressed little concern for the debilitating effects of opium addiction on their subjects. Only when world opinion was focused on the practice in the 1920s was any move at all made to eradicate the trade and sale of opium. The process of elimination was, however, very slow, and the government was still in the opium business when Japanese forces arrived in 1942.

The Bugis Diaspora

*T*he role of the Bugis was characteristic of the period without strong Indonesian states. They embarked from a democratically pluralistic periphery of the Archipelago to build new networks which did not need to be upheld by state power.

Malay kampung in Makasar where a small number of Javanese and Malays lived.

Fishing for trepang, or sea cucumbers. During the 19th century voyages were organised in response to the high demand for trepang by the Chinese wangkang fleets visiting Makasar yearly.

The Bugis

The southwest arm of Sulawesi embraced three related peoples active as seafarers, the Makasarese in the southwest, the Mandarese in the northwest, and Bugis, the most numerous, occupying most of the remainder of the peninsula. These people shared a similar written script and a highly pluralistic political system in which local authorities were anchored in supernaturally endowed regalia (*arajang*) and descent from a variety of mythical ancestors, each separately descended from heaven (*tomanurung*). In the period 1600-1669 the city of Makasar and its Gowa-Tallo ruling dynasties dominated the region politically and economically. Resentful Bugis of the Bone kingdom therefore allied with the VOC to destroy Makasar in 1669. This event had at least two consequences. First, Bone became the most important kingdom in southwest Sulawesi until the 19th century. Second, it led to the Bugis diaspora, particularly of the men of commercial-minded Wajo, which had been allied with Makasarese Gowa rather than Bugis Bone in the war. The Bugis became noted both as effective warriors and enterprising traders throughout the Archipelago.

In Java

Two Bugis warriors achieved fame during the troubled years of Mataram, the principal Javanese kingdom of the 17th century. First, Aru Palakka, the King of Bone and an ally of the Dutch during its war with Makasar in the 1660s, assisted the Dutch in their involvement in Javanese politics and the affairs of Sultan Amangkurat I. Second, Karaeng (Prince) Galesong, one of the warriors

BUGIS WARRIORS
Bugis warriors, as reflected by the Dutch illustrator of Johan Nieuhof's published travels. After Arung Palakka's death many Bugis fought with Jonker as mercenaries for the Dutch, or even entered the ranks of the Mataram forces. Later, in the formation of the army of Mataram, a separate company of Bugis called the Pasukan Daeng was always included.

of Makasar and an enemy of Aru Palakka, assisted the rival of Amangkurat I, Prince Trunajaya from Madura. In 1675 Karaeng Galesong built his headquarters in Pasuruan (Eastern Java). Until his death around 1679, Galesong and his men roamed the north coast of Java assisting the Madurese warriors of Trunajaya. On many occasions they fought against Palakka and the Ambonese warriors of the VOC led by Kapitan Jonker.

In the Straits of Melaka

Another group of Bugis migrated to the Riau Archipelago (Straits of Melaka), headquarters of the Sultan of Johor since the mid 17th century. In 1679 a Bugis warrior, Daeng Mangika, and his men offered their assistance to the fugitive king, Ibrahim. From that time on the Bugis became involved in the politics of the kingdoms of the Malay peninsula. Daeng Parani, another warrior, succeeded in making himself viceroy (Yangdipertuan Muda) of Sultan Abdul Jalil of Johor at Riau in 1722.

Up until the end of the 18th century Bugis warriors were always appointed as viceroys of Johor. Daeng Parani was followed by his younger brother Daeng Marewah. Another relative, Daeng Chelah, whose son Raja Luma was appointed Sultan of Selangor, succeeded his uncle at Riau, followed by Daeng Kamboja. The last Bugis viceroy in Johor was a nephew of Daeng Kamboja, Raja Haji. From their headquarters in Riau the Bugis expanded their influence to a number of kingdoms on the peninsula. From time to time they controlled the tin kingdoms of Perak and Kedah. In the kingdom of Selangor they were unchallenged and eventually became kings themselves, starting with Raja Luma. Their economic base in the peninsula was the export of tin.

The political pattern began to change in the mid 18th century when Sultan Sulaeman of Johor allied himself with the Dutch at Melaka. By promising concessions on the tin mines to the Dutch, Sulaeman used them to balance the power of the Bugis. Daeng Kamboja was then forced to move from Riau to Linggi. The Bugis risked all in an attack on Dutch Melaka in 1756, but were badly defeated. Two years later three Bugis leaders, Daeng Kamboja from Linggi, Raja Tua from Klang and Raja Abdul from Rembau, tried to make their peace with the Dutch and Sultan Sulaeman. Raja Haji, the successor of Daeng Kamboja, tried every means to uphold Bugis power in the Straits, even murdering Sulaeman. In 1784 a large fleet was sent from the Netherlands under Admiral van Braam, defeating and killing Raja Haji of Melaka. From then on the political influence of the Bugis on the peninsula declined, though their position in Selangor continued. Many nobles of the kingdom today trace their ancestry back to the Bugis warriors.

AREAS OF BUGIS TRADE AND SETTLEMENT

In Eastern Waters

Since the emergence of Makasar as an emporium, traders from south Sulawesi became the middlemen in the spice trade from Maluku. Even though Makasar was conquered by the Dutch in 1669, their boats (*padewakang*), were always able to evade the blockade of the Dutch fleets protecting the monopoly on spices from Maluku.

Apart from trading in spices, the Makasar-Bugis traders also developed into the main inter-island traders in the eastern waters of Southeast Asia. In time two different trade patterns emerged among the Bugis. The first was the 'formal trade', using legal passes issued by Dutch authorities. The settlements of these traders in the cities of Maluku, like Ambon, Ternate, and Tidore were known as *Kampung Makasar*, although a small number of Javanese and Malays also lived there. In Ambon, besides trading, their leaders were used by the government as intermediaries when dealing with Muslim villages in central Maluku.

The second pattern was the 'informal trade', avoiding the formal trade routes controlled by the Dutch. Those who traded in this way, regarded as 'smugglers' by the Dutch, must have been more numerous than those who sailed with government passes. Most of them settled in the coastal area of north Seram which was still unoccupied by the Dutch. Those who settled in the villages on the islands east of Seram (Seram Laut and Gorong islands) had a longer history in the area as they had been visiting there since the early 17th century without the Dutch being able to stop them.

The Bugis trade network in the islands of Maluku was an extension of their settlements in various places in the Nusa Tenggara islands such as Bali, Lombok, Sumbawa, Sumba, and Timor. The 'informal trade' of the Bugis was important in two ways. First, many traders tended to marry locally and became in fact trade agents for their compatriots who visited the area once a year. Sea products were their principal interest, especially trepang (sea cucumbers) which were much in demand by the Chinese. The second importance of the Bugis presence in the eastern waters was their influence on local culture. The fact that they circulated such 'foreign' goods as iron, weapons, textiles, and rice was important to the development of the material culture of the area. Further, the influence of their house styles was strong in some settlements in north Seram. And most importantly, they brought Islam to the marginal islands of Maluku. Although Makasar was controlled by the Dutch from 1669, Bugis traders kept operating from the port city. A group of Bugis from Mandar, for instance, operated as far as Cambodia. Amanna Gappa, their *Matoa* (chief) in Makasar, rewrote the maritime laws of Melaka in the form of an elaborate Bugis maritime code.

Another trading activity organised from Makasar was the 'trepang' trade to the northern coast of Australia. Studies made by historians and linguists point to the fact that many loan words in the local Aborigine languages of the Northern Territory are of Bugis or Malay origin. In particular words denoting kinship, maritime activities, trade commodities, art, ornaments, parts of the body, and flora and fauna are positively identified as being Bugis or Malay.

Australian aboriginal drawing of an Indonesian (perhaps Bugis) prahu, visiting Australia for trepang.

« *Makasar man and wife, drawn for Nieuhof's voyages of the 1650s.*

A Bugis boat (padewakang). These small, fast vessels often evaded Dutch patrols.

Dualisms and Unities in Maluku

*T*he micro-island world of Maluku was held together as a system less by hierarchic power than by a complex web of ritual relationships. Although there were myths which linked the cultures of the different islands into the single conceptual world of Maluku, numerous dualities characterised relations between major groups within this system.

Royal korakora (galleys) of Tidore and Ternate, 17th century. From François Valentijn's Ouden Nieuw Oost-Indien Dordrecht *(Amsterdam, 1724-6).*

» *Muslims performing a ritual chant in Makian.*

⌐ *A Visit to the Sultan of Ternate, as illustrated by Paulus Lauters after C.W.M. van de Velde, from* Gezigten uit Neelands Indie *(Amsterdam, 1843-45).*

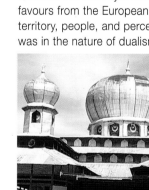

A mosque in Makian, one of the peripheral clove - growing islands in north Maluku.

Ternate and Tidore

The idea of 'Maluku' was apparently an old one, having been mentioned in the 14th century Majapahit epic, the *Nagara-krtagama*. However, the islands making up Maluku remained unclear. When the Portuguese first arrived in Ternate in the early 16th century, the term Maluku was applied to the five small clove producing islands of Ternate, Tidore, Moti, Makian and Bacan. The term 'Maluku' later came to include all areas in eastern Indonesia which were dominated by these small island kingdoms. Thus in time Maluku at its furthest extent represented an area extending westward to Butung and southeast Sulawesi, eastward to the Birdshead in New Guinea, northward to northern Sulawesi, and southward to the Aru-Kei islands.

A number of dualities characterised relations between major groups throughout the Maluku region, the most important of which was between Ternate and Tidore, two of the original Maluku entities. By the beginning of the 16th century, they were the two dominant kingdoms vying for supremacy in the area. What motivated this rivalry was a dualism which was regarded as essential for the maintenance and preservation of Malukan society. This dualism was expressed in the manner in which marriage partners were exchanged between the two royal houses, in competition for favours from the Europeans, and in conflicts over territory, people, and perceived studied insults. Yet it was in the nature of dualism that such conflicts had a

sacral function which was deemed essential to assure the well-being of the whole community. Therefore, despite the antagonisms between these two kingdoms, neither sought the destruction of the other. One Tidore ruler captured the essence of this rivalry by expressing the wish that both kingdoms should continue to exist, for the demise of either would mark the end of Maluku.

Dualisms and Rivalries

While Ternate and Tidore played out their dualism throughout the region, other dualisms and rivalries were evident in particular Malukan areas. These dualisms were expressed in the 'unities of five' and the 'unities of nine' (*Uli Lima* and *Uli Siwa* in Ambon; *Pata Lima* and *Pata Siwa* in West Seram; *Tutu Lima* and *Tutu Siwa* in East Seram, etc.). These divisions were a basis for alliances with the outside world. When the Ternatens extended their influence into Hitu on the northern peninsula of Ambon, they allied with the *Uli Lima*, who became Muslim and the enemy of the Portuguese. The Portuguese, on the other hand, linked themselves with the *Uli Siwa* groups in the southern peninsula, who became Christian and the enemy of the *Uli Lima* and the Ternatens. This type of arrangement became typical throughout Maluku, where the 'unity of five' would ally with one outside group with its particular political and religious ideas, and the 'unity of nine' would ally with another group representing the opposite ideas. In Maluku during the period from the 16th and the 19th centuries, the 'five-nine' dualisms frequently divided along both Christian-Muslim and coastal-interior oppositions.

Because of the importance of dualisms in Maluku, many of the historical narratives of the area based on political events are sometimes confusing to outside observers. What Europeans regarded as rebellions and political conflict often masked deeper cultural preoccupations. Such was the situation between Sultan Mandar Syah of Ternate (1648–75) and Sultan Saifuddin of Tidore (1657–89). After the ousting of the Portuguese from Ternate in 1575, a new sequence of alliances developed. The Spanish conquest of Ternate in 1606 led to an alliance between Tidore and the Spaniards. To counter Tidore's new strength, the Ternatens turned to the Dutch in 1607 and forged an equally powerful alliance. The balance was maintained till the middle of the century, when neglect of the Spanish outpost

in Maluku made the latter an uneven match for the ever strengthening Dutch East India Company.

The final departure of the Spaniards in 1663 left Tidore in what should have been an unequal relationship with Ternate. But the dualism demanded that some form of balance be maintained, and this was done through a sagacious decision by Sultan Saifuddin of Tidore to abandon the Spaniards a few years before their departure and to begin to court the Dutch. What occurred during the reigns of Sultan Saifuddin of Tidore and Sultan Mandar of Ternate was therefore a classic dualist sparring in which triumphs were marked by signs of favour shown by the Dutch governor toward one or the other monarch. So intense and subtle became this struggle that Malukans referred to Saifuddin as 'Tossa' and Mandar as 'Rossa' to indicate that both were from the same ball of wool.

Prince Nuku's Rebellion

Another more famous example of the cultural imperatives underlying political events is the case of Prince Nuku's 'rebellion'. In 1681 Ternate lost a war with the Dutch East India Company and was forced to become its vassal (*leen*) two years later. Tidore, on the other hand, retained its independence until 1779 when its ruler was deposed by the Dutch. With both Tidore and Ternate having been made vassals of the Company, the belief repeatedly expressed by Sultan Saifuddin of Tidore in the 17th century became widespread; as long as the two kingdoms

of Ternate and Tidore continued to survive, there would be peace and prosperity in Maluku. The domination of both kingdoms by the Dutch East India Company seems to have been interpreted by many as a sign of the demise of Maluku.

The phenomenal success of the Tidore Prince Nuku in drawing all different groups to his camp in defiance of the Dutch and their appointed rulers was principally due to his ability to translate Malukan grievances into cultural terms understood by all. He explained that the stability and harmony in Maluku had been disturbed by the undermining of the four major pillars (the kingdoms of Jailolo, Bacan, Ternate and Tidore) and finally by the demise of the dualism of Ternate and Tidore. Nuku's appeal was obviously understood, for it enabled him to resist the Dutch successfully for more than two decades and to retain power until his death in 1805. The case of north Maluku is not unique. Many other areas of present day Maluku continue to function in accordance with dualist imperatives, and political events can often be understood more fully within a dualist framework.

Remnant of walls of the Dutch Fort Victoria in Ambon.

☞☞ *Interior of a Christian Church in Ambon. Christianity came to south Ambon through the Portuguese who linked themselves with the Uli Siwa groups.*

The mosque of Ternate with its characteristic multi-layered roof, early 19th century. From H.D.T. Willink's Landschappen en Volkstypen van Nederlandsch-Indie *(Haarlem, 1883).*

Slavery and the Slave Trade

Slaves represented the lowest social category in many Indonesian societies, but what that really meant varied with time, place and context. In some cases, slaves were tribute paying retainers of powerful lords, living their own lives with their own families and farms; in others they were half starved, abused labourers or chained commodities for trade.

Two domestic slaves in a wealthy Dutch household.

⤚❯❯*A slave auction in Batavia.*

❯❯❯ *A romanticised European image of merchants selling slaves in Timor. A copper engraving from* Voyages et Naufrages Celebres *(Paris).*

A slave of Lombok with his belongings, 1865.

Economic Roles

Slaves could be drawn from their own community, through debt — the need for money for trade, rituals or gambling, or as punishment. But they could also be seized from other societies, in war, pirate raids or opportunistic kidnapping. Slaves could simply be an economic resource; sometimes this meant that they lived apart and maintained themselves while providing a surplus for their owner, or they could be in trade, even making long journeys with their master's (and perhaps their own) capital. Others provided the necessary labour for economic enterprises, such as the pepper gardens of Banjarmasin, the textile workshops of Bali and Selayar or the 19th century expansion of coffee and coconut production. In Maluku for example, the *orang kaya* used their many 'slaves' to harvest cloves from trees they had hired from farmers who had planted them. But slaves were also valued as unproductive signs of wealth and status. This was particularly evident in aristocratic or Dutch East India Company households, where retinues of musicians and concubines lived far more comfortably than most free people.

An example of the many uses and ambiguous status of slaves is given in a list of people controlled by the Bugis nobleman Aru Teko in 1701. Of the nearly 800 people, more than half were legally free but mostly debt-bondsmen, obliged to work for the Aru; of the slave remainder, almost a third had no legal slave status but were 'stolen' from Sumbawa. The Aru used them in various ways; a mixed group of slaves and freemen worked for him as fishermen, but most slaves or Sumbawan captives lived in his compound at Ujung Tanah near Makasar. This group included many single men (probably armed retainers). Elsewhere in south Sulawesi he also had mixed groups sending him tribute, plus a village allocated to him by the king as a reward for services. There was no clear division in residence or function between slave and free; distinctions in status and treatment formed a hierarchy in which the lowest rungs might reasonably be translated as slave.

Demographic Element

We can, however, make several generalisations about slavery and the slave trade. Firstly, slavery was an instrument of labour mobility and demographic change in Indonesia before the early 20th century. Slaves were used for labour, but also as agricultural pioneers, and as sexual partners and mothers, to

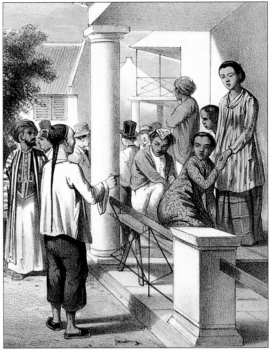

create new Indonesian settlements or to maintain and reproduce immigrant communities, such as those of Europeans, Chinese and Arabs. This demographic element is linked to economic frontiers and the balance of power; slaves tended to be drawn from inland communities to the coasts, and from east to west Indonesia. In the 15th and 16th centuries war torn Java was a major exporter of slaves to the Asian market (Melaka, Siam, Pasai and Brunei); in the early 17th century the Dutch drew many slaves from India. By the later 17th century we see patterns of slave trading by Bugis, Malays and mestizos with Makasar, a major transfer point, exporting around 3,000 people a year to

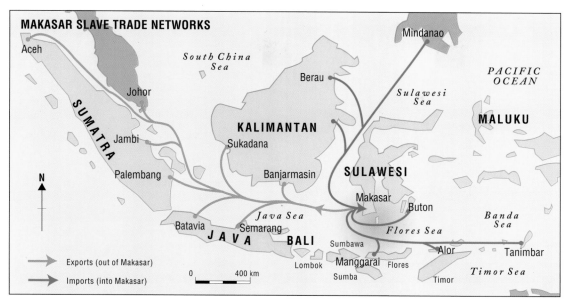

MAKASAR SLAVE TRADE NETWORKS

Exports (out of Makasar)
Imports (into Makasar)

0   400 km

A Toba Batak enslaved in Asahan, east coast of Sumatra. Having fled his long-term owners and been recaptured, he is being held in stocks prior to sale.

Batavia alone. In the later 18th century the feared Sulu pirates seized thousands in their raids.

Categories of Slave

A second point is the distinction often made between 'inside' and 'outside' slaves, between those who lived and worked within the household of the master, and those who maintained themselves outside. While the latter had more 'freedom', they were also often severely exploited, while the more dependent 'inside' slaves were integrated into the lower levels of the family. Indeed, when these were women who bore the children of their masters, they could achieve considerable status; Dutchmen, for example, usually freed the mother of their offspring, and acknowledge-ment of paternity gave the children legal European status. Such freedom was not always welcomed; in January 1679, the slave Elizabeth of Bengal, mother of two children, was legally reinstated as a slave at her own request, having found life as a free woman much too hard.

Worse off, however, than the 'outside' slaves were the 'trade slaves'. An 18th century Dutch slave trader in Makasar, Jacob Bikker Backer, bought most of his 'commodities' from local traders, and kept them in stone cellars and chains until he had a good stock; he reckoned on a 10 per cent death rate. Trade slaves were not considered to be people, being external to, or beyond the ties of society. In the *Hikayat Abdullah,* the author describes the arrival of

slave traders in Singapore in 1823. A Bugis had about 300 slaves for sale, including many women and girls; these were bought by Chinese, Indians and Malays 'who took them to wife'. Most were Bugis and Balinese, but people from Mandar, Manggarai, and the more Melanesian east were also mentioned. Malay traders also came from Siak, bringing in cargoes from Minangkabau in Sumatra and Pekan Baru in the Malay Peninsula. Abdullah was shocked by the beatings, the filth and the sexual licence of the trade. His outrage was shared by his patron Raffles, whose interregnum in Indonesia (1811-1816) laid the abolitionist movement's foundation.

The End of Slavery

The chronology of the slave trade before the 19th century is complex, because of the importance of local variation. There are trends in the development of the long distance trade, linked to the expansion of commerce and commodity production, but any changes which may have taken place in local communities' use of slaves are harder to establish. As the Dutch gradually extended their control over Indonesia from the 1830s to the 1910s, so they encountered, documented, and reluctantly moved to abolish the slave trade, aided by steamships and political contracts. This was done in a series of hesitant steps between 1818 and 1860; hesitant because the varied realities of Indonesian slavery — political subjugation, subordinate family member, abused being of non-human status — conflicted with the moralistic simplicities of anti-slavery campaigners like van Hoevell, whose depictions of such scenes as a 'slave auction in Batavia' mobilised public opinion in the Netherlands. Nonetheless, slavery remained a reality in many societies into the 20th century; travellers like the Sarasin brothers in Sulawesi took photographs of chained slaves being brought to market in 1895.

At best slaves could be the most trusted assistants of powerful men, more honoured and rewarded than most free men; at worst captive slaves were used as human sacrifices in a number of societies in Kalimantan and the east.

A Banda orang kaya, his arms carried by a slave, published by de Bry.

A 19th century Dutch image of a slave woman bathing, by E.A. Hardouin, in Ritter's Java (1855).

Two chained Toraja slaves brought to market in 1895, photograph by Sarasin.

Revolt of the Chinese and the 'Chinese War'

*T*he revolt by, and massacres of the Chinese in 1740 are often seen as gruesome, but isolated incidents. The effects, however, were far-reaching. It took years for the local economy of Batavia to recover, and to re-establish a measure of trust between the Chinese and the VOC. On Java the effects were catastrophic. The revolt triggered a war which tore the fragile fabric of the Javanese state asunder. When it was finally patched together in 1757, the body politic of Java had disintegrated.

Scene of the massacre of the Chinese in Batavia on 9 October 1740, an 18th century engraving.

Places attacked by the Chinese and the Javanese.

0   100 km

CHINESE ATTACKS ON THE DUTCH, 1740s

All Dutch posts, from Tegal in the west to Pasuruan in eastern Java, were attacked in the 1740s by the combined forces of the Chinese and the Javanese.

A wealthy Chinese trader carried by Javanese in a palanquin. In the 18th century the Chinese comprised more than half of the population in Batavia. They were also well represented in the economic life of the city. The revolt, therefore, surprised many Javanese (C.W. Mieling after van Pers, The Hague, 1853-62).

The Revolt

An increasing influx of Chinese from the end of the 17th century onwards, combined with a deteriorating economy, bred unemployment and banditry, especially in the countryside around Batavia where most of these immigrants found work in the sugar industry. Exhaustion of soil and forests had already depressed this industry, but the slump in exports caused by the closure of the Persian market in the early 1720s brought on a crisis. The Chinese were the main victims. Not only were the sugar mills almost wholly Chinese owned and worked by Chinese labour, but also a large part of the Chinese community depended indirectly upon this industry. Unemployment and banditry created an unmanageable problem.

Unlike the organised Chinese community within the town, the Chinese in the countryside constituted an amorphous mass which was kept under control by police brutality and corruption. Repression was the only answer the VOC found for the problem. At first, it had tried to limit the number of incoming Chinese and remove those without an official permit. The arbitrary enforcement of this policy and the enormous corruption in the sale of permits only worsened the situation until, on July 25, 1740, it was decided to arrest all wandering and suspicious looking Chinese, irrespective of whether they had a valid permit. If found without a livelihood, they were to be deported to Ceylon.

The resolution was enforced with unprecedented brutality, arbitrariness, and corruption. Unrest spread through the Chinese population and turned to panic on the rumour that Chinese being deported to Ceylon were in reality going to be drowned at sea. Illegal and legal residents fled to the woods where they banded together and armed themselves. Before anyone realised it, Batavia was besieged by bands of primitively armed Chinese. Then the panic spread to the European population, and led to the infamous massacre of the Chinese within the town on October 9 and 10, 1740. An estimated 10,000 Chinese in and outside the town perished in the massacre and the attacks. The survivors withdrew to Bekasi. In June 1741, they were dislodged and moved on to central Java.

The War on Java

The Chinese revolt sent a shockwave through central Java. Since the founding of Batavia, the Chinese and the VOC had collaborated closely. Batavia had literally been built by the Chinese. Not counting the slaves, they comprised more than half of the population, and the economic life of the city, in as far as it was not purely VOC business, depended on them. In Java the revolt was viewed as a sign from God spelling the end of the VOC.

For Sunan Pakubuwana II the revolt provided a chance to redefine his relationship with the VOC. Though elevated to the throne in 1726 with the help of the VOC, he had become thoroughly frustrated by the VOC's heavy handed political interventions and economic encroachments. They had thwarted all his attempts to strengthen his grip on his realm. The so–called help of the VOC did not seem worth its costs, especially since the VOC refused to help him against the recalcitrant Pangeran Cakraningrat of Madura.

When the VOC requested his help against rebellious Chinese from the sugar mills around Pati, Kudus and Demak who, by June 1741, besieged Semarang, the Sunan procrastinated. One faction, led by Patih Natakusuma, urged him to seize the opportunity and join the Chinese. Others showed less enthusiasm. They were worried more about their own position and the chances which a war might give to their opponents than about the VOC. Only Cakraningrat of Madura chose the side of the VOC. He invaded eastern Java and massacred the Chinese on his way. On July 20, 1741, Patih Natakusuma broke the deadlock in Kartasura by engineering an attack on the VOC fortress. This *fait accompli* seemingly swung the Javanese behind the Chinese. Reinforced by the arrival of the Chinese bands which had fled from Bekasi, the Javanese forced the fortress to surrender. They then joined the siege of Semarang, while another army was sent against Cakraningrat. For a while it looked as if the Javanese and their Chinese allies would succeed. From Tegal to Pasuruan, all VOC posts were besieged while Rembang and Juwana were overrun. However, Semarang held out. By sending the yearly return fleet via Semarang, the VOC managed in early November to break the siege. In the same month, Cakraningrat defeated the Javanese armies sent against him. The turning point of the war had been reached.

Critically exposed, Pakubuwana II approached the VOC. In revenge, the remnants of the Chinese and their Javanese supporters fell on Kartasura. On June 30, 1742, they occupied the kraton and elevated a grandson of Sunan Amangkurat Mas to the throne, while the hapless Pakubuwana II fled to Ponorogo. From there he attempted a counterattack with the few regents still loyal to him. Cakraningrat, however, headed him off and took Kartasura in November 1742. All over Java the war turned into a free-for-all struggle, usually determined by local feuds. The VOC, meanwhile, concentrated on recovering the coastal areas. Once that was completed, it pressured Cakraningrat to vacate Kartasura. On December 20, 1742, Pakubuwana II was reinstated on the throne of Java.

By reinstalling Pakubuwana II, the VOC hoped to avoid a lengthy war in the interior. Moreover, his gratitude would make him amenable to its wishes. It took, however, until November 1743 before a semblance of order was restored and the VOC could dictate a peace treaty. The golden opportunity of the Chinese revolt had turned into a nightmare. However, it was not over yet. What had started as a 'national effort' against the VOC had turned against the Sunan and then degenerated into local usurpations and struggles. Now it reached the core of the state, or what was left of it, when the Sunan's own brothers rebelled and carried on the war until the division of the realm in 1755. The only beneficiary appeared to be the VOC, which gained a firmer foothold in Java as a result of the war. Nevertheless as late as 1761 the forger of the compromise of 1755, Nicolaas Hartingh, still wondered whether it had been worth the cost.

BASIC CAUSE OF THE CHINESE REVOLT
The increasing influx of Chinese from China combined with a deteriorating Batavian economic situation were the basic causes of the Chinese revolt. The policy devised to deal with this problem–the first measures date from 1690– simply tried to limit the number of incoming Chinese and remove illegal immigrants. The arbitrary enforcement of this policy, however, and especially the enormous corruption involved in the sale of permits, only worsened the situation, until it finally erupted in 1740. These tensions were exacerbated by a worsening of both the basic problem and the policy devised against it. A 19th century Javanese depiction of an episode in the 'Chinese War' of 1741-2. From Museum Sono-budoyo, Babad Pacina.

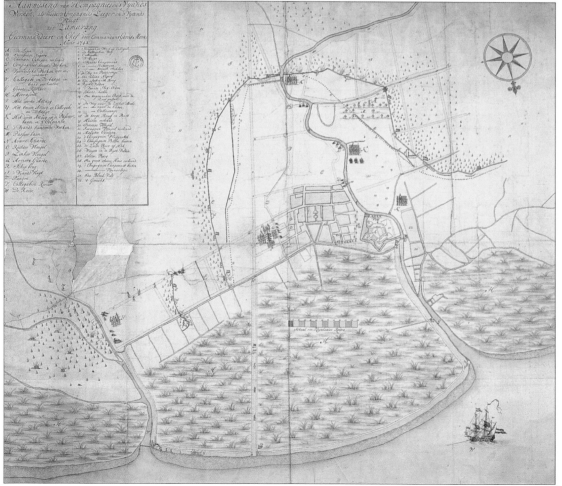

A contemporary map drawn by Commander Gerrit Mom, indicating the positions of his troops attacking the Chinese who retreated from Semarang, 1741 (ARA, Afdeling Kaarten en Tekeningen, VEL-1262).

Chinese immigrants, from an engraving after Charles Wirgman in the Illustrated London News. In the 18th century many Chinese immigrants worked in the countryside around Batavia.

Riau-Lingga Writers

*I*n response to political displacement and the threat of social change, the nobles of Riau-Lingga were inspired by the writings of al-Ghazali to foster the Muslim sciences and follow the ideals of Islamic kingship. The desire to record the past history of the kingdom, to educate their children and to entertain their peers, motivated literate men and women to compose texts, many of which survive in Riau, and in collections in Indonesia, Malaysia and Europe.

Some of the books from Yang Dipertuan Muda Raja Muhammad Yusuf's library, now in the Penyengat mosque.

⚘ *A 19th century Dutch impression of Penyengat island as seen from Tanjung Pinang, Riau.*

Yang Dipertuan Muda Muhammad Yusuf (ruled from 1858 to 1899) with his followers.

Historical Context

By the 19th century, the kingdom of Riau-Lingga was all that remained of the famous 15th century Malay court of Melaka. During the 18th century, the Malay sultans of Riau, descendants of the rulers of Melaka, had been forced to share power with a group of Bugis mercenaries from south Sulawesi who married into the royal family and were given the title of Yang Dipertuan Muda (Junior Ruler). The Bugis were skilled in commerce as well as war, and were active in the tin and opium trade which flourished during the mid to late 18th century. Conflict over control of trade in the Straits of Melaka brought serious clashes with the Dutch East India Company, and eventually resulted in the Bugis and Malays having to accept a Dutch presence in Riau. There followed a re-arrangement of the kingdom into a Malay Sultan centred court on the island of Lingga to the south, and a Bugis dominated centre on the small island of Penyengat, across the water from the Dutch post at Tanjung Pinang.

It is common to present the 19th century history of Riau-Lingga as a period of immense change and decline. However, compared with the situation during the 18th century when the kingdom was under regular attack from east Sumatra — and there was constant internal dissension as Bugis and Malays negotiated a *modus vivendi* — the acceptance of a permanent Dutch presence and the division into Riau and Lingga spheres of influence resulted in peace, and for a time prosperity. The trade which had formerly centred on Riau gradually shifted to Singapore, but Malays and Bugis still participated in the network and Riau became then, as now, a beneficiary of Singapore's efficient organisation of trade. When the Dutch finally deposed the Malay Sultanate in 1911 and ended the kingdom in 1913, most nobles were able to move permanently to Singapore or the Peninsula and re-establish their lives there.

Penyengat

The leading families of Riau, and to a lesser degree Lingga, profited greatly from the general renewed commercial vigour of the 19th century. They invested their profits in substantial building projects on Penyengat island which was developed as a gracious centre for the Yang Dipertuan Mudas and their relatives. Travel was also funded by trade and the first pilgrimage to Mecca was undertaken in 1828 by Raja Haji Ahmad and his son Raja Ali Haji. Their *hajj* signalled a quickening interest in Islam, the introduction of religious brotherhoods and commitment to the teachings of the great Muslim scholars, particularly the 12th century Persian theologian, al-Ghazali. Scholars from the Middle East who visited Singapore were brought also to Penyengat, to advise and teach, some staying for months. Money, travel and literacy provided

the impetus and the opportunity for some Penyengat nobles to collect books and manuscripts and to compose their own texts.

Literary Activity

Raja Ali Haji (c. 1809-1873) is the best known of the writers of Penyengat. With his father, he compiled the *Tuhfat al-Nafis*, a wide ranging history of Malay and Bugis interaction over almost two centuries. The work is remarkable because it specifically names the accounts, both written and oral, which have been used as sources, and it is concerned to organise its material chronologically and methodically. Raja Ali Haji's writings are representative of the variety of works which Penyengat authors composed. Besides history, he composed manuals for correct administrative practice in a kingdom, verses of moral guidance (*Gurindam Duabelas*, 1847), a grammar of Malay for the instruction of children (1851), and a two volume, but incomplete, encyclopedia of Malay language and custom (*Kitab Pengetahuan Bahasa*) which was begun in 1858. Each of these works has a table of contents, is systematically organised and is written to establish and preserve 'correct' Malay language, custom and behaviour, because Raja Ali believed that neglect of language and established tradition would cause the downfall of a kingdom. Following al-Ghazali, he believed that it was the function of the ruler to provide the material and spiritual conditions necessary for his subjects to observe all the tenets of Islam and to prepare for the world to come.

In the late 1880s some of the Penyengat writers formed the *Rusydiyah* Club, a cultural and religious study group which had its own printing press. Another press operated on the island of Lingga and published official documents as well as works for entertainment. Several members of the *Rusydiyah* Club later wrote for the Muslim reformist journal *al-Imam,* which was distributed from Singapore throughout the Malay speaking world, and became a voice for modernist Islam.

The Legacy

The reputation of Riau-Lingga as a centre which best preserved the 'high' Malay language of Malay courtly tradition, and Raja Ali Haji's reputation as grammarian and historian, attracted European scholars to come and study there. They compiled their own dictionaries and made copies of Riau texts as exemplars of 'good' Malay. As a result of their espousal of Riau Malay, it is this version of the Malay language which they chose to propagate as the unifying language of the Dutch East Indies. In due course it became also the basis of the national language of the Republic of Indonesia.

It is not so well known, that descendants and relatives of Raja Ali Haji continued to be specialists in Islam and to compose texts up to the time of the Second World War. Raja Haji Abdullah, a grandson of Raja Ali Haji, who was active in the 1920s, is still remembered in the Riau-Lingga area, and seems to have inherited some of his grandfather's extraordinary talents. He was fluent in Arabic, studied in Mecca, served as a judge in the religious court on Penyengat, and he was also respected for his knowledge of magic. He is said to have possessed a skull which could predict events, and a pen which could write by itself. In addition, he was a painter, sculptor and writer.

Many of the early 20th century writings from Riau-Lingga were published by the Ahmadiah Press in Singapore, which was also run by relatives of Raja Ali Haji. The Press was still operating in the 1980s. Another relative established a school, the Madrasat Muallimin, on Penyengat in the 1930s, to educate young Muslim men and women about their religion and the ways of the modern world. On Lingga, also in the the 1930s, one of the descendants of the Malay sultans composed a brief history of the Malay royal line of Riau-Lingga, a text which offers an alternative view of Riau history from Raja Ali Haji's *Tuhfat al-Nafis*.

The Japanese Occupation of the Riau-Lingga Archipelago caused a break in the writing tradition of the area, but in the 1950s several local histories appeared. It was at this time that the first attempts were made by local writers and scholars to produce an inventory of all books and manuscripts in the islands. Support was offered by the Indonesian Ministry of Education and Culture, and the official centre for Riau studies was located at the Universitas Riau, at Pekan Baru in southern Sumatra. In 1983 a group of individuals, some with direct links to Raja Ali Haji, established the Yayasan Indera Sakti (Indera Sakti Institute), on Penyengat, to preserve historical remains and buildings as well as texts and manuscripts. The institute cooperates with foreign scholars to document and research the cultural heritage of Riau and Lingga which now extends back for over two centuries.

« *A page from one version of Tuhfat al-Nafis, catalogued as Sejarah Raja-Raja Melayu dan Bugis, is held in the library of Dewan Bahasa dan Pustaka, Kuala Lumpur. One of the most factual of Malay histories, Tuhfat al-Nafis is a fine example of the blending of Islamic, Malay, Bugis and western influences at Penyengat.*

Grave of Raja Ali Haji (top).
19th century mimbar, or pulpit in Penyengat Mosque (center).
Mosque on Pulau Penyengat (bottom).

Jambi and Palembang: Friends and Rivals

*H*istorically, Jambi and Palembang have had a close relationship in which rivalry and friendship were mingled. While their royal families often intermarried, there was considerable competition in trading concerns. Both areas were well situated along the Melaka Straits, and both vied to supply passing traders with products from the ocean and the tropical rainforests.

Upstream groups in south Sumatra developed their own script for writing Malay, known as ka-ga-nga. Texts were written on bamboo, horn, rattan, and on the folded bast of certain trees.

»» Panglima Dalam (Rawas). An upland chief of Palembang dancing.

The Heyday of the Pepper Trade

The downstream rulers also competed to attract the loyalty of interior groups. The Batang Hari in Jambi and the Musi River in Palembang reach far into the interior, and their tributaries provided avenues connecting the sparsely inhabited coastal areas or *ilir* with the more populous and fertile interior (*ulu*). During the 17th century the pepper trade brought Jambi a superiority over its neighbour, but over the next 100 years this declined and Palembang, made prosperous first by the tin trade, reasserted its supremacy.

The economic importance of southeast Sumatra is indicated by the fact that both Jambi and Palembang were conquered by Demak sometime during the late 15th century. By the end of the 16th century both Jambi and Palembang had regained their independence and Jambi in particular had become well known for its pepper. This was grown on the upper reaches of the Batang Hari, primarily by Minangkabau migrants who brought it down to be sold at the *ilir* port of Tanah Pilih. Until the early 17th century the major overseas purchasers were Chinese and Portuguese, but in 1615 both the Dutch and English East India Companies established a post at Tanah Pilih, opposite the royal residence. Hoping to gain a monopoly over the pepper trade, the Dutch tried to negotiate a contract with neighbouring Palembang. However, relations soon soured and in 1659 Palembang was attacked and burned. The Dutch were now able to monopolise Palembang's pepper and in 1685 this was extended to Jambi following the English departure.

Jambi's Declining Prosperity

For both Jambi and Palembang the 17th century was a period of prosperity, when they were able to free themselves from Java's overlordship. Javanese influence remained strong, however, and in the court the Javanese language was still used until the end of the 18th century. Meanwhile, successive rulers attempted to extend their control into the interior, and to increase their authority over important pepper producing districts. The rivalry between them became more pronounced, for under Sultan Agung (died 1679)

Jambi had gained particular fame with its royal family linked by marriage to the rulers of Johor, Makasar and Banten. Jambi's prosperity, however, began to wane during the late 17th century, primarily because of the decline in pepper prices and the disadvantageous Dutch contract. A second reason was the difficulty of retaining control over the upstream districts as increasing numbers of Minangkabau men arrived to mine gold along the interior rivers. They often refused to acknowledge the authority of the downstream rulers. Relations between upstream and downstream worsened when pepper prices dropped. Rebellions became more frequent, and from 1687 until 1709 Jambi was divided, with a Dutch supported ruler downstream and a rival king based at Mangunjaya (near modern Muara Tebo). Although the country was then reunited under one ruler, Jambi was no longer able to maintain the wealth of earlier times. The association with the Dutch East India Company broke down, and in 1768, following an attack by Jambi, the Dutch post was withdrawn. In the following years the Jambi royal house became more closely associated with the Bugis-Malay court of Riau.

Palembang's Tin Trade

In Palembang the 18th century was a period of growth and expansion. A short-lived civil war was soon resolved in favour of a prince who assumed the throne in 1724 under the title Sultan Mahmud Baharuddin (1724-57). During his reign tin mining on the island of Bangka was expanded, as Chinese miners were encouraged to settle and open new sites. A contract was signed which gave the Dutch East India Company a monopoly over tin as well as pepper, but much of Bangka's tin was secretly traded with neighbouring ports. The wealth that came to Palembang during this period allowed its court to sponsor art and craft work, and the area became especially famous for its lacquer and for silk weaving.

In the early 19th century civil war broke out in both Jambi and Palembang. *Ulu* and *ilir* were divided under the control of rival princes and their followers. In 1833 the Jambi ruler, hoping for Dutch support against his opponents, signed a contract with the Netherlands Indies government at Batavia. From the middle of the century opposition to the Dutch was centred upstream, under the leadership of Sultan Taha. In 1904 Sultan Taha was captured and the Dutch imposed direct control. In Palembang, where the tin trade was economically so important, European involvement was much greater and direct control came earlier. Sultan Mahmud Badaruddin II attacked the Dutch lodge in 1811, encouraged by the English, who were enemies of the Dutch Napoleonic regime. During the following decade both the Dutch and the English attempted to assert their sovereignty over Palembang and thus gain access to its rich economic resources. In 1824, however, the last Palembang ruler was deposed and sent to Batavia. For 50 years the Dutch preserved the shell of the indigenous government, but this was replaced by direct control in 1864.

Though the old connections between Jambi and Palembang are now less obvious, memories of old links are still preserved in legends and folklore. Economically the region remains important, and the oil of Palembang (now in the province of South Sumatera) helps make it among the richest of Indonesia's provinces.

« The City of Palembang under attack by the Dutch fleet in 1659. The Chinese and Portuguese houses ❶, are depicted on the lower (southern) bank. To the right of the picture a defensive chain has been placed across the river between two forts ❷ and ❸, the defenders attempted in vain to burn the Dutch ships by floating blazing vessels down river into them. From J. Nieuhof (1732).

« Part of the royal burial complex at Lemabang, dating from the reign of Sultan Mahmud Badaruddin (1724–57).

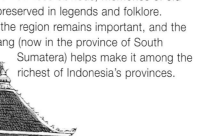

During the 17th and 18th centuries Minangkabau migrants developed gold mines in Jambi's interior. Here a woman digs for gold using traditional methods.

The Mesjid Agung, or Great Mosque of Palembang, originally built during the reign of Sultan Mahmud Badaruddin, from H.D.T. Willink (1883).

It also attracted migrants, notably Arabs from the Hadhramaut in the Yemen, several of whom intermarried with the royal family. Palembang rulers acted as sponsors for Islamic teachers and writers, and during the reign of Sultan Mahmud a great mosque was built, part of which still stands today. He also ordered the construction of a new palace (*kraton*), and the royal burial complex of Lemabang is an impressive testimony to his reign.

Increased European Intervention

The late 18th century was a difficult time in southeast Sumatra as maritime trade declined because of increased piracy in the Melaka Straits. Jambi's seaborne commerce did not recover and as the flow of Minangkabau migration continued, Jambi effectively became a Minangkabau vassal. Palembang's tin trade was also threatened by piratical trading, particularly by the Ilanun from the southern Philippines. Many Chinese miners left Bangka because of these recurring attacks. Smallpox epidemics were frequent, killing thousands of people. Relations with the Dutch were strained because Palembang's commerce found other outlets as the Dutch East India Company declined.

Chinese Mining Kongsis

China's prosperity, and its demand for metals in the mid-18th century raised expectations in Southeast Asia. There, deposits of gold and tin were in sparsely populated terrain, and local labour scarce. In about 1740, some sultans brought in Chinese miners; the Sultan of Palembang imported workers for the tin of Bangka, while the Sultans of Mempawah and Sambas recruited Chinese to mine gold in west Kalimantan.

THREE MAJOR KONGSI FEDERATIONS IN THE 1820s

Sambas River
• Sambas

SANTIAOGOU

• Singkawang

DAGANG
• Monterado

Great River

LANFANG
• Mempawah
• Mandor

N

Pontianak •

0   50 km

KALIMANTAN

An old photograph of Chinese tin miners in Bangka. In the 18th century the Chinese began to dominate the mining of tin and gold in Indonesia, activities previously the preserve of locals.

Settling a dispute. Chinese coolies fighting in a mine -'The coolies are a wild set of men and a scene such as that depicted is not an infrequent occurrence', from the Graphic (1895).

Chinese Gold and Tin Mining

Through the miners' kongsis, organised as share-holding brotherhoods, Chinese not only developed mining effectively, they became politically independent. Chinese mining technology and organisation greatly increased production, and therefore, profits. The Chinese used simple machines and water power to clean the ore, and mobilised, through kongsis, larger numbers of men to work a site. Supplying food, opium and other provisions at inflated prices, the sultans took a share of the metal produced in payment.

A kongsi was any common undertaking in which members held shares. Kongsi members chose their own headmen, clerks, and cooks, and, after smelting the ore, delivering the metal, and paying off their debts, divided their profits. The term 'kongsi' could also mean the quarters where the mine head and the workers lived. Europeans sometimes referred to kongsi bosses themselves as 'kongsis' or 'Congsees'.

Mining areas were isolated and insecure, and for defence, politics, or economic efficiency, the kongsis often expanded their power at the expense of that of the sultans. In Bangka, their involvement in smuggling provoked the Sultan of Palembang to discharge one Chinese headman. Finding, however, that

the tin was no longer being produced at all, the sultan was forced to reinstate him. Palembang finally lost control of Bangka during the British period (1811-16), and the Dutch subsequently absorbed the Chinese mining kongsis into state run tin production.

Gold Kongsis in Kalimantan

In west Kalimantan, sultans had even more difficulty controlling trade from their river mouth capitals, for other passages to the sea were convenient for transporting gold and smuggling supplies. Kongsis controlled much of the upland area north of the Kapuas river, between Pontianak and Sambas, by the end of the 18th century. They also formed alliances or 'federations' which increased their control and absorbed most of the smaller kongsis. After 1818, when the Dutch tried to assert their authority the larger three federations were virtually independent of the sultans, absorbing most of the smaller kongsis. In 1822, the Dutch made peace with the Lanfang Kongsi of Mandor (which bordered the territory of the Sultan of Pontianak), appointing its leader as *Kapthay* (great Kapitan) in the following year.

Unable to profit from the miners, the Sultan of Sambas, on whose territory the kongsis Dagang (Thaykong) and Santiaogou (Samthiaokioe) were situated, resorted to preying on navigation. When the Dutch suppressed piracy, they offered the sultan income from opium and salt farms in compensation,

THE FEDERATIONS OF THE LANFANG KONGSI IN MANDOR, 1822

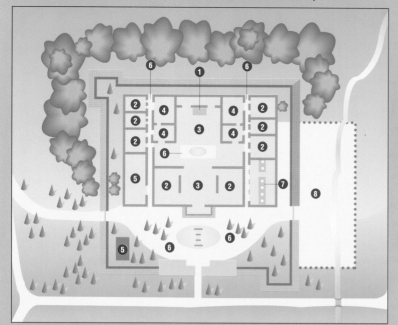

❶ Toapekong   ❸ Great hall   ❺ Store rooms   ❼ Cooking area

❷ Captains and   ❹ Guest rooms   ❻ Open areas   ❽ Sleeping quarters
   writers rooms

The kongsi house was more than a headquarters for the mine. It was a home to the mine boss (*Kapthay*) and other officials ❷, and living quarters for the bachelor miners ❽. The enclosure included storehouses ❺, kitchens ❼ and quarters for visitors ❹; gardens and pigsties were nearby. Most important was the great hall, both assembly room and temple ❸, with an open inner court and small pond ❻ in front of the altar and Toapekong ('Earth God') ❶. Defence was important; a palisade of earthworks and ironwood posts, some nine feet high, surrounded the quarters. In 1852 a visitor noted that the kongsi house of Mandor has stood for 80 years and would certainly last many more. The front courtyard ❻ also had a pond and bridge, perhaps of symbolic importance for the initiation of the miners, who became members of a common ritual 'brotherhood'.

Miners with families, farmers, and tradesmen usually lived in the pasar, a short distance away. There, wooden shop houses were built in rows at ground level; fire was always a hazard. Shop owners might hold shares in the kongsi as suppliers of capital, labourers, or provisions. In all, the pasar was about 400 metres long; the mines themselves were a distance from the settlement.

After an engraving in P.J. Vett, Borneo's Wester–Afdeeling, Vol.II, 1822.

Chinese miners smelting tin.

Tablets of the dead in the temple of Singkawang in West Kalimantan. A last relic of powerful Dagang?

of states. Farming settlements grew up to complement mining activities and federations established market places, improved paths linking settlements, collected tolls on the tributary rivers, maintained a standing army, and organised religious life. In addition to Toapekong or Dabogong, the 'Earth God', they especially worshipped Guan Di, patron of warfare and of merchants.

Changes Brought by Kongsis in Kalimantan

The introduction of Chinese miners changed the balance of power. On the other hand, the Sultans of Sambas and Mempawah lost some of their ability to profit from the upland peoples, the Dayak, who could ally with

Toapekong or Dabogong, the God of Earth and Riches, from the temple in Pangkalpinang, Bangka, an old tin mining area.

but the kongsis were already smuggling these products themselves. Why should they pay monopoly prices for goods they could obtain more cheaply elsewhere? The powerful Dagang Kongsi of Monterado remained intractable, although the Dutch repeatedly tried to make their authority felt. Its rival, the Santiaogou Kongsi, sought protection from the Dutch. Dagang then attacked, and most of Santiaogou's population fled to Sarawak. Between 1850 and 1854, the colonial power blockaded the coastline, assembled an adequate force to attack Monterado, overcame the recalcitrant miners' resistance, and dissolved the Dagang Kongsi. The last surviving kongsi was Lanfang, established in 1777. Already in debt and faced with depleted ore sites, Lanfang was abolished by the Dutch in 1884, on the death of the last *Kapthay*.

Kongsi Activities

As a result of the need for food supplies, communications, and defence, kongsis took on the attributes

the Chinese to avoid Malay domination. The sultans tried to use the Dayak to control the Chinese, but the Chinese formed alliances with the local people, often taking their women as wives. In battles with the sultans and the Dutch, some Dayak also fought on the Chinese side. The sultans gained and then lost income from the mines, finally depending on Dutch help. Kongsi battles over gold sites and water supplies contributed to unrest. When the Dutch subdued Dagang, gold was becoming scarce, for west Kalimantan was never the El Dorado they had hoped to find. For the sultans, the Chinese miners may have seemed like 'Trojan Horses', but they brought positive features as well. In both areas there are sizeable Chinese minorities whose activities in agriculture contributed to the livelihood of the entire population.

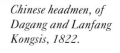

Chinese headmen, of Dagang and Lanfang Kongsis, 1822.

The Last Flowering of the Javanese State

*T*he wars which had plagued Java for so long at last ended between 1755 and 1757. In 1755, the rebel king Mangkubumi agreed to the Treaty of Giyanti with the VOC and reached a reconciliation with Pakubuwana III (1749-88) of Surakarta. Mangkubumi took over half of the kingdom, established his new court in Yogyakarta and took the title and name Sultan Hamengkubuwana I (1749-92). In 1753 the flamboyant Mas Said surrendered to Pakubuwana III, and was installed as the subsidiary prince Mangkunagara I (1757-95).

The water palace of Taman Sari (meaning 'fragrant gardens') was built as a pleasure garden, an aquatint by J. Jeakes (London, 1815). Accessible by water from the kraton, it contained sunken bathing-pools and various chambers, and a structure called Sumur Gumuling, which some people claim was intended as a mosque. Legends also link the palace with the Goddess of the Southern Ocean, a means by which the Sultan sought to establish his legitimacy as a monarch of the House of Mataram. (inset) Part of Taman Sari as it appears today.

Years of Peace

Throughout the remaining years of the 18th century, intrigues amongst the Javanese aristocracy continued. But it seems that the aristocrats felt the cost of the 80 years of frequent warfare from the 1670s to the 1750s to have been too high. There was not a major war in Java again until 1825, although there were some minor clashes. These seven decades were probably the longest period of peace in Java since the 15th century, perhaps the longest ever in the history of the Javanese state.

The Dutch East India Company was slipping rapidly towards bankruptcy and wished no more involvement in wars in Java. It was a relief that such warfare came to an end, removing both the occasion and the need for VOC intervention. As a result, the Javanese elite had greater opportunity to shape their own destiny than had been true for a century.

Court Culture

In Sultan Mangkubumi (Hamengkubuwana I) of Yogyakarta, the Javanese dynasty at last had a ruler of wisdom and stature, who saw in the circumstances of late 18th century Java an opportunity to restore the fortunes of the bloodied dynasty. He ruled his new kingdom firmly, supported by all those lieutenants who had been at his side

during the nine years of civil war. But Yogyakarta was only one of two courts: in Surakarta Susuhunan Pakubuwana III (1749-88) still ruled. After the end of the civil war, courtiers began to return to Surakarta and it, too, began to gain a grandeur which had not been possible during the years of fighting.

In both courts, cultural life was patronised by the kings. Sultan Mangkubumi himself is credited with personally composing several *wayang wong* (dance drama) texts. Javanese literature blossomed in this period. Long poems of an Islamic religious character, romantic adventures and other works survive from the courts of both Surakarta and Yogyakarta. One Javanese source tells of Mangkubumi himself quoting from a Javanese chronicle as a means of instructing his sons. This literature was an important repository of cultural paradigms which guided the Javanese courts in their regained power and splendour.

Twice a week there were tournaments at court, where courtiers exercised the martial skills which were increasingly unnecessary in an age of peace, but the equestrian knight remained a central cultural paradigm of the courts. They jousted on horseback. They performed stylish dances with weapons, which also drilled soldiers in how to fight with lances or other arms.

Political Conflicts

The cultural and political restoration of the Javanese state was only seriously threatened when Pakubuwana III's life came to an end. His son, who succeeded in Surakarta as Susuhunan Pakubuwana IV (1788-1820), began to dispose of many old court officials and to ignore senior members of the royal family. He surrounded himself with a small circle of new religious scholars (*santri*) whose doctrinal affiliations are not known with confidence. Their enemies accused them of not being orthodox Muslims. At least they told the new king that they had supernatural powers and could reduce Yogyakarta to a status inferior to that of Surakarta.

Such ideas threatened the vital interests of Sultan Mangkubumi, of prince Mangkunagara I and of the

Tigers were set to fight buffaloes on the great squares before the courts. The Javanese saw these contests as a metaphor for relations between themselves and the Europeans, with the buffalo representing themselves and the tiger the VOC. The slow but powerful buffalo almost always succeeded in defeating the tiger, which was quicker but had less stamina (J.J.X. Pfyffer zu Neueck, Skizzen von der Insel Java, Schaffhausen, 1829-32).

VOC, which correctly saw a balance between Yogyakarta and Surakarta as essential to its own continuing presence on the north coast of Java. The Javanese enemies of Pakubuwana IV's *santris* did all they could - including providing exaggerated stories of their perfidy - to persuade the VOC to act, despite its reluctance to be involved militarily in central Java again. In November 1790, combined forces from Mangkunagara I, Yogyakarta and the Company besieged the Surakarta court and demanded the surrender of the *santris*. Finally the king gave in, his new favourites were sent into exile and the old elite was re-established in control of Surakarta. No fighting had been necessary, to the relief of all.

Forebodings

At the death of Sultan Mangkubumi in 1792, Yogyakarta was probably the most powerful

Javanese state since the time of Sultan Agung a century and a half before. But three matters boded ill for the future. First, the next generation of the Yogyakarta royal family would not match the wisdom and ability of the old sultan. Second, European power in Indonesia was about to revive and reach a level never before seen there. And third, the fact that the Javanese state was divided into the two kingdoms of Surakarta and Yogyakarta, and the subsidiary Mankunagaran principality meant that the Javanese royal elite could not stand together in facing the new challenge of a more powerful Europe.

The Pendapa Agung, the great reception hall, in the Palace of the Mangkunagara in Surakarta. The Pendapa with a ceiling painted with cosmic symbols is among the largest and most majestic in Java (KITLV, Netherlands).

The Yogyakarta kraton, designed and built in stages between 1756 and 1790 by Yogya's founder, Sultan Hamengkubuwana I, is a splendid example of traditional Javanese court architecture (Demmeni, published by Toeristenbond voor Nederland, 1900s).

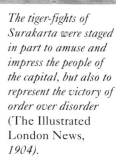

KRIS FROM SURAKARTA
Naga sasra kris, identified by the gold naga (serpent) inlay on the blade, said to have been made in the Surakarta palace in 1800. All kris must have blades with an odd number of curves; this fine example has 11. It was purchased from a Mr Groenveldt for 150 guilders in December 1947; the seller claimed that it was one of a set of 20, made in emulation of the pusaka of the Surakarta court.

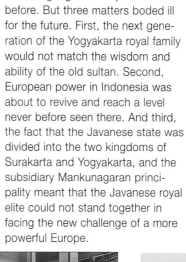

The tiger-fights of Surakarta were staged in part to amuse and impress the people of the capital, but also to represent the victory of order over disorder (The Illustrated London News, 1904).

South Sulawesi After Arung Palakka

*T*he Dutch took control of Makasar (Ujung Pandang) for purely commercial reasons, and had neither the desire nor the capacity to control its hinterland. Dutch interference in succession disputes was sufficient only to prevent a hegemonic Bugis or Makasar power emerging again.

↘ *Arung Palakka's tomb, at the Gowa royal burial site in the outskirts of Ujung Pandang. It is regarded as sacrally highly potent among local inhabitants.*

· » *A 20th century Bugis arung (lord) and his courtier. These are descendants of Bugis warriors who supported Arung Palakka.*

Salakoa crown from Gowa-Makasar, 16th century. The possession of royal regalia (pusaka) was a powerful factor in succession disputes.

The Fall of Gowa and Wajo

The Bungaya Treaty, signed between the Makasar twin kingdoms of Gowa-Tallo and the VOC in 1667, set the groundwork for the realignment of power in south Sulawesi. It is a significant document because problems were structured in a south Sulawesi manner.

The local word used for 'treaty' in the document was *ceppa* (Bug.) or *cappa* (Mak.), which means 'to take part in something'. The treaty also mentions by name a number of the many small states which comprised south Sulawesi. Local traditions of the coming of heavenly beings-*Tomanurung* (Bug.), *Tumanarung*, (Mak.)-and the existence of sacred objects-*gaukeng*, (Bug.), *gaukang* (Mak.) identified with specific communities, encouraged the proliferation of smaller states. The Bungaya Treaty did not interfere with their existence, but simply realigned them with the new local overlord, Arung Palakka. Nevertheless, the conquest of Gowa-Tallo in 1667 and of Wajo in 1670 by the combined forces of the Dutch East India Company and Bone-Soppeng under Arung Palakka had major consequences for these kingdoms. The utter devastation of Gowa and Wajo had resulted in a flow of refugees out of south Sulawesi to various parts of the Archipelago and even to mainland Southeast Asia. This stream of refugees did not abate during the reigns of the Bone rulers Arung Palakka (1672-96) and of his chosen successor La Patau (1696-1714). One compelling reason for the exodus was the increasing practice in south Sulawesi of selling the enemy as slaves to the Dutch East India Company. In the 17th century and the first half of the 18th century Dutch demand for labour was met by 'kuli slaves' principally from Bali, Banda, Timor, and Sulawesi.

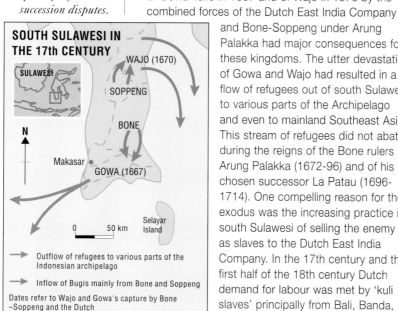

SOUTH SULAWESI IN THE 17th CENTURY

WAJO (1670)
SULAWESI
SOPPENG
BONE
N
Makasar
GOWA (1667)
Selayar Island
0   50 km

→ Outflow of refugees to various parts of the Indonesian archipelago

→ Inflow of Bugis mainly from Bone and Soppeng

Dates refer to Wajo and Gowa's capture by Bone –Soppeng and the Dutch

The large movements of people out of their homeland left many of the Gowa and Wajo areas desolate and the governments weakened. This invited incursions by the victorious Bugis, mainly from Bone and Soppeng, who began to settle in some of these vanquished lands. With many Gowa and Wajo leaders either forbidden to govern or in exile, the people had to tolerate rulers who were placed in power either by Arung Palakka and later La Patau or by the Dutch East India Company. Only after the passing away of these two Bone rulers did the situation in south Sulawesi begin to show the signs of long suppressed discontent.

Bontolangkasa

Controversy surrounding the selection of a successor to the Gowa ruler in 1709 revealed the deep rifts in the society. While the Dutch and La Patau chose one contender, the Gowa nobles and members of the council known as the Bate Salapang preferred another. A struggle known in Makasar as 'the family war' (*bundu'pammanakang*) occurred but was quickly resolved in favour of the Dutch and Bone choice. Yet this favoured ruler, too, later displeased the Dutch and was removed in 1712. The new ruler chosen was again opposed by the Gowa leaders, among whom was Karaeng Bontolangkasa, a person of high birth who felt aggrieved at not having been offered the Crown. He therefore left south Sulawesi to settle in Sumbawa. When he finally returned in 1723, the situation in Gowa had not improved, and the Dutch were still playing kingmakers. Bontolangkasa took advantage of the frustration and deep discontent in Gowa society to lead a movement to oust the Dutch. He seized Gowa and became its ruler in April 1739.

La Maddukkelleng

When he began to organise the Gowa people, Bontolangkasa was able to gain the support of similar movements in Bone and Wajo. Arung Kaju of Soppeng plotted to overthrow his wife the reigning Queen of Bone, but he was discovered and had to leave to save his life. He and his followers formed a large group fighting alongside Bontolangkasa. However, his strongest ally was La Maddukkelleng Arung Sengkang of Wajo. Like Bontolangkasa, he had spent time in exile as a result of having been accused of insulting the royal family of Bone. He was called back from exile in Pasir in east coast Kalimantan, and when he reached Wajo in 1763 he was raised to be the Arung Matoa (ruler of) Wajo. La Maddukkelleng then began a campaign to remove the Bone settlers from Wajo, and while he was occupied with this, Bontolangkasa and Arung Kaju proceeded to attack the Dutch positions in Maros, the ricebowl north of Makasar. Thus began a series of battles in which the people of Wajo and Gowa, aided by certain discontented Bone elements, sought to harness the long suppressed population for a final struggle to evict the Dutch from south Sulawesi. Despite their early successes, they were unable to withstand the combined Bone and Dutch forces. Gowa was seized in July 1739, and two months later Bontolangkasa died of wounds sustained in the fighting. La Maddukkelleng continued to resist until his death in 1765.

I Sangkilang

The campaigns of Bontolangkasa and La Maddukkelleng, though ultimately unsuccessful, made a strong impression on the minds of the people of south Sulawesi. In 1776 a person from Gowa, known by the people as I Sangkilang, appeared and claimed to be a former ruler who had been exiled to Ceylon. Despite his dubious story that the ship transporting him to Ceylon had foundered and had enabled him to escape, the people wanted to believe him because he promised to remove the Dutch from their lands. This appeal had proved to be effective for Bontolangkasa, La Maddukkelleng, and now for I Sangkilang because the people traced the cause of their suffering to the defeat of Gowa in 1667 at the hands of the Dutch.

I Sangkilang successfully attacked the Dutch at Maros, thereby helping to swell the number of his followers. Though he was soon forced out of Maros, he succeeded in conquering the Gowa capital, deposing the king, and being made the new ruler in 1777. Dutch efforts to dislodge him from Gowa failed because of his solid support among the people. With the arrival of the English in eastern Indonesian waters soon thereafter, the Dutch were too preoccupied to launch further campaigns. I Sangkilang was able therefore to maintain his position until his death in 1785.

The Dutch in Control

After I Sangkilang's death the Dutch seized Gowa's regalia and presented it to the ruler of Bone. With both regalia in his possession, the ruler of Bone wished to unite the two kingdoms, but the Dutch feared that this would make them too formidable to control. Toward the end of the century the Dutch became less willing to tolerate any opposition whatsoever for fear that this would lead to English intervention. The Dutch therefore made certain that whoever was chosen to be ruler of any of the south Sulawesi kingdoms would be submissive to Dutch wishes. The English interregnum in 1811-1816 did little to change the situation, and opposition to the Dutch for much of the 19th century came principally in the form of the occasional figure, like I Sangkilang, who claimed to represent a former champion of the people.

The remains of the palace built by Arung Palakka at Bontowala (near Makasar): a mosque and graveyard, as depicted by J.C. Rappard from Het Kamerlid van Berkenstein in Nederlandsch-Indie (Leiden, 1888).

The Dutch Governor's residence within Fort Rotterdam in Makasar.

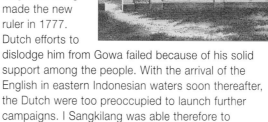

FORT ROTTERDAM
The fort's original name, Ujung Pandang, can be variously translated as 'the furthest visible point' (as seen from the south) or as 'Screwpine Cape', from the screwpine pandanus palm which grew at this point, and was used in making mats.

The Dutch fort also became known as Benteng Panyu (turtle) because it looked like a huge turtle crawling to the sea. From the time of its construction in the 1670s, Fort Rotterdam was the centre of Dutch power in central Sulawesi.

The palace of Buitenzorg ('Beyond Care', sans souci), or Bogor. This palace was established as a retreat by Governor-General van Imhoff in 1745. Thomas Stamford Raffles was the first Governor of Java to establish his principal residence there, but subsequently its mild climate and stately gardens attracted many 19th century Dutch Governor-Generals to make it their main residence in preference to Batavia. This picture by J. Gordon, 'Prise du Parc' was painted in 1843, after an original by A.J. Bik.

ESTABLISHMENT OF DUTCH POWER IN THE 19th AND 20th CENTURIES

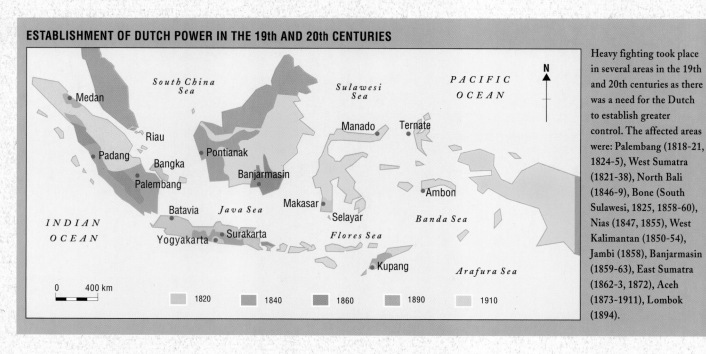

Heavy fighting took place in several areas in the 19th and 20th centuries as there was a need for the Dutch to establish greater control. The affected areas were: Palembang (1818-21, 1824-5), West Sumatra (1821-38), North Bali (1846-9), Bone (South Sulawesi, 1825, 1858-60), Nias (1847, 1855), West Kalimantan (1850-54), Jambi (1858), Banjarmasin (1859-63), East Sumatra (1862-3, 1872), Aceh (1873-1911), Lombok (1894).

Founder of Singapore, author of the first (and some would say the best) serious book in English on Java, opponent of slavery, upholder of English enlightenment values, and proconsul first of Java then of British Bencoolen (Benkulu), Thomas Stamford Raffles (1781-1826) looms larger than life in Southeast Asian history-especially in British eyes. The Dutch tended to see him as an outrageous troublemaker, and some Javanese princes saw him as a brutal aggressor. But the judgement of history is likely to be that, taken together with that of his Napoleonic predecessor Marshall Daendels, Raffles' regime marked (according to Ricklefs writing in 1993) 'a colonial revolution, a new policy which called for European assumption of sovereignty and administrative authority throughout Java, and which aimed to use, reform or destroy indigenous institutions at will'.

At the age of 30 Raffles was named Lieutenant-Governor of Java after a British force took over the colony in the name of the exiled Dutch king in 1811. Raffles had risen meteorically as agent of the Governer-General of India for the Malay States, and had spared none of his remarkable energy in convincing Lord Minto that Britain's destiny was as enlightened rulers of the Archipelago. In Java he ruled with unprecedented vigour if not always success, attempting to make Java a modern colony staffed by officials (rather than heriditary princes) and paid for by a land tax. He publicised the ancient monuments of Java, but was very harsh on the independent-minded princes of Yogyakarta.

When, to his disgust, Java was returned to Dutch rule in 1816, Raffles continued his attempts to extend British influence from the unpromising British pepper colony of Benkulu, long moribund before his term as Lieutenant-Governer there (1818-23). There he curbed slavery, reformed agriculture, launched the *Malayan Miscellanies*, mounted expeditions to Pasemah, Minangkabau, the Batak area, and Nias, signed a treaty with Aceh, and of course founded Singapore as a permanent base for British influence. Finally, he was inexhaustible in collecting and copying manuscripts, and established a secure base for the study of the Malay world in Britain, and more generally in Europe.

NINETEENTH CENTURY PRESSURES

The 18th century ended with the collapse of the VOC after its lifeline to Amsterdam was cut during the Napoleonic Wars. For Indonesians this was a time of opportunity as the VOC monopolies were replaced by a freer system of trade, in which English and American private traders provided the crucial external stimulus. This brought new wealth especially to Acehnese, Minangkabaus and coastal (*pesisir*) Javanese. Arab traders from the Hadhramaut were among those taking advantage of the new opportunities, and traffic to the Middle East became easier. Ideas of Islamic reform followed the routes of trade and pilgrimage, including the militant Wahabbism of the Padris in Sumatra. The ideas of the French Revolution and the English Enlightenment also found their supporters as the Archipelago became caught up in the European turmoil. A Napoleonic Governor — Marshal Daendels — (1807-11) was replaced by the English Government (in Java) of Stamford Raffles (1811-16). The English and the Franco-Dutch each encouraged Indonesian princes to defy their rivals, giving rise to a period of some fluidity.

The British restored all their possessions in Indonesia to the Dutch in 1816, except Benkulu which was surrendered in exchange for Melaka in the 1824 London Treaty. But the informal influence which the VOC had through its commercial strength was lost to the economically weak Netherlands colony. Dutch colonial profits now came more from estate agriculture than from trade, so that a greater degree of control was required.

After the upheavals of 1795-1816, Dutch power had to be established over most of the Archipelago by force (see map, left), even in central Java where Daendels' and Raffles' interference had created a turbulent situation. With the exception of the damaging Java War of 1825-30, however, Java was in a condition of relative peace after the Giyanti Treaty of 1755. Rapid population growth began about a century earlier in Java than elsewhere in Indonesia, so the 19th century saw Java's population shoot ahead of all the other islands combined.

An awareness of weakness and impending crisis can be sensed in much of the literature of the period. Frequently it sought to explain contemporary defeats in terms of moral decline. Even when moralists appealed for a return to older values, however, they perceived themselves as their ancestors could not have, as an embattled collectivity seeking a new form of identity with which to compete in an increasingly threatening world.

Pepper and the Revival of Aceh

*F*rom the 1790s to the 1870s Aceh emerged once again as a major pepper exporter, producing nearly half the world's supply of pepper. The revitalisation of pepper production was initiated by local rajas controlling a 75 mile stretch of the west coast between Trumon and Kuala Batu.

A pepper vine, Piper nigrum, *from Kohler (1887).*

ʾʾ Captain Thomas Forrest at the Acehnese court in 1784.

The seal of Sultan Jauhar Alam Shah of Aceh, 1795-1824.

A view of the South Front of Fort Marlborough, West Sumatra, by J.C. Stadler (1799).

Pepper Planters and Workers

New vines brought from the Malabar coast of India grew well in the sloping and well-drained coastal plains and river valleys of Aceh. In this part of Sumatra, production of pepper rose from 2.13 million pounds in 1797 to an estimated 18.6 million pounds in 1822. As the west coast developed it attracted migrants from Aceh and Pidië. Some were from the older pepper areas forced to move due to soil exhaustion. Others sought to escape the sultan's trade control which was characterised by low commodity prices and high taxes. Life in the pioneering pepper districts was tough. The majority of the migrants ended as paid labourers enduring loneliness and mostly hardship. The celebrated *Hikayat Ranto* describes vividly the life of an immigrant Pedirese cultivator in the pepper-growing west coast of this period.

The Ulubalangs

There was also the class of planters who were ruling chiefs, and Lebai Dappah and his family in Singkil best typified these early entrepreneurs. Originally from Aceh proper, they pioneered new pepper plantations and encouraged planters from neighbouring regions to sell through Singkil. New wealth enabled Lebai Dappah to extend control over additional ports which he turned into flourishing pepper centres. Of these, the most important was Susoh.

Coastal chiefs such as Lebai Dappah were important in maintaining political order along the coast. New pepper wealth became a source of occasional tension in the area as coastal chiefs competed for trade and contested disputed pepper districts. These *ulubalangs* also had to cope with the demands of the sultans who claimed duties on all pepper exported.

Coastal *ulubalangs* particularly Lebai Dappah also had to respond to expanding British and Dutch commercial interests in the region. In the late 18th century there was a reappearance of British presence. An increasing number of private and Company ships, some based in Madras, arrived to obtain pepper for the growing China trade. Two outposts, Natal and Tapanuli established in the 1750s, collected pepper from the Acehnese coast for Bengkulu and for passing British ships. Over time, some understanding was reached between Lebai Dappah and local British officials demarcating their respective spheres of influence and regulating trade practices.

It was the commercial role of the *ulubalangs* through whom all trade were conducted which was crucial. The *ulubalangs* were the producers and, as ruling chiefs, the ones relied on to enforce and honour all contracts made. Through them a freer trading condition in the west coast was created as against the monopolistic control of Acehnese rulers and European companies elsewhere.

American Pepper Traders

The arrival of American traders led to a more competitive condition in the Acehnese west coast. The first of the American ships turned up in Sumatra in 1790. From then until 1860, American ships based largely in Salem and Boston, made an estimated 967 voyages to Sumatra. They carried away more than 370 million pounds of pepper worth about 17 million dollars. This represented almost half of all pepper produced in Aceh in the period. Low operating costs and faster ships enabled American traders to compete with the British and Dutch in the European pepper market. American trade in the Acehnese west coast worried the British. In the 1818 pepper season 35 American ships turned up, a number larger than at any one year prior to the blockade. Bengkulu authorities sought to check American trade and had on occasions detained American ships on alleged violation of British trading laws. Sir Stamford Raffles,

who took office in April 1818 as Lieutenant-Governor, alerted London and Calcutta to the seriousness of American competition. More ominous, according to Raffles, were reports that an American at the Acehnese capital was probably negotiating for a permanent American presence there.

First Phase in the Pepper Industry

Meanwhile, efforts by Sultan Johar Alam Shah (1795-1823) to enforce collection of duties on the pepper and betel nut trade led to strong opposition from the *ulubalangs*. The sultan, seeking to curb the growing political influence of the enriched coastal ports, complained to Penang and Bengkulu that unregulated trade in the west coast particularly involving American traders had cost him serious loss of royal revenue. Rebelling *ulubalangs* eventually overthrew the sultan in October 1814 and the son of a Penang Arab trader was installed instead.

On developments in Aceh, British opinion was divided. Penang insisted on trade unhindered by Acehnese central control. Raffles disagreed, arguing that a weakened court rendered the sultanate vulnerable to Dutch expansionist plans. Concerned about the effects of the civil war on British trade and worried about Dutch intentions, Raffles and John Coombs were sent to negotiate a treaty with the claimant most likely to prevail. On 22 April 1819, the mission recognised Johar Alam Shah, and through a treaty offered him assistance in exchange for factory facilities and an undertaking to exclude American and European powers from Aceh. The treaty was relied on later to gain, in the 1824 London agreement, Dutch acceptance of Aceh's independence and British trade in Sumatra.

Second Phase

Under Sultan Muhammad Shah (1823-38), a second phase in the pepper industry took place when production shifted to the region north of the west coast districts. Production in the old pepper region had begun to decline. Soil exhaustion and root disease attacking the pepper vines were the main reasons. New plantations were opened further to the north such as Pate, Rigas, Teunom, and Meulaboh. Production of pepper reached 13 million pounds (100,000 pikuls) in 1839.

The shift was also due to the growing importance of Penang and Singapore as transits for Acehnese pepper. Since the founding of Penang, pepper was carried to the island by hundreds of small Acehnese boats. A larger volume was transacted by ships of Chinese and British merchant houses in Penang. Penang and Singapore assumed more importance following the withdrawal of the British from Bengkulu in 1824 and the decline of American pepper trade in Sumatra.

Third Phase

The third phase of pepper production began with the opening of new plantations along the north eastern tip between Lhokseumawe and Tamiang in 1850. Political stability and the granting of a degree of autonomy by Sultan Ali Ala'ad-din Mansur Shah (1838-70) encouraged the *ulubalangs* to expand pepper production. The two principal pepper producers in this district were Simpang Ulim and Idi Rayeuk, each exporting an estimated 4.6 million pounds (35,000 pikuls) per annum. Together with Julok Rayeuk, Peureulak and Peudawa Rayeuk, this region produced 13.3 million (100,000 pikuls) annually. The population in the eastern region of Aceh swelled to an estimated 100,000 in 1873 through arrival of workers from other parts of Aceh. Pepper enriched many *ulubalangs* through income from taxes levied on the produce, from a monopoly of trade, and from ownership of the pepper plantations.

Pepper became less important in the Acehnese economy towards the last quarter of the 19th century with the fall in its price and production decline due to soil exhaustion. But east Aceh, long linked to overseas markets through pepper trade, was able to shift first to tobacco and later more successfully to the profitable rubber and oil palm cultivation. Thus the decline of the pepper industry ended a phase of economic activity sustained largely by the enterprise of Acehnese coastal *ulubalangs*, American traders, and private merchants from Natal, Penang and Singapore.

PEPPER PLANTATIONS IN NORTH SUMATRA

Banda Aceh
Pidie
Lhokseumawe
Simpang Ulim
Peureulak
Meulaboh
SUMATRA
Susoh
Tamiang
Trumon
Singkil
Tapanuli
0   100 km
Natal

N

Numerous pepper plantations were opened along the north eastern tip of Sumatra in the mid-19th century.

PRICE OF PEPPER

The pepper trade was profitable for the west. Pepper was bought at an average of $6.22 per pikul of 133 1/3 pounds in the west coast of Sumatra and with expenses it worked out to six cents per pound. At its height in 1812 and 1813, the price of pepper averaged between 30 to 40 cents per pound. Nevertheless, pepper prices went through regular cycles of boom and depression. They were also affected by international conflicts. During the British blockade of the Sumatran coast in 1811-1815 pepper prices fell to four dollars per pikul as a result of the pepper being left uncollected. (Picture below) Harvesting Pepper, from Liebig Card.

Dipanagara and the Java War

Although the Dutch had been in Indonesia since the late 16th century, it was only in the 19th century that they embarked on a concerted attempt to expand their colonial authority. This eventually resulted in Dutch control of the whole of present-day Indonesia. Throughout the Archipelago, this expansion was fiercely resisted, nowhere more so than in Java where the Dutch were forced to fight a bitter five–year struggle against the Javanese known as the Java War (1825–30).

Dipanagara in 1807 (1785-1855).

⟿ *From the* Babad Dipanagara; *two encounters between Javanese and Dutch forces. From the Koninklijk Instituut voor Taal- Land- en Volkenkunde, Netherlands.*

Marshal Herman Willem Daendels (1762-1818).

Early Years

The Javanese leader was Pangéran (Prince) Dipanagara (1785-1855)-a Sanskrit derived name meaning 'the light of the country'-the eldest son of the third sultan of Yogyakarta. Dipanagara had grown up at his great-grandmother's country estate at Tegalreja, just outside Yogyakarta, where he mingled with wandering students of religion (santri) and ordinary Javanese villagers. In his autobiography, the Babad Dipanagara, the prince spoke of how 'he was strictly educated in his religious duties. Moreover, the estate at Tegalreja soon became very full, for many people came to visit there. All sought food and the santri sought religious knowledge. There was much devotion and prayer...'. According to his uncle, Mangkubumi, 'even as a child, the prince loved to wander off alone into the mountains and forests. (He lived) with the poorer santri in their religious schools (pondhok)..... and dressed as a common man so that few people recognised him.'

During these wanderings he met his future religious adviser, Kyai Maja, who was to join him during the Java War. A deeply religious man, Dipanagara was seen by many Javanese as the Ratu Adil, the 'Just King' and reincarnation of the Hindu god, Vishnu, who would sweep through Java and establish a just kingdom after a period of moral decline. A portrait sketched by a Yogya court artist in 1807 shows a tight-lipped determined face with powerful downcast eyes and a slightly flattened nose,

a face aglow with cahya, intense charisma and spiritual power. The prince's features set him apart from other Javanese, deriving from his Madura and Sumbawa ancestry ancestry, an ancestry which also accounted for his fiery temper. Once he was reported to have struck the Yogyakarta prime minister (patih) across the face with his shoe, so enraged was he at the patih's commercial dealings with the Dutch.

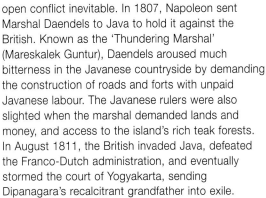

Resentment of European Rule

The attitude of the European colonial settlers and administrators made open conflict inevitable. In 1807, Napoleon sent Marshal Daendels to Java to hold it against the British. Known as the 'Thundering Marshal' (Mareskalek Guntur), Daendels aroused much bitterness in the Javanese countryside by demanding the construction of roads and forts with unpaid Javanese labour. The Javanese rulers were also slighted when the marshal demanded lands and money, and access to the island's rich teak forests. In August 1811, the British invaded Java, defeated the Franco-Dutch administration, and eventually stormed the court of Yogyakarta, sending Dipanagara's recalcitrant grandfather into exile.

The prince witnessed these events and became convinced of the need to restore Java's fortunes before the island fell completely under European dominance. For a time he served as senior advisor to his father, the third sultan and did his best to ease some of the burdens imposed on the Javanese peasantry.

But, in 1816, the Dutch returned, more intent than ever on recouping the financial losses they had suffered during the Napoleonic wars. To them, Java was a potential source of income, a milch-cow for the impoverished Dutch state. Taxes became ever more extortionate, with Chinese tax collectors manning tollgates and supervising local markets and opium dens. Soon many Javanese peasants were indebted to them for they alone had the cash to pay government taxes. Even wealthy Javanese suffered, for the Dutch took advantage of the confused economic situation to rent lands from impoverished Javanese nobles and exploit the unpaid labour of their tenants.

Rebellion

The time was ripe for a man of Dipanagara's abilities and social position to lead an uprising. Time and again he had remonstrated with the Dutch and their Javanese allies to alleviate the burdens on the

PANGERAN DIPANAGARA

Charcoal sketch of Dipanagara by A.J. Bik, Baljuw (Magistrate) of Batavia and guardian of the prince, during his period of confinement in the *Stadhuis* (Batavia) between 8 April and 3 May 1830. It shows him dressed in the 'priestly' garments which he wore during the Java War, namely a turban, an open-necked kabaya (cotton shirt) and a loose outer robe (*jubah*). A sash hangs over his right shoulder and his pusaka kris (heirloom dagger), Kangjeng Kyai Bandayuda, is stuck in his flowered silk waist band. The slightly sunken cheeks which accentuate the prince's high cheek bones were the result of successive bouts of malaria from which he had been suffering since his wanderings in the jungles of Bagelén at the end of the war.

Ali Basah Sentot Prawiradirdja, commander of Dipanagara's Turkish–style armed forces. From Kepper's Wapenfeiten.

Hendrik Merkus Baron de Kock (1779–1845), Lieutenant Governor–General of Java and supreme commander of the Netherlands Indies forces during the Java War. From 20th Century Impressions of Netherlands India, *1909.*

Batik print showing Dipanagara, while in exile at Manado, writing his diary and attended by his wife. The bottom left section portrays the prince having a vision of a Javanese spirit. From the Snouck Hugronje Collection of the Leiden University Library, Netherlands.

Javanese people. All his efforts were rebuffed. The prince now started meeting with local religious leaders and village heads. His meditations in lonely mountain caves ceased to be abstract musings and became a preparation for spiritual and military leadership. As he confided to his friend, the senior Yogya religious official (Pengulu), 'Thanks be to Allah! (For) what do men in life wait for, if they are not awaiting some exceptionally great task?'. Soon afterwards, he had a vision of the Ratu Adil who empowered him to lead his armies in battle against the Dutch.

Following an incident in July 1825 when the pro-Dutch *patih* had tried to build a road through Dipanagara's estate, the prince left Yogya and set up the standard of revolt. He addressed open letters to every important priest and leader in central and east Java calling the people to arms 'to fight in the countryside and restore the high state of the true religion (*ngluhurken agami Islam*)'. The response was immediate; from the hot plains around Surabaya to the rich ricelands of Bagelen and Banyumas, the flag of revolt flew high. Petty Dutch officials and Chinese tax-collectors were murdered, and for a time it seemed that the Dutch authority in central Java would collapse.

Capture and Exile

In areas cleared of officials, Dipanagara declared tax amnesties and the end of forced labour, provided his troops were given sanctuary. Indeed, the modern Indonesian word for liberty, *merdeka* derives from the tax-free areas, known as *merdikan* by the local population at this time.

In July 1826, shortly before a major battle just outside Surakarta which turned the tide of war against the Javanese, Dipanagara wrote to the Dutch Governor-General begging him to acknowledge defeat. All he demanded from the Dutch was recognition as the spiritual ruler and protector of

religion in Java. In return, he was prepared to allow the Dutch to remain as traders and settlers, provided they restricted themselves to their old trading bases on the north coast. Realising that they could never regain their position in Java if Dipanagara remained at large, the Dutch decided to embark on a course of treachery. The prince was invited to 'confer' with the Dutch commander, Hendrik Merkus de Kock, at Magelang during the fasting month (*puwasa*) of 1830. On Sunday, 28 March, Hari Raya Idulfitri, he was taken prisoner and sent into exile, first in Manado (1830-33) and then in Makasar (1833-55) where he died of natural causes on 8 January 1855.

His capture spelt the end of the Java War and the beginning of a period of full-blown Dutch colonial rule in Java which lasted until the Japanese occupation of 1942-45. But the prince's name lived on in Java; many uprisings throughout the island in the 19th century hailed him as a spiritual leader and liberator. Eventually, in August 1945, the Indonesians declared their independence from the Dutch, Dipanagara's name was used by the central Javanese army division, which fought the Dutch in much the same terrain as Dipanagara had done in 1825-30. Thus, nearly a century after his death, the prince finally triumphed over the Dutch and he is now revered as Indonesia's first national independence hero.

The Rise of the House of Karangasem

With the fall of the Gelgel dynasty in the mid-17th century, the Balinese state fragmented and supra-village political power came to be vested in a number of lords, or Rajas, each of whom headed a dynasty consisting of his immediate as well as his extended family. Each Raja exercised absolute power within his principality. However, they faced constant challenges from family members and their powerful chiefs.

Ratu Agung-Agung Ngurah Karangasem, the dominant figure of Lombok-Karangasem from 1838 to 1894, in Batavia, 1895, after his capture by the Dutch.

Anak Agung K'tut Karangasem, 1894. Son of Ratu Agung-Agung Ngurah Karangasem. Crown Prince of Lombok, Karangasem.

Members of the Balinese ruling class of Lombok (seated), c.1880, with their armed followers. Rifles were very widespread in Lombok, some imported by English traders and others manufactured on the island.

The Rajas of Karangasem

The Rajas and chiefs were forever trying to increase their wealth and power and, if possible, to achieve all island hegemony. These ambitions meant frequent intrigues, shifting alliances and almost constant warfare. Although the struggle for hegemony proved ultimately futile, one of the rival dynasties, the House of Karangasem, came close to achieving the reunification of the Balinese world.

In the 1670s, a few decades after the fall of Gelgel, the Rajas of Karangasem first entered the stage of history as independent actors. Prudently avoiding conflict in Bali itself, they began to make a concerted effort to bring the neighbouring island of Lombok under their sway. Time after time, they sent raiding parties across the Lombok Strait. In west Lombok the Karangasem warriors joined forces with local Sasaks whereupon the Balinese-west Sasak fighters made their way across Lombok's central forest to do battle with the Makasarese who, a few decades earlier, had established themselves there. After a few years of intermittent fighting, the Balinese-west Sasak forces succeeded in driving out the Makasarese, whereupon they began to assert control over the Sasak villages of eastern Lombok. The east Sasaks resisted these encroachments as

best they could but gradually they lost ground and by 1740 Karangasem rule was firmly entrenched over the entire island.

Conflict within Karangasem

Although the conquest of Lombok greatly increased the wealth and power of the lords of Karangasem, strife within the dynasty prevented the Rajas from turning this advantage into increased influence in Bali. One problem was that the chiefs whom the Karangasem Rajas had appointed to rule over Lombok increasingly began to assert their independence. Another problem was that the Lombok chiefs, who soon styled themselves 'Rajas', were unable to maintain unity within the ranks of their own descent group. This progressive fragmentation meant that by the beginning of the 19th century the Rajas of Karangasem had lost control over Lombok, whilst in Lombok itself the House of Karangasem had split into two rival factions, one based in the West Lombok town of Cakranegara and the other in the nearby town of Mataram.

The tensions between the two Lombok branches of the House of Karangasem simmered for many years until, in January 1838, they resulted in open warfare. Initially, the war seemed an unequal contest because with about 20 times as many followers than the Raja of Mataram, the lord of Cakranegara was clearly the more powerful of the two potentates. Two factors, however, worked in Mataram's favour. Firstly, the Raja of Mataram received support from his relatives in Bali and consequently, thousands of Karangasem warriors were ferried across the Strait to bolster his forces. Secondly, Mataram had control of Ampenan, Lombok's best port, which meant that it could more easily export its surplus rice, and import rifles, gunpowder and other war materials, from Singapore. Largely for these reasons, Mataram gradually gained the upper hand until, by June 1838, Cakranegara's military position had become

hopeless. Deserted by all but his relatives and a handful of devoted followers, the lord of Cakranegara chose the traditional death of a defeated Raja (*puputan*). In accordance with Balinese custom, the Cakranegara faction, dressed in white, set fire to the palace and, with the Raja at the centre, rushed outside in a furious charge at their foes. The Mataram forces, who had expected the assault, cut down all assailants with rifle fire, the lance and kris. Cakranegara had fallen.

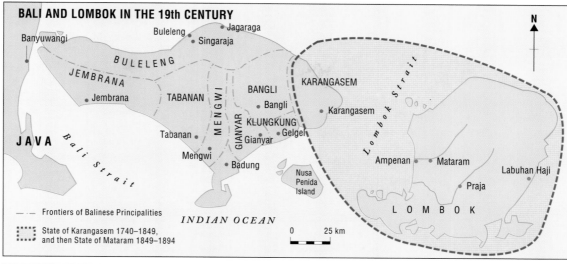

BALI AND LOMBOK IN THE 19th CENTURY

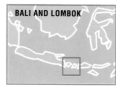

BALI AND LOMBOK

The pleasure gardens of Narmada (left) and Lingsar (right). These were built by Ratu Agung-Agung Ngurah using some of the wealth he obtained from a flourishing export trade during the 19th century.

The Reunification of Lombok

Although Mataram's victory meant the reunification of Lombok, it did not spell the end of strife within the House of Karangasem. The problem now was that the Rajas of Mataram refused to recognise the supremacy of the lords of Karangasem who, for their part, continued to view Lombok as a conquered province. The enmity which resulted from these conflicting ambitions blinded the belligerents to the dangers posed by the Dutch who, in the 1840s, were beginning to extend their influence. In fact, the Rajas of Mataram as well as those of Karangasem sought to enlist Dutch support for a war against their arch enemies, an endeavour in which Mataram was eventually successful. Consequently, in May 1849, a fleet of Dutch transport ships ferried thousands of Lombok warriors across the Strait, Balinese as well as Sasaks, who, assisted by several local chiefs, quickly overthrew the Rajas of Karangasem. And, as had happened at Cakranegara 11 years earlier, the defeated Rajas dressed in white and surrounded by their relatives and loyal followers, perished in a suicidal attack. Karangasem, too, had fallen.

The End of Conflict

Mataram's second victory finally ended the strife within the House of Karangasem and ushered in a long period of greatness for the Balinese dynasty. This period, which lasted for more than four decades, was dominated by Anak Agung G'de, the young prince who, after the death of his father in the 1838 war against Cakranegara, rose to become *de facto* Raja of Mataram. Although Anak Agung G'de's elder brother formally succeeded to the Mataram throne, after 1838 no decision of substance was taken without his consent and approval. Anak Agung G'de was the architect of the alliance with the Dutch which in 1849 had resulted in the annexation by Lombok of

Karangasem. He appointed two trusted nephews to rule Karangasem. He established an alliance with the central Balinese principality of Bangli by which he achieved a stable balance of power in the Balinese world. In 1876, after the death of his elder brother, he became Raja of Lombok-Karangasem also in the formal sense under the name of Ratu Agung-Agung Ngurah Karangasem.

Lombok-Karangasem

Ruled by Ratu Agung-Agung Ngurah, Lombok-Karangasem became in the late 19th century the richest and most powerful kingdom in the Archipelago. The Raja used the considerable wealth he derived from the flourishing export trade in rice to rebuild the Cakranegara palace on a grand scale. He established deer parks in the foothills of Mount Rinjani where the princes and chiefs could hunt; and, in the vicinity of the court in west Lombok, he laid out a number of stunning pleasure gardens, the most impressive of which were the gardens at Gunung Sari, Lingsar, and Narmada. Whilst much of the Raja's wealth was spent on luxury projects, some of it was put to more productive uses. The Raja, for instance, extended the irrigation system and paid a great deal of attention to road construction and town planning. European visitors to Lombok invariably expressed their admiration for the paved, shaded road from Ampenan to Mataram, Cakranegara and Narmada. Visitors were astonished also at the size and orderly lay out of Mataram and Cakranegara, towns in which the roads were wide, straight and shaded and where at night the main streets were lit by lanterns. In short, Lombok-Karangasem was a viable state, a state which, if history had been a little kinder to it, might well have survived into the 20th century.

Anak Agung Jilantik Karangasem, 1894. Nephew of Ratu Agung-Agung Ngurah.

The Padri and the End of Minangkabau Monarchy

*I*n 1803 three pilgrims returned from the Holy Land to their birth places in the Minangkabau region. Having observed the success of the puritan Wahabi movement in the Holy Land they were determined to intensify the process of integration of Islamic doctrines into the Minangkabau social fabric and cultural orientation. This signalled the beginning of the transformation of the Minangkabau social system and religious orientation.

WEST SUMATRA

N

Fort de Kock (Bukittinggi)

Bonjol

Fort van der Capellen (Batusangkar)

Lake Maninjau

Pariaman

Lake Singkarak

Padang

0   50 km

Mentawei

SUMATRA

The mosque at Pariaman, one of the main entry points along the west coast of Sumatra through which Islam made its way into the Sumatran highlands.

The Network of Surau

The three pilgrims came at the right time, because Tuanku nan Tuo from Koto Tuo (in the Agam district) and his students had already launched a relatively moderate reform movement. The three returning haji saw that some of those involved in it preferred more radical methods of reform. They supported these radically inclined reformers and helped to transform the nature of the religious conflict — from civil strife to intra-village *(nagari)* warfare. By the end of the century the network of *surau* (religious schools), with its earliest centre at Ulakan on the west coast, had been firmly established in both the coast and highlands of Minangkabau. Some of the *surau* under the leadership of their respective *tuanku* (teacher) had also emerged as the centres of special branches of Islamic knowledge. Since only those who were considered to have mastered the three most important branches, namely *tauhid* (the unity of God), *fikh* (law) and *tasauf* (mysticism) could be recognised as *tuanku*, it can be imagined that each centre of learning would attract students from all over the region. The three branches of knowledge, however, could only be properly learned if the students had adequate training in other branches, most notably Arabic, Quranic recital and exegesis, and *hadith* (Prophetic tradition). The movement of students became, therefore, a relatively widespread phenomenon.

Tuanku Nan Tuo's Reform Movement

Tuanku nan Tuo, whose *surau* was widely recognised as the centre of the Shatariyah mystical school or *tarekat* in the Minangkabau highlands, began his movement as a reaction to the unresponsiveness of the Minangkabau holders of power (the *adat*-chiefs or the *penghulu*) to the increased mobility, either between the scattered centres of religious learning or between the coastal area and the interior. This took place in a period when major economic changes were occurring in the Minangkabau interior, as trade relationships with the coast, under the domination of the Dutch, flourished. But the shallow knowledge about religious obligations of the men in power, according to Tuanku nan Tuo, and their weak commitment to religious ethics made them not only unaware of the new opportunities, but also caused them to ignore the safety of the travellers, a major offence in the Minangkabau segmentary political tradition. By emphasising strict adherence to religious obligations and social harmony Tuanku nan Tuo's reform movement was also aimed at securing safe journeys for travelling merchants and religious students.

Padri Movement

The radical reformers, however, were impatient to transform the Minangkabau social system and religious orientation. By using the networks of former religious students, these young *tuanku* who came largely from the Agam district, managed to expand their sphere of influence to the other parts of Minangkabau. Their movement, since then known as the Padri, not only challenged the authority of the old *tuanku* who, on the basis of religious law, condemned the use of force against fellow Muslims and the legitimate political position of the *penghulu*, but also threatened the centuries old Minangkabau monarchy, with its centre in Pagarruyung. In a supposedly peaceful gathering between the Padri leaders and the royal family, fighting broke out. Although the old king, Sultan Alam Muning Syah, managed to escape, a number of the royal family members were killed. The sacred royal family, structurally set apart from the Minangkabau matrilinial social system, was on its way to extinction.

The Dutch Intervention

It was Dutch intervention (1821) into the intra-*nagari* warfare, however, that finally put an end to the sacred Minangkabau royalty. Under the pretext of helping the monarchy against the Islamic zealots, the Dutch, who had re-taken

Padang from the British, intervened in the purely internal affairs of Minangkabau. After taking control of the seats of the Minangkabau royal family, the Dutch made the newly installed king, Sultan Alam Bagagar Syah, Regent of Tanah Datar. During a short lull in the war in 1832, after the first fall of the last bastion of the Padri, Bonjol, the Dutch suspected that their former allies, the Sultan and other *adat*-chiefs and *tuanku*, were conspiring with the Padri leaders to expel the Dutch. While the others were hung, the sultan was exiled to Java. The Minangkabau monarchy had ended just as colonial warfare began. In January 1833, the whole of Minangkabau rose against the Dutch

occupying army. Tuanku Imam Bonjol, leader of the Padri in Bonjol, and who by the time of the first occupation of Bonjol (1832) had returned political power to the *penghulu* of Bonjol, resumed his leadership and emerged as the spiritual leader of the independent struggle. It took more than four years of heavy fighting before the Dutch army managed to re-occupy the forts of Bonjol. Tuanku Imam Bonjol was captured and exiled to west Java, and subsequently to Ambon, and Minahassa (North Sulawesi), where he died. With the fall of Bonjol (1837) the Minangkabau region became part of the Netherlands Indies.

View of Padang hill as published by Marsden (1810). The resumption of Padang by the Dutch from the British in 1816 signalled the beginning of Dutch intervention in the internal affairs of Minangkabau.

Penghulu from the Lake Singkarak region, Minangkabau, c.1825.

The plain white costume of the Padri reformers, who condemned all vain show.

The house of a rich merchant at Kota–Baroe. A wood engraving by A. Sargent after H. Catenacci from Le Tour du Monde Noveau Journal des Voyages *(Paris, 1880).*

꜒꜔ *Tuanku Imam Bonjol. He became the spiritual leader of the independent movement against the Dutch in the Minangkabau region.*

The styles of dress favoured by Padris (left), and more traditional Minang dress (right).

Islamic Networks as Alternative Identity

In the 19th century Muslim hopes of renewal turned away from the rulers, who progressively lost their battles with advancing colonial troops. The autonomous networks formed by tarekat, by pesantren, by teacher–pupil relations, and by the annual pilgrimage to Mecca, became more important as means of holding the religious community together. They provided a new vision of brotherhood, a programme of reform based on a purer adherence to shari'a law, and sometimes a chiliastic hope of divine help to restore an Islamic order free of kafir rule.

An Islamic school (Jean Demmeni, photo poster, published in 1911 by Kley Nenberg and Company). In the 1880s there were reportedly 15,000 Islamic schools and about 230,000 pupils.

The Palembang School

One of the principal centres of Islamic scholarship in 18th century Indonesia was tin-rich Palembang. Sultan Mahmud Badruddin (1803-21) was himself a reputable scholar, while several of his predecessors were important patrons of the *ulama*. Palembang was also one of the centres of the Hadhramaut Arab diaspora which spread throughout the Archipelago in the last decades of the 18th century. Usually concentrating on trade, financing and religious education, several of these Arabs married into the ruling families of Sumatra, Java and Borneo, and provided one of the means by which reformist ideas from the Middle East made their way to the Archipelago. Their numbers increased during the 19th century, so that by 1885 20,000 Arabs were registered in Netherlands Indies enumerations.

The weakening of Dutch control over shipping routes from the mid-18th century may also have made it easier for Indonesian Muslims to visit Mecca and the other holy places, not only for the obligatory pilgrimage but also for prolonged study. One prominent *ulama* from Palembang who did so was Abd al-Samad (al-Palimbangi), who spent most of the period 1760-90 in Mecca and Ta'if, translating two of the major works of al-Afghani into Malay, and thereby making available to Malay readers of the 19th century a great source of Islamic orthodoxy. Abd al-Samad also became a disciple in Mecca of the Sufi Shaikh Muhammad Samman (1719-1775), and subsequently a proponent of the Sammaniyah *tarekat* dedicated to commemorating and reciting the miraculous deeds of that master.

Tarekat and Pilgrimage

The Sammaniyah was one of the new vehicles for religious devotion in the Archipelago, especially Sumatra, in the early decades of the 19th century. New energy also came to the older ritual and mystical communities (*tarekat*), the Syattariyah, Qadariyah and Khalwatiyah, all known in Sumatra and Java since the 17th century. In the second half of the 19th century these *tarekat* were surpassed by the Naqshabandiyah, which spread to Indonesia from Mecca in this period as a relatively orthodox Sunni vehicle, despite its roots in central Asia of the 14th century. In Minangkabau and Banten, in particular, it launched a reform movement against what it considered to be the heterodox practices of the other *tarekat*, especially the Shattariyah. It was thought to be behind a number of movements against the Dutch in this period. In Minangkabau about one third of the adult population were thought to be attached to the various *tarekat* orders in the 1880s, while in Singapore the Dutch Consul was alarmed to find an active and anti-Dutch Naqshabandiyah movement with 500 members. The pilgrimage to Mecca became markedly less onerous in the course of the 19th century, as shipping links became more regular and Dutch obstructions eased.

Islamic Revolts

Anxious Dutch officials probably exaggerated the extent to which hajis, 'priests' and envoys from Mecca or Istanbul were behind every anti-Dutch movement in 19th century Indonesia. But in a pre-nationalist era identification with Islam was undoubtedly an important motive for cooperation and resistance. In the early 1850s this kind of opposition was largely centred in Banten and south Sumatra. When a Banten revolt in the Cilegon area was crushed in 1850, several of the *ulama* associated with it fled to Lampung and helped inspire resistance there. Then in 1855 Sultan Taha came to the throne of Jambi and began to seek Turkish support for his struggle with the oppressive Dutch. He was replaced by a Dutch expedition of 1858. Soon thereafter, in the years 1859-63, a movement against the Dutch and their unpopular client Sultan of Banjarmasin arose in southeast Kalimantan, and quickly acquired an Islamic character. The Banjarese guerrilla fighters motivated themselves with *tarekat*-inspired recitations (*ratib*), and perceived their headquarters as another Mecca.

The outbreak of war between Holland and Aceh in 1873 provoked further attempts at solidarity against the aggressor, and the first serious interest by Turkey in the Archipelago for centuries. Aceh had renewed its ancient fealty to the Ottoman sultan in 1850, and again in 1868 and 1873, in the hope of

ACHEEN STREET MOSQUE

The Aceh community in Pinang was active in arousing support among Muslims throughout the Archipelago for the Acehnese struggle against the Dutch from 1873. The wealthier members of the community concentrated around the Acheen Street mosque (right) and the 'Gudang Aceh', then the tallest building in Pinang and owned by the pepper–exporting ruler of Simpang Ulim in East Aceh.

obtaining Turkish protection. The best the 'sick man of Europe' could do was to offer Turkish mediation to end the war, but enthusiasts in Mecca, Pinang and Singapore did alarm the Dutch with a series of letters throughout the Archipelago urging Muslims to support the Aceh cause. In 1881 a high-level mission from Mecca gave rise in south Sumatra and Banten to hopes that infidel rule would end with the Islamic century (A.H. 1299). Many of these factors-*tarekat*, *pesantren*, returning pilgrims and the hope of intervention from Turkey-came together in the Cilegon rebellion which took the lives of many Bantenese and a few Dutch in 1888.

Minangkabau Reformism

In Islamic areas newly placed under Dutch rule, such as Minangkabau, Dutch efforts to maintain the status of officials who served under them were often counterproductive. The social and cultural influence was gradually eroded of both the territorial chiefs (*penghulu*) and the *adat*-religious hierarchy, the *imam* and the *khatib-adat*. The autonomous role of the *ulama*, most of whom were *tarekat* leaders, on the other hand, was becoming more important. The post-Padri period can be described as one of rapid expansion of both the *surau* networks and the *tarekat* brotherhoods.

The growing influence of the religious teachers and their *tarekat* had direct impact upon the reformulation of the Minangkabau cultural world. It was now defined as a world where *adat* and religion ruled. '*Adat* applies, religion designs', as an aphorism puts it. This new definition of self, depicted by *tambo* ('history', probably re-written by *tarekat*

leaders) and *kaba* ('story'), and popularised by the numerous *adat*-sayings, not only established Islam as the legitimate basis of change, but also made the understanding itself the focus of intellectual conflict. In the 1890s another wave of reform took place. This time it was instigated by a *syariah* orthodox movement which put more emphasis on the application of religious law in both social and personal lives. Launched from Mecca by Syaikh Achmad Chatib al-Minangkabawi, the new movement emphasised the strict application of religious law. This Minangkabau *ulama*, who was also an *imam* of the Syafiite school of law in the Haram mosque of Mecca, not only questioned the doctrinal validities of the *tarekat* orders, but also the very foundation of Minangkabau matrilineal inheritance law. The frontal assaults on both *adat* and religious establishments not only created anxieties, but also more importantly forced his former students, who had returned to Minangkabau after sojourning in Mecca, to resolve these legal discrepancies and to reformulate a new basis of reform.

In the mid-1900s these young *ulama*, who were known as the *kaum muda*, began their 'modernist' movement. Without ignoring the orthodox foundation of their movement, which aimed at the purification of religion from unlawful 'innovations', the *kaum muda ulama* offered legal and sociological solutions to the discrepancies between Islamic law and the Minangkabau social system and established Islam as the ideological basis of social change. More than any other social and cultural forces, the *kaum muda*, with their extensive networks of modern Islamic schools, organisations, and publications, finally made Minangkabau one of the most important centres of the Islamic nationalist movement.

*A haji as depicted by Auguste van Pers (*Nederlandsch Oost-Indie Typen, *The Hague, 1853–62). Returned pilgrims from Mecca, known in Indonesia as haji, were at the centre of many movements of renewal and even rebellion. The respect with which they were regarded also put them in a strong position to lead.*

Hadhramaut merchants, like this man portrayed coming ashore in Java in the 1850s, were much more influential than their numbers would suggest, especially those who claimed descent from the Prophet through the title Sayyid. This is a rare lithograph executed by Lemercier after a drawing by Ernest Alfred Hardouin, from Ritter's Java, 1855.

New Crops for World Markets

*B*y the late 18th century, new export crops were beginning to replace spices in the Indonesian region's participation in international commerce. The principal ones were coffee, indigo and sugar. With this shift to new crops, the region's export economy came to be focused increasingly on the island of Java.

Coffee

At the beginning of the early modern period, Java had been best known for its production of rice, appreciable quantities of which, around 1800 had been exported from central Java to the rest of the Indonesian region and to other parts of Southeast Asia. Around 1800, however, rice's importance as an export had given way in terms of value to coffee, and was soon to be entirely supplanted by a combination of coffee, indigo and sugar. The bean bearing bushes which produce coffee were introduced to Java by the Dutch at the end of the 17th century. From the mid-1700s onwards they were disseminated in Java, Sumatra and other islands, initially by the Dutch East India Company and its agents, with a view to creating a profitable staple for its trade to Europe.

In the mid-19th century, coffee became the most extensively grown and, for the government, most profitable crop grown under the auspices of the Cultivation System. This system, devised during the 1830s, enabled the 19th century Dutch colonial government to secure supplies of valuable export produce through the forced labour of the Javanese population. Following piecemeal dismantlement (which began in the 1860s and was finally completed early in the 20th century) coffee was grown both by Indonesian smallholders and on estates owned and managed by European colonists. It maintained an important place among Indonesia's exports for the remainder of the colonial era.

Indigo

Indigo, which is a dyestuff made from steeping vegetable matter in water and working the resultant precipitate into a paste or drying and compressing it into hard, soap-like cakes, had a rather different history. During the 18th century, the indigo plant had been grown for local use in much of the Indonesian region. It was used locally in the manufacture of coloured cloth and in batik. In the 1780s, however, there began an interlude, lasting for something over a hundred years, in which attempts were made to develop indigo into a large scale industry geared to expanding international markets. The popular 'navy blue' uniforms of the 19th century British navy, for example, owed their colour to this vegetable dyestuff.

The expansion of Indonesian indigo production for world markets reached its apogee in Java under the Cultivation System in the mid-19th century. By the century's end, however, international sales of indigo were increasingly undermined by the production of chemical dyes in Germany and elsewhere. Ultimately, the history of indigo production came full circle; the dyestuff reverted to the kind of handicraft production which it had originally been, and which had enjoyed a continuous existence beneath the overlay of export oriented manufacture.

Cane Sugar

Of the three new crops for world markets, cane sugar was by far the most significant and controversial. At the outset of the early modern

CULTIVATION SYSTEM

The Dutch *Cultuurstelsel* (Cultivation System) was introduced into Java in 1830 by van den Bosch. It was designed to increase revenue from crops for a colonial government strapped for cash following the Java War (1825-1830).

The government and the 'contractors' who processed the the agricultural produce of the system made a great deal of money. The results were less favourable for the three-quarters of a million Javanese households involved.

Douwes Dekker's novel *Max Havelaar* — written in 1860 — did much to alert public opinion in the Netherlands to the abuses of power and the cruelties which underlay the System. Its dismantlement took 20 to 30 years and was dictated not so much by 'humanitarian' ideals, but by the System's very success in implanting large-scale export production into the heartlands of rural Java. Dutch firms and plantation companies took over where the Government left off. The gross brutality of the System's worst years was replaced by more subtle pressures on Indonesian labour.

such factories by 1850, and by the century's end their number had almost doubled.

This development, however, was at a cost. The factories and their predominantly Dutch owners and managers dominated the surrounding countryside and shaped agriculture to their own, rather than Indonesian, requirements. For some sectors of the rural population, sugar may have brought work opportunities which, as numbers grew in the countryside, were otherwise increasingly hard to obtain. For many small landholders, on the other hand, sugar was at once an opportunity and a threat. With the dismantling of the Cultivation System, landholders were no longer forced by the government to grow cane for the factories. Instead, by the 1880s, factory managers had moved into the business of renting peasant land for cane production (in addition to which, they also took over from the state the recruitment of labour for the planting, harvesting and haulage of cane). What notional 'freedom' existed for the peasant landholder to enter into such arrangements with the sugar factories was rapidly eroded, however, by mounting indebtedness in late 19th century village Java, and by whatever 'traditional' authority continued to be exerted by village headmen (and other, large land holder groups in the countryside) who often worked in collusion with the sugar industry.

Under such conditions, there took place a distortion of development priorities, brought about by concentration on an export staple which was prone, as in the 1880s and again in the 1930s, to disastrous slumps on the world market. Such 'boom and crisis' conditions (allied to the predominance of Dutch metropolitan ownership) augured ill for the long-term creation of Indonesian capital from agriculture such as was occuring elsewhere in Asia, most notably in Japan.

Sugar cane, Saccharum sp., by Churchill, 1704.

period, and until well into the 19th century, the sweetener most popularly used in the Indonesian region was made from the sap of the palm tree. Since its inception, cane sugar was an industry which grew in response to overseas markets (it was not until the second half of the 20th century that Indonesian consumers came to constitute the largest and eventually sole market for its output). These markets were predominantly Asian in the 17th and 18th centuries, but in the 19th century became largely European and north American (by the early 20th century, however, the industry again achieved most of its sales in Asian markets).

Manufacture of sugar in Indonesia in the early modern period was almost exclusively confined to Java, where there were rich volcanic soils and a ready supply of labour. This combination, together with its alliance with a sympathetic colonial government, had brought the Indonesian industry to the forefront of the world sugar economy by the late 19th century. Only Cuba produced and exported more cane sugar than did the Java industry in its colonial era heyday. From the 1830s onward (and entirely supplanting an earlier industry which had grown up in the 17th century in the environs of Jakarta) the most fertile and populous parts of central and east Java began to be covered by a network of large and increasingly industrialised sugar factories. There were some hundred

Indigo, Indigofera sp., *published by W. Marsden, 1783.*

The industry's raw material came from plantations established on land rented annually from peasant landholders of the surrounding districts. This rare photograph shows these landholders gathered together to be paid their rentals by members of the factory staff (From KIT, Netherlands).

A large female workforce was engaged in planting out rooted cane shoots (bebiet), the last stage of fieldwork (From Koninklijk Instituut voor Taal-Land- en Volkenkunde, Netherlands).

Dutch Rule and the Population Explosion

*D*uring the late 18th and 19th centuries, well in advance of the other islands, Java showed unprecedented population growth rates. Fertility had always been high, but endemic diseases, epidemics, famines and wars had caused such high mortality that the overall growth rate of the population was very low. Under Dutch rule, mortality owing to wars, smallpox and famines dropped gradually, with a much higher growth rate as a result.

A Javanese family. In the 19th century Javanese women had, on average, seven children.

⟶ Volcanic eruption in Maluku as depicted by Pierre van der Aa from Voyages Remarquables *(Jean Albert Mandelslo, 1727). Volcanic eruptions had an indirect influence on fertility and mortality rates, as harvests were destroyed leading to food shortages and famine.*

⟶ The flooding of kampungs near Kota Tagai. Such calamities caused harvest failures, which, in turn, led to epidemics (Van Rees, Nederlandsch Indie, 1883).

Population Growth

Prior to 1800, long term population growth was very slow in almost all areas of Indonesia. Precise figures are absent, but it is unlikely that the average annual growth rate for the whole Archipelago between 1400 and 1800 was higher than 0.1 or 0.2 per cent. However, these low rates, measured over a period of four centuries, mask considerable differences between groups, places and periods.

Most scholars accept that hunter-gatherers of the humid tropics (Sumatra and Kalimantan) used to have low fertility rates. Their mortality was perhaps somewhat lower than that of shifting cultivators and sedentary peasants, but still so high that rates of natural increase (births minus deaths) were very low. Sedentary peasants (Sumatra, Java, Bali and Sulawesi) are associated with high fertility rates. As their mortality rates, particularly infant mortality were also quite high, the resultant natural increase was very low. However, among the sedentary groups, short bursts of relatively high growth rates (on average one per cent or more per annum), sometimes lasting one or a few decades, can be observed. This could occur when a period was relatively free of wars, epidemics, famines and 'acts of God' (volcanic eruptions and earthquakes). Such a period, however, was usually preceded and/or followed by a long series of very bad years, during which the growth rate was negative. Thus, periods of high and negative growth cancelled each other.

Mortality

There were several factors which influenced fertility and mortality rates. Starting with mortality, one can distinguish endemic disease, epidemics, famines, 'acts of God', and wars and raids. It is not always easy, or even possible, to separate these influences during historical periods of high mortality, because they often operated together at the same time. Wars, for instance, were often the cause of harvest failures, which, in turn, facilitated famines which in their turn led to epidemics through lowered resistance to infection and disease. Nevertheless, it can be said that 'acts of God' rarely had more than a local significance of moderate proportions. Most epidemics probably did not add much more than 20 per cent to the normal levels of endemic mortality, when measured over a longer period of time. Famines were mostly of regional importance only,

and although they were far from rare, their impact on long term all-Indonesia death rates could not have been great. Wars and raids probably added more than other factors to the 'normal' death rate. Their frequency in all types of societies in early modern Indonesia was high, and the mortality that followed in their wake was entirely out of proportion to the low number of direct deaths in battle, because they were usually accompanied by epidemics and famines. On the contrary, most damage was done by wars in sedentary peasant societies.

Fertility

Fertility rates were not, as is often assumed, a natural given. In all Indonesian societies prior to 1800 on which we have data, fertility was way below maximum

'natural' fertility. In Java around 1800, women had, on average, seven children, but the number of children that reached maturity was much lower than the number born, due to high infant and child mortality. There are no indications that other Indonesian societies had higher average fertility rates. On the contrary, in many of these societies the number of births per woman was probably lower. This was partly the result of a low fat content of the diet, and partly caused by conscious attempts to limit the number of conceptions and births.

Increasing Growth Rate

It is well known that after the Second World War, the rate of natural increase in Indonesia was quite high, reaching levels of two per cent and above (per annum). In Java after 1757, we witness the beginning of a period of transition from very low to higher growth rates, arriving, at the end of the 19th century, at a level of 1.5 per cent and above. As fertility rates remained at the same level, and even dropped somewhat after 1850, the gradually increasing growth rate must be attributed to diminishing mortality. The following factors were responsible for the lower death rate.

In 1757 the last war of succession in Java was over. There would be wars after that date, particularly the Dutch expeditions in east Java (1760s and 70s) and the Java War (1825-1830), but nevertheless it was the beginning of a relatively peaceful period. This factor alone would have been sufficient for a lower death rate. In the 19th century this effect was reinforced by several other factors of which the successful struggle against smallpox was the most important one. On average, smallpox alone was responsible for a mortality of some four per cent prior to the 1820s, representing ten per cent of the total death rate. Although variolation — vaccination with human smallpox matter — had already started in Java in 1779, and real vaccination with cowpox matter in 1804, an effective and well administered programme did not begin until the 1820s. Initially, this programme met with some passive or active

resistance in a number of areas, as not all people were convinced of the good intentions of the colonial govern- ment, which had made vaccination obligatory. Given the bad expe- riences of the Javanese pea- santry with higher taxes and corvee services, such reactions were not surprising. Slowly but surely, however, when the vaccination programme had proven itself to be harmless and effective, resistance gave way to acceptance in most of the areas concerned. By 1860 the point was reached where 50 per cent of the Javanese population was vaccinated, by which time smallpox was no longer a 'big killer'. Much less could be done about other epidemic (and endemic) diseases. A new form of cholera was particularly vigorous between 1820 and the 1850s, and typhoid fever raged in central Java during the late 1840s. Malaria, both in its endemic and epidemic form, probably spread to new areas in Java before it could be checked at the end of the century with quinine and the drainage of mosquito breeding areas. Local and regional famines had become rare, apart from the late 1840s. Due to improved communications, the impact of local harvest failures was less serious at the end of the century than at the beginning, because transport of rice surplus from other areas had become much easier. Relatively serious crop failures during the years 1900/2 and 1921, however, were evidence that widespread hunger had not been overcome by 1900.

A sanatorium at Lendanglaya.

A Military Hospital, 18th century as depicted by Rach. Hospitals such as this played a key role in keeping epidemic and endemic diseases under control.

POPULATION ESTIMATES OF INDONESIA AND MEAN ANNUAL GROWTH-RATES, 1800 AND 1930, PER ISLAND OR GROUP OF ISLANDS (x 1,000)			
	1800	1930	growth/year in per cent
Java	7,500	40,900	1.3
Sumatra	3,500	7,700	0.6
Kalimantan	700	2,200	0.9
Sulawesi	2,000	4,200	0.6
Lesser Sunda Islands	1,600	3,400	0.6
Maluku	400	900	0.6
Total	15,700	59,300	1.0

In all the major islands outside Java the factors lowering the death rate, both the 'pax Neerlandica' and the vaccination programme, became effective much later than in Java. In places such as northern Sumatra, central Sulawesi, Borneo and Bali–Lombok, war-related deaths were still high as late as the first decade of the 20th century, not least the effect of the Dutch conquest itself. Hence Java's population grew far more rapidly than that of other islands in the 19th century, giving rise by 1900 to the extreme population imbalance which has since marked Indonesia.

Chinese Revenue Farmers

*U*ntil the 20th century, colonial finances depended substantially on revenue farming — the lease of the right to collect taxes on behalf of the government. 'Farms' included sale of opium, alcoholic beverages, tobacco, gambling and pawnshops. In the early 19th century, there were also farms for markets, toll gates, slaughtering animals, and collecting birds' nests. Nearly always, revenue farmers were ethnic Chinese; this saved hiring a bureaucracy and conveniently deflected resentment of colonial practices to members of a conspicuous minority.

REVENUE FROM OPIUM TAX FARMS IN THE OUTER ISLANDS, 1835–1912

— Total revenue from farm fees

- - - of which from Sumatra's East Coast

f (guilders) million

1835 45 55 65 75 85 95 1905 15

Source: Diehl, F.W., 'Revenue Farming and Colonial Finances in the Netherlands East Indies, 1816–1925', in Butcher, J. and Dick, H. (eds.) The Rise and Fall of Revenue Farming: Business Elites and the Emergence of the Modern State in Southeast Asia. London: Macmillan, 1993.

A Chinese officer or 'Captain of the Chinese' was the headmen of the local Chinese community in Indonesia in the 19th and early 20th centuries, from Tijdschrift voor Nederlandsche Indie *(1853),* Koninklijk Instituut voor Taal-, Land- en Volkenkunde, *Netherlands.*

Tax Farmers

The Chinese officers, 'Captains of the Chinese (Kapitan Cina)', and 'Majors' and 'Lieutenants', too, were headmen of the local Chinese communities, and they also acted as their spokesmen. Initially they wore mandarin dress, later the Dutch fitted them out with gold-braided uniforms, symbolising their close relationship with the colonial power. Just as the officers exercised control over their communities, the farmers could prevent tax evasion and smuggling. However, other Chinese resented their power.

Revenue farmers were keen rivals, and competitors could ruin an opium farmer by smuggling in his territory. On the other hand, successful bidders had to provide guarantors for the farms. They usually recruited other prominent Chinese in kongsis or syndicates to raise capital and help control their territories.

Opium Farming in Java

In many parts of Southeast Asia, opium, alcohol and gambling were considered 'Chinese vices'. In Java, however, ordinary peasants consumed opium, mostly in small amounts, and it was widespread among Javanese. Their network of dens and agents penetrated the interior of central and east Java. The last farms were abolished in 1904.

During most of the 19th century, the colonial government tried to restrict the movements of the Chinese; they had to reside in special quarters and obtain passes in order to travel in the countryside. In contrast, the opium farmers and their agents could travel freely in the rural areas. They used their presence in the villages to expand activities such as money-lending.

Revenue Farming in the Outer Islands

In Sumatra and Kalimantan, revenue farming was linked with the Chinese.

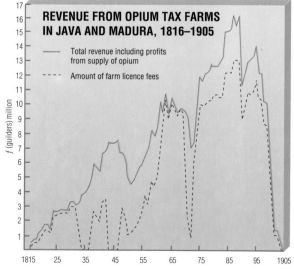

REVENUE FROM OPIUM TAX FARMS IN JAVA AND MADURA, 1816–1905

— Total revenue including profits from supply of opium

- - - Amount of farm licence fees

f (guilders) million

1815 25 35 45 55 65 75 85 95 1905

Source: Diehl, F.W., 'Revenue Farming and Colonial Finances in the Netherlands East Indies, 1816–1925', in Butcher, J. and Dick, H. (eds.) The Rise and Fall of Revenue Farming: Business Elites and the Emergence of the Modern State in Southeast Asia. London: Macmillan, 1993.

Consumers of the major farm products such as opium, pork, alcohol, or gambling were usually Chinese, most often coolie labourers. The Chinese-run gambier plantations of Riau or the tin mines of Bangka, founded in the 18th century were essentially not profitable unless coolie wages could be 'recycled' by providing them with these goods at exorbitant prices.

Revenue farmers could be mine or plantation investors as well. When the opening of east Sumatra's tobacco plantations with western capital brought a great demand for labourers, the farmers, often Chinese officers such as the brothers (Majors) Tjong Yong Hian and Tjong A Fie of Medan were on the spot. The great influx of Chinese, and later Javanese coolies made this a lucrative farm area until the opium farm there was closed in 1911. The Tjongs had extensive interests in the salt revenue farm in Bagan Siapiapi (the centre of salted fish production in the Archipelgo), in plantations, and in commercial activities in Penang, Singapore and China.

The End of Revenue Farming

Revenue farmers were rich and powerful, but not necessarily popular, even among ethnic Chinese. A satirical poem by 'Boer Sing Hoo' (a pseudonym) describes the auction of central Java's opium farms in 1889. The poem ridicules the event as a kind of circus, while the author barely disguises the participants by giving them the names of animals-Ox, Horse, Crocodile and Dragon.

At the end of the 19th century, westerners too voiced their objections to opium as an addictive and impoverishing habit. Other voices favoured limiting the influence of the Chinese on the village economy. Batavia began to enforce pass and residence restrictions more strictly in 1897 and 1900, and gradually withdrew the opium farm. The result, however, was that economic troubles fell on both former revenue farmers, and on the peasants themselves, who were now cut off from markets and credit. Soon, the government lifted restrictions on Chinese travel and residence, and Chinese moved into Java's intermediate trade again.

As the colonial state replaced tax farmers with bureaucrats, economic development brought revenue from other sources than 'sin taxes'. Revenue farming had enabled some Chinese to become fabulously rich, others had slid into bankruptcy when competitors forced up the price for the farm or smuggled in their territory or when economic depression, as in the 1880s, reduced sales. With the

end of the farms, many wealthy families sank into oblivion. In contrast, Oei Tiong Ham, whose immigrant father had bankrolled his successful bid for the opium farm of Semarang (Central Java) in 1889, used his profits to lay the foundation for wide-ranging modern enterprises.

CONCENTRATIONS OF OPIUM USE AND OPIUM FARM PROFITS IN THE RESIDENCIES OF JAVA

Chinese workers at a plantation, after a painting by L.Székely.

A Chinese pedlar with his coolie, a coloured lithograph from J.J.X. Pfyffer zu Neueck, c. 1830.

high
medium
low
forbidden areas

0   100 km

A group of Chinese gambling, by C.W. Mieling after Auguste van Pers (1853–62).

The Chinese revenue far–mers became valued visitors at the court. They were classic cultural brokers between the indigenous courts and the urban Chinese commercial communities. Revenue farming also produced numerous affluent Chinese such as Tjong Yong Hian (top) and Tjong Ah Fie (bottom) who constructed elaborate residences of their own, from 20th century Impressions.

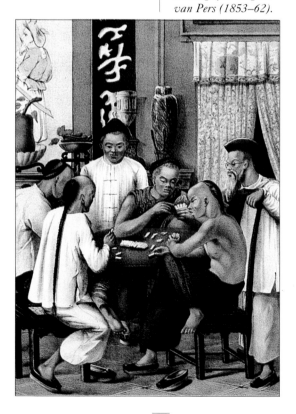

Nineteenth Century Javanese Culture

*U*nder the orderly appearance of colonial Java, with its palace-centred hierarchies and its stately adhiluhung literature, was a growing restlessness and erosion of these certainties. In the larger context of Javanese society, beyond the walls of the kraton and kabupaten, the popularity of Ratu Adil (Just King) myths was evidence that all was not well. Although without leadership protest movements remained scattered and ineffective, they were ominous for the 20th century.

DUTCH RESIDENT AND SULTAN OF SOLO

A formal portrait of the Dutch Resident, de Vogel and the Sultan of Solo, Pakubuwana X. As prescribed by court protocol, the Sultan here holds the arm of the Resident, to guide him into one of the palace staterooms. The Sultan's opulent dress, indicative of his status, consists of a batik sarong decorated with the royal *parang-rusak* ('broken blade') pattern, intricately-decorated dagger called kris, and formal European-style trousers, jacket and medals (Jean Demmeni, photo poster, published in 1911 by Kley Nenberg and Company).

»» *The hierarchic proprieties of 19th century Java. Raden Adipati of Madura with retainers on his alun–alun, with mosque in background, as depicted by C.W. Mieling, 1853–62.*

Colonial and Pre-Colonial Java

The period of Dutch rule in Java properly speaking lasted little more than a century from the end of the Java War in 1830 until the Japanese invasion of 1941. Even so, this was long by the standards of previous dynasties of Java, whose tendency to disintegrate had given rise to expectations that each ruling house would fall at the end of the (Javanese) century. The time of Dutch rule was in many ways Java's 'longest' century, a relatively stable and controlled period in which the pattern of modern Javanese culture was set. Some comparison of this long century with earlier Javanese periods is essential to an understanding of Java's intellectual, social and cultural history.

Though pre-colonial dynasties fell with relative frequency, each collapse was a social catastrophe. A change of dynasty usually meant a shift of royal capital, and since the densest settlement was found around the capital each shift entailed a great upheaval of population. It would hardly be an exaggeration to speak of pre-colonial Java as a series of 'nomadic' peasant settlements. By contrast colonial Java witnessed the expansion of bureaucratic control over all spheres of Javanese life, rapid increases of population, and the gradual rolling back of the tropical jungle to the mountain peaks. The *pax Neerlandica* brought not only peace and order (*rust en orde*) but an end to the battles of princes and the intrigues of political factions in the *kraton* (palace). This new order, together with the rise of a plantation economy made Java what it is today.

Dutch Official and Javanese Aristocrat

At the end of the Java War the *bupati* (territorial chiefs, or in Dutch *regenten*) of the 'outer' Javanese lands (*mancanegara*) supported Dutch annexation of their lands, forgetting any loyalty they owed to the Mataram princes in their four kratons, just as the *bupati* of the coastal regions (*pesisir*) had before them. Even the four princes themselves forgot their earlier vows to rule in Java. With the aid of Dutch scholars and officials this Javanese elite of *bupatis* and princes directed much of their attention instead

to creating the refined high culture of aristocratic Java, often referred to as a *halus* (refined) or *adhiluhung* (beautiful sublime) culture. The process also involved, however, a miniaturisation of Java.

Dutch rule was based on a dualistic system, whereby a bureaucracy of Dutch officials (*Binnenlandse Bestuur* or B.B.) governed through the intermediary of the local Javanese elite composed of princes and their families in the royal domains of Surakarta and Yogyakarta, and the *bupati* throughout the remainder of Java. The *bupati* ruled within his *kabupaten* in a reflection of the princely rule of the four *kraton* of Surakarta and Yogyakarta, but reported directly to his superior, the Dutch Assistant-Resident. Collectively, together with the officials beneath them, this hereditary Javanese ruling class became known as *priyayi*, or *pangreh-praja*.

Central Javanese kraton compounds had in front of them a big square (*alun-alun*), in imitation of the traditional royal centres. Prison, mosque, market and government offices were constructed around this centre of palace and *alun-alun*. In bureaucratic terms also each *kabupaten* came to resemble the princely kratons. Like the princes they were assisted by a vizier *(pateh)*, and by a hierarchy of territorial chiefs descending from *wedana* to assistant *wedana* and finally *lurah* (village chief). Ceremonial umbrellas, sacred kris and many other paraphernalia of authority (*pusaka*), as well as the hereditary principal, made each *kabupaten* of Java a miniature princely land. For the first time in history perhaps, every Javanese was subject to princely authority and aristocratic high culture.

Protest Movements

Though colonial 'peace and order' dominated the reports of government officials and much of the scholarly discourse of the time, it represented only one side of Javanese social reality. Java did not change overnight from extreme instability and looseness of social structure to the complex hierarchy of official order. The pre-colonial political jungle continued to exist beneath the calm and controlled surface.

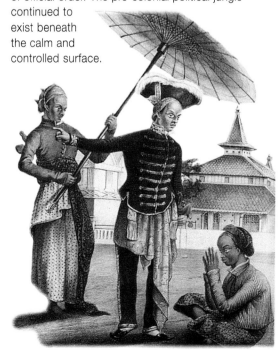

126

ROYAL PROCESSION, YOGYAKARTA
Although the *kraton* ceremonial cycle has been greatly scaled back in post-independence Indonesia, many of the elaborate rituals and royal processions such as this one in Yogyakarta continue to be practiced. For the Javanese of today, as in the past, they constitute living proof of the divinity of the Sultan and the influence of his court.

PENDAPA AGUNG, SURAKARTA
The Pendapa Agung (Istana Mangkunagaran) of Surakarta is among the most majestic in Java. Begun by Mangkunagara II at the end of the 18th century and completed in 1866, the *pendopo* is also said to be the largest in Java. Like the kraton of Surakarta, the *pendopo*'s design is rich with cosmological significance.

Between 1830 and the early 20th century there were more than a hundred rebellions, protest movements, demonstrations and strikes. Although colonial authorities tended to classify all as rebellions against legal authority, they represented a range of social unrest from full-scale rebellion to simple requests for the redress of grievances. The most radical often took the millenarian form of *Ratu Adil* (Just King) movements, seeking a totally new order under a prince of justice who would put all to rights. Inspiration often came from the widely known Joyoboyo prophecies of the coming of a new age of prosperity and justice under such a *Ratu Adil*. King Joyoboyo had ruled with legendary justice in eastern Java in the 13th century. The period of his life and prophecies were to be followed by four successive cycles of decline, injustice, pestilence and civil war. 'Silver money disappeared from villages to be replaced by bad coins', according to one early 19th century version of the prophecies. When the bottom line of human suffering was reached then a just king would appear to announce a new dawn of justice and prosperity in Java. These prophecies represented a form of mass mobilisation, and their currency always increased before a major rebellion. These post-1830 movements, though numerous, were always on a local scale, occurring within a single village or at most a district. Another sign of a narrowing of vision within the 19th century was the absence of risings against the princes of Java as such. The titles of the new *Ratu Adil* bore no resemblance to those of ancient kings, tending at best to call themselves by some such local appellation as 'Sultan of Ponorogo'.

A Blurring of Power Relations

The *adhiluhung* culture which reached such high development by the late 19th century included a totalitarian conception of royal power emanating from the person of the king. This concept of power as essentially passive, concentrated and indivisible has been brilliantly analysed in a famous essay by

Benedict Anderson. This must be seen as a construct of the 19th century, however, not as an ideology with its roots in pre-colonial Java. Among the Javanese texts analysed by Anderson is the *Suluk Gatholoco*, a very anti-Islamic poem dating from the late 19th century. In it the hero Gatholoco, hideously built and yet the perfect man, asks the Islamic scholars to answer a riddle about the Javanese puppet theatre (*wayang*) as representing the cosmos. Which is older, the puppeteer (*dalang*), the puppets (*wayang*), the oil lamp which casts the shadows (*blencong*), or the screen (*kelir*)? In this 19th century text the Muslim scholars all answered wrongly, and only Gatholoco knew that the right answer was the lamp, without whose flickering flame nothing could be seen. Yet as G.W.J. Drewes has pointed out, in earlier Javanese manuscripts of the 15th and 16th centuries dealing with the Muslim *walis*, it was the puppeteer which was seen as the correct answer to the same riddle. The refined culture of colonial Java appeared to have blurred the concept of power by shifting it away from the masterful puppeteer, since that kind of power was now in Dutch hands.

Similarly the Javanese *babad* literature of this late period appears to have been preoccupied with stately royal processions, where the older literature described battles and conflicts. There are elaborate descriptions of the processions between Kartasura and Surakarta, processions at royal weddings, and even processions at meetings between Javanese princes and Dutch officials.

Works by Prince Mangkunagara IV (r.1853-81) of Surakarta, such as the *Serat Weddhatama*, discuss the art and ethics of ruling rather than its substance. It was more civil than the *Babad Tanah Jawi* of previous centuries, but less realistic. Although the great poet Ronggowarsito (1802-73) wrote the fashionable forms of *adhiluhung* literature on commission from the Dutch, he experienced his 'world as one turned upside down'.

The role of the courts in the continuity of Javanese culture is most visible in the arts such as the gamelan.

The warriors of the courts of Yogyakarta and Surakarta became more renowned in the 19th century for their elegance rather than their effectiveness.

New Technologies and New Perspectives

*C*ulturally, the 19th century is a bridge to the modern world. In the latter part of the century Indonesia experienced a heady mix of economic development, urbanisation and a revolution in communications. By the end of the century the key cultural institutions which would lead Indonesia into modernity were in place.

In the late 19th century, rail first began to replace horse drawn transport in Java.

Post offices in major towns and postal service made communication over distances possible in Indonesia from the late 19th century.

» Head postman, telegram carriers and postman.

Post and telegraph office, Weltevreden, by C.T. Deeleman (1860).

Imagining a Wider World

The printing press, the steamship and railroad, and the telegraph all contributed to the change in the way that time and space were imagined, and how this imagination was communicated. Multi-ethnic urban environments and print communications also began to change the way individuals saw themselves in society.

As the 19th century progressed, steam power made transport quicker and more regular both by sea and by land. The opening of the Suez Canal in 1869 meant that both Europe and the Muslim holy land became more accessible. By 1880, the Archipelago was crowded with small steamers, and scheduled steamship services dominated the European run. In the 1860s, rail first began to replace horse drawn transport on the trunk routes of Java. Both steam shipping and the railways made a regular public postal service possible, and this was in operation, with pre-paid postage stamps and post offices in the major towns of Java in 1862. Within a couple of decades, it had suddenly become possible to communicate over distances and to travel with far greater ease and confidence.

The wider horizons, greater physical mobility, and non-traditional environment of urban life supported a new kind of literature. Its epitome was the travelogue. The earliest were written in Malay by Abdullah bin Muhammad al-Misri (1823) and Abdullah bin Abdul Kadir (1838). Description of travel was an old theme, but these accounts were cast in the first person. They communicated the perspective of idiosyncratic individuals, who were urban men, marginal to traditional society.

The same interest is reflected in the first European novels translated into Indonesian languages. The first was Defoe's *Robinson Crusoe*. Malay versions were published in Singapore (1855) and in Batavia (1875 and five subsequent editions). A Javanese version appeared in 1881. *Robinson Crusoe* promotes European Christian supremacy through a story of exploration and individualism. Its account of an ordinary individual coping in an environment of social isolation is a metaphor for urban man. The well-received Malay translations of Ida Pfeiffer's journey around the world (1877) and through the Indies Archipelago were doubly challenging because of the gender of their protagonist.

Printing and the Press

The expansion of commercial agriculture, and particularly of sugar in Java, required an industrial infrastructure of mills and railways which fed the North Java ports of Semarang and Surabaya. The rapid growth of these urban commercial centres, coupled with their hinterland transport networks and the postal system, underpinned the great communications revolution of the 19th century, the appearance of the newspaper.

The technology of printing came early to the Indies, in 1659. But only in the 19th century was any substantial amount printed in Indonesian languages by the Protestant mission stations in the Straits Settlements (1817), Ambon (1819) and Batavia (1822). The audience was limited and the Dutch authorities, appreciating the dangers of the technology, kept printing out of independent hands until 1848. The situation changed in 1855 with the launch of a Javanese weekly newspaper in Surakarta. *Bromartani* was edited by the Eurasian, G.F. Winter. It reported parochial news of births, deaths, sales and auctions, court events, government decrees and appointments, along with articles on agricultural improvement and excerpts from literary works.

The following year a Malay newspaper, *Soerat Kabar Bahasa Melaijoe*, was launched in Surabaya. This was the trail blazer for many commercial newspapers based in the north Java ports during the rest of the century. At first the focus was on advertisements, current market prices and shipping information. The twice-weekly *Bintang Timor*, which appeared in Surabaya in 1861, was the first newspaper which took up reporting on local issues including social and economic conditions, and published 'news from the mail' relating to Europe and

China. The readership of these early Malay and Javanese newspapers reflected the limited distribution of literacy and western style education. It was largely urban, comprising especially Chinese and salaried *priyayi*. In their first decades, newspapers were printed by Eurasians, with Chinese coming to dominate ownership during the 1880s, and indigenous ownership becoming significant only in the 20th century.

Printing in Indonesian languages accelerated in the late 19th century. A lithographic speed printing machine, from Faber and Schleicher.

New Consciousness

The psychological potency of the new medium should not be underestimated. The immediacy of current reporting was enhanced by the telegraph. After 1870 the major urban newspapers were translating news from a telegraphic cable pool run by the government. Letters to the editor were a popular feature, as were articles submitted by readers. In 1869 *Bintang Timor* invited its readers in various parts of Java to send in news and articles in exchange for free subscriptions to the newspaper. In these ways newspapers fostered a sense of solidarity among their readers, who jointly experienced the news, and could communicate with one another.

The newspaper and magazine thus set a pattern for a new kind of social relationship which depended not upon personal networks or neighbourhood obligations but upon the shared interests of individual subscribers. Voluntary associations took a more concrete form in 1872 when *priyayi* clubs were formed to buy books and subscribe to Malay and Javanese newspapers. Later, major voluntary associations like the Chinese Tiong Hoa Hwe Koan (1900) and the indigenous Sarekat Islam (1911) used newspapers as extensions of their membership, initiating a persistent feature of the Indonesian press.

Rise of Malay Urban Culture

At first it was difficult to find a widely understood language medium. Some early newspapers included pages in Javanese as well as Malay. *Selompret Melajoe* of Semarang (1860) provided glossaries of difficult Malay words for the benefit of, particularly, its Chinese readers. The successful commercial newspapers relied upon the language most current in the thriving port cities, the so-called low Malay which was used by natives, Chinese, Arabs, as well as Eurasians, Europeans and the lower levels of the Dutch administration. The penetration of inland Java by the global economy brought in its wake newspapers and printed books in low Malay, and as the century progressed Malay gained greater currency. In the 1890s bilingual newspapers in Javanese and low Malay were appearing in Surakarta and Yogyakarta. Low Malay, in Dutch script, was the pre-eminent vehicle for the new literature of journalism and translation which conveyed new ideas and values.

Opening to Wider Horizons

Chinese publishers put out both newspapers and books. From 1883

the new medium was used extensively for Malay translations of popular Chinese historical romances and classics. These translations spoke to Chinese Peranakan who were rediscovering their Chinese identity, stimulated by an influx of new arrivals from China (the Chinese population of the Indies more than doubled between 1860 and 1900), and by telegraphic reports of affairs in China. The press allowed all Indies Chinese, whether speakers of Chinese, Malay or Dutch, to follow the Sino-Japanese War keenly. The press also carried telegraphic reports on contemporary events in the Middle East and Turkey, including the Russo-Turkish War, which allowed Indonesian Muslims a greater sense of participation in a wider Islamic community.

Thus, the newspaper press, and the printing of books, greatly increased individual access to information and transformed it into an industrial commodity. This made individual choices between a wider range of identities possible. In the 19th century these revolutionary changes did not reach far beyond the urban and aristocratic elites, but they unleashed forces of modernity which have continued to gain ground to this day.

NEWS OF A CHANGING WORLD

Newspapers such as those shown below brought local and international news to subscribers in the major towns of Java. Their elite readership was as ethnically mixed as the fast-growing urban centres in which they were published.

Successful newspapers published news, letters from readers, and serialised literature alongside advertisements, shipping lists and market reports. The frequency and regularity of the newspaper let its readers share a sense of being up-to-date in a rapidly changing world.

Long-barreled guns with octagonal bore were made in the highlands of west Sumatra in the 18th and early 19th centuries and saw use in the Aceh wars. The technology was introduced to Indonesia by the Portuguese. Picture (right): not to scale.

In Indonesia, one of the areas of technology most open to foreign influence has always been weaponry. The long Europeanised kris is from the Riau Archipelago. The floral silverwork is characteristically Malay, though the proportions of the weapon are European. Picture (left): not to scale.

THE END OF AUTONOMY

Colonialism came exceptionally early to some parts of Indonesia, as the spices of Maluku had drawn Europeans to establish strongholds and monopolies in the area. It had however come exceptionally late to other areas protected by Indonesia's intense pluralities. A few states such as Aceh had always retained a proud independence, buttressed in the 19th century by the proximity of British rather than Dutch ports. Other upland societies protected themselves from outside influence by their very statelessness, which left little for an outside power to seek to manipulate.

Dutch power expanded cautiously in the middle of the 19th century, after the exhausting battles to subdue first Dipanagara and then the Sumatran Padris. The Sumatra Treaty with Britain in 1871 provided a new impetus to substantiate on the ground the claims over the whole Archipelago which Holland was now making. However, the disastrous experience during the first five years of the Aceh War put out of the question any further demands on Dutch resources for 20 years. Expansion could occur only where it was relatively peaceful and profitable. When the combination of General van Heutsz and Christian Snouck Hurgonje 'solved' the Aceh problem with a policy of relentless force at the end of the century, the momentum of these successes finally carried the Dutch forward to all the other corners of the Archipelago.

By this time the weapons of Europe had far outstripped the capacity of the small remaining Indonesian states to mount effective resistance. Aceh and Lombok had acquired European-style ships, and rifles were widespread in the Archipelago. The more fundamental European achievements of scientific method, mass education and printing, and orderly representative government, could not so readily be copied without fundamental reconstruction of Indonesian societies. This would occur only with much pain in the following century. This Dutch offensive marked the end of the colourful variety of political forms in the Archipelago. Though some titles, palaces and rituals were retained, there would be no doubt after 1910 that it was Dutch-colonial administrative, financial, technical and eventually educational systems which determined the development of all these colourful societies in a similar direction. The 'last stand' of the Acehnese, Gayos, Batak, Balinese, Bugis and other polities was often heroic and poignant, but it would require a very differently-educated later generation to see in them anything other than bitter defeat.

Aceh and the Perang Sabil

*T*he longest war in the history of Dutch colonialism was required to incorporate the proud Sultanate of Aceh into Netherlands India. Although Aceh had a history of close relations with other states, it remained as the only large Archipelago state to have avoided ever signing a treaty accepting Dutch sovereignty. Acehnese distinguished themselves by a heroic resistance for more than 30 years, based first on self-defence but later on an aroused spirit of Islamic martyrdom.

»» The bombardment of Aceh by the Dutch fleet, from The Illustrated London News.

The Mesjid Raya or the 'Great Mosque' of Kutaradja, built by the Netherlands India Government in 1879 as a token of peace. It was extended with two additional bays in 1936. From H.D.T. Willink's Landschappen en Volkstypen van Nederlandsch–Indie *(Haarlem, 1883).*

Unsuccessful Dutch Campaigns

Britain had guaranteed Aceh's independence in a Treaty of 1819, and Turkey had been reminded in the 19th century of the protection it had extended to Aceh in the 16th century. In the colonially-dominated climate of 1871, however, Britain and Holland signed a treaty withdrawing objections to Dutch annexation of all Sumatra, after which war came quickly.

The war began when Dutch troops attacked the Aceh capital on 26 March 1873, only four days after arriving from Batavia with instructions to impose Dutch sovereignty either by negotiation or force. Put together hastily in the belief that Aceh was in the process of negotiating a defensive alliance with the United States, France or Turkey, this force of 3,000 men retreated ignominiously a month later, having lost its commander in the fighting. The Dutch now believed their tarnished honour had to be avenged by a military conquest, which was commenced in November 1873 with a second expedition of 13,000 men.

The royal palace was taken in January 1874 in the midst of a cholera outbreak which took thousands of victims on each side, including the young Acehnese Sultan, Mahmud. Frustrated in the attempt to strike a deal with a chastened sultan, the Dutch now proclaimed their own rule over the whole of Aceh, even though they controlled only the capital. Six years and thousands of deaths later Dutch troops had subjugated the valley of the Aceh river while Dutch naval blockades had persuaded the *ulubalang* (territorial chiefs) of Aceh's long coast to sign treaties of submission. Exhausted morally and financially by the war, the Dutch declared it over in 1879, appointed a civil Governor, and built the Mesjid Raya (Great Mosque) as a symbol of reconciliation. When the Acehnese demonstrated their continued defiance with a mounting wave of guerilla raids, the Dutch responded in 1884 by withdrawing all their forces within a strongly fortified 'concentrated line' around the capital. Many Acehnese felt that God had given them the victory.

Inspiration of the Holy War

The resistance which flamed anew in this period was inspired particularly by *hikayat*, or poetic tales. Many of these emphasised that those who died fighting the Dutch were *syahid*, Islamic martyrs. According to the *Hikayat Perang Sabil* (Tales of Holy War) the martyrs would go immediately to heaven where their sins would be forgiven by God, and they would enjoy bliss

as beautiful angels became their wives, catering to their every need.

The Dutch military regarded such texts as extremely dangerous and burned all the copies they found. Fortunately however a civilian official expert in Acehnese, H.T. Damste, rescued a number of copies as keys to understanding the Acehnese mentality. Several remain in the Leiden University Library, transcribed on instructions of the Islamicist Christiaan Snouck Hurgronje.

The long and ruinous 'Dutch War' or 'Infidel War', as the Acehnese called it, reinforced their conviction that Islam was at the centre of their identity as a people. While the *ulubalangs* had led the earliest phase of resistance, inspiration from the mid-1880s onward was primarily in the hands of religious scholars such as Teungku Chik di Tiro Muhammad Saman. Through sermons, letters, and texts such as the *Hikayat Perang Sabil* they mobilised Acehnese to form guerilla bands of *Muslimin* who faced death with courage.

Holy War in Islam is *jihad fi sabili'l-lah* (war in the path of Allah), or in Malay *perang sabil*. The most quoted verse of the Qur'an was 111 al-Taubah, which reads in translation: 'Lo! Allah hath brought from the believers their lives and their wealth because the garden will be theirs. They shall fight in the way of Allah and shall slay and be slain. It is a promise which is binding on Him in the Torah and Gospel and Qur'an. Who fulfilleth His convenant better than Allah? Rejoice then in your bargain that you have made, for that is the supreme triumph'. One religious teacher from the central theatre of war, Syaich Abbas Ibnu Muhammad, enunciated in his 1889 treatise *Tadhkirat ar-Rakidin* the central doctrine that Aceh was Dar-al-Islam except for the area controlled by the Dutch which had become Dar-al-harb. It was the moral duty (*fardhu'ain*) of all Muslims, including women and children, to fight to recover this infidel-ruled land for the Dar-al-Islam. This ideology of the Holy War had emerged in Aceh as early as the 17th century, but was revitalised by religious teachers at times of crisis, of which the end of the 19th century was the most acute.

Final Dutch Offensive

During the first 25 years of a very unpopular war, Dutch policy changed constantly and was carried out by 14 different Governors. In 1898 a policy of ruthless conquest was decided upon, however, and placed in the hands of General J.B. van Heutsz as Military-Governor. He was advised by the Islamic scholar Snouck Hurgronje. Van Heutsz was succeeded by three other forceful military figures - J.C. van der Wijck (1904), G.C.E. van Daalen (1905) and H.N.A. Swart (1908). Lightly-armed and highly mobile units of the Marechaussee (*marsose* to the Acehnese) pursued the war party relentlessly into the forests and swamps which had previously given them

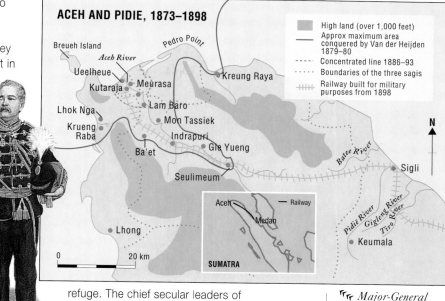

ACEH AND PIDIE, 1873–1898

High land (over 1,000 feet)
Approx maximum area conquered by Van der Heijden 1879–80
Concentrated line 1886–93
Boundaries of the three sagis
Railway built for military purposes from 1898

Breueh Island
Pedro Point
Aceh River
Ueelheue
Kutaraja
Meurasa
Kreung Raya
Lhok Nga
Lam Baro
Krueng Raba
Mon Tassiek
Indrapuri
Ba'et
Gle Yueng
Seulimeum
Batee River
Sigli
Pidië River
Gigleng River
Tiro River
Keumala
Lhong

Aceh — Railway
Medan
SUMATRA

0   20 km

refuge. The chief secular leaders of resistance, Sultan Muhammad Daud, Tuanku Raja Keumala, Tuanku Mahmud and Teuku Panglima Polem Muda Perkasa, surrendered in the course of 1903. The *ulama*-inspired resistance effectively ended after ten more years of fighting.

Islamic Adjustments

Having fought the Dutch in terms of a holy war, Acehnese leaders had to rethink their world view when it became apparent that such resistance had failed. Many of them moved in a similar direction to the outstanding Indian intellectual, Sayyid Ahmad Khan, who explained the obligation of *jihad* in terms of a military struggle against religious oppression. If Islam was not oppressed and Muslims were free to practice their faith, as was the case in both British India and Netherlands India, then there was no obligation on Muslims to take up arms.

The Acehnese leaders knew that they had given their best in the holy war, but failed. Further resistance would only destroy the country, its people and its religion. They therefore felt justified in making peace (*taslim*), like their co-religionists in India, and concentrating their efforts on strengthening their religious faith and institutions. Though Aceh was defeated, the spirit of freedom was still alive in its people, as was manifested again in the 1940s.

Major-General Karel van der Heijden, the most successful of the early Dutch commanders, who conquered most of the Aceh River valley in 1879-80.

Two pages from the Hikayat Perang Sabil, from the collection of the University of Leiden, Netherlands (Cod.Or. 8667).

Dutch Fort in Aceh, from The Illustrated London News, *1878.*

Foreign Penetration of North Sumatra

*E*arly descriptions of the Batak people as 'isolated' in the rugged, mountainous interior of Sumatra, were only accurate from the perspective of the outsider who found the terrain impenetrable, and the inhabitants inhospitable. The Batak, however, were able to descend to both of Sumatra's shores to actively take part in the pre–colonial trade. The lives of the Batak changed radically during the 19th century.

Toba Batak marketplace.

A Christian grave in Tomok, Samosir Island shows the combination of Batak and Christian motifs.

Missionary Ginsberg and elders of the Batak Church (19th century). Toba men publicly announced their conversion to Christianity by cutting their hair and removing their headgear.

Social Organisation

Certain features were common to the social organisation of all seven of the Batak ethnic groups. Each was characterised by exogamous patrilineal clans divided into autonomous village units. These villages were small in Toba, numbering just a few houses. However, they were larger in Karo and in the southern regions of Angkola and Mandailing where, in the mid 19th century, the inhabitants of a single village could number up to 400 people. Each village was led by a raja or a chief, whose office was passed down through the patriline.

Batak society was structured around two opposing forces; the need, in the interests of self-protection, to create alliances, and simultaneously the need, also in the interests of self-protection, to distrust all outsiders to the village. Uneasy relations between villages and territorial units were expressed in endless intrigue and virtually ritualised inter-village warfare. Supra-village political arrangements were under constant negotiations and achieved only ephemeral expression.

The Sisingamangaraja

The imperatives of colonial bureaucracy forced the development of an identifiable 'Batak region', creating a stable supra-village political, economic and social organisation for the first time in Batak history. There was also widespread opposition to the Dutch. However, the Batak spiritual and social leader Sisingamangaraja XII proved no match for the Dutch when he attempted to organise armed resistance. Dutch troops pursued him relentlessly until they killed him in a shoot-out in 1907. With his death, all significant opposition to the Dutch regime was brought to an end.

Alliances

The strongest alliances between social units in the Batak society were forged by marriage ties. The elaborate ritualised exchanges between wife-giving and wife-taking groups located them in a dense web of ongoing mutual obligations. Political strength was reckoned, at least in part, by strategic marriage alliances. It is no wonder, therefore, that blessings were counted in sons and daughters.

Another kind of inter-village and inter-regional alliance was expressed through the exchange of goods. The Batak were active traders albeit in some regions more than others. Their wild interior was criss-crossed with ancient footpaths linking territories and trading centres. Territorial alliances regulated safe passage to and from the markets on market days.

Early European Impact

The centrally located Lake Toba provided a convenient locus of trade for Batak society. Its shores were and still are dotted with strategically located markets serving also as relay stations in long distance trade. As trade accelerated under colonial rule and plantations expanded, the increasingly powerful Malays, who were in control of the trade and the plantations, pushed the Karo out of their coastal territory and up into the mountains. The Karo rebellion of 1872 was quelled by the Dutch who sided with the Malays. The Karo did not relax their resistance and accept Dutch and Malay

power until well into the 20th century.

In the middle of the 19th century, the southern Batak political elite were wearing Malay trappings of power. In the 19th century, the Dutch colonial forces helped the southern Batak resist the destructive invasion of the Minangkabau Islamic Padri sect. The Dutch themselves did not leave after the war. Ironically, the subsequent sweeping Malayanisation of this region was underwritten by the colonial presence.

Toba Batak men publicly announced their conversion to Christianity by cutting their hair and removing their headgear. Missionaries were active in the Batak region early in the 19th century, with the Rhenish Mission under the leadership of I.L. Nommensen booking greatest success. The Rhenish Mission shifted its operations to the interior, to the Silindung Valley, in 1863. This was to become an important centre of Christian and colonial power; it had always been an important centre of Batak trade. The Toba Batak converts formed a bulwark against Malayo-Muslim forces on every side. Christianity offered the Toba Batak new means to attain social prestige and new terms for its expression.

BATAK LANGUAGE GROUPS AND TRADE CENTRES

N

KARO
Belawar
Kutacane
Medan
Berastagi
Kabanjahe
SIMALUNGUN
Sidikalang
Ambarita
Pem. Siantar
Strait of Melaka
PAKPAK
Tomok
Parapat
Singkil
Samosir Island
Balige
Porsea
Laguboti
Barus
Tarutung
Rantau Parapat
Sibolga
TOBA
NIAS
ANGKOLA
Padang/ Sidempuan
MANDAILING

● Trade Centres

0   100 km

SUMATRA

Karo Batak women pounding rice - Karo society was more egalitarian prior to colonialism. The egalitarian multi-family dwellings eventually gave way to single-family dwellings, and diversification in the economy led to greater economic differentiation amongst the people.

The Karo chief, Pa Mbelgah and his family - including the skulls of his ancestors. The photographer wrote that the Karo 'treated me with friendship... they did not see in me one of those Europeans who had taken their land from them by force and ruled them according to foreign laws.'

The longest canoe on Lake Toba. Lake Toba formed a natural forum of communication among the Toba Batak. The important lakeside villages all had large dugout canoes for both trade and warfare.

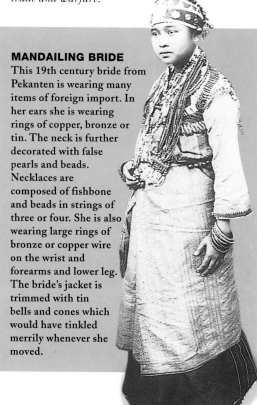

MANDAILING BRIDE

This 19th century bride from Pekanten is wearing many items of foreign import. In her ears she is wearing rings of copper, bronze or tin. The neck is further decorated with false pearls and beads. Necklaces are composed of fishbone and beads in strings of three or four. She is also wearing large rings of bronze or copper wire on the wrist and forearms and lower leg. The bride's jacket is trimmed with tin bells and cones which would have tinkled merrily whenever she moved.

The Fall of the Bugis States

Bugis battle flag combining Islamic and pre-Islamic motifs.

Over the centuries there has been a peculiar bond between the Bugis and the Dutch. In the 17th century they fought side by side against the Makasarese, resulting in a Bugis domination over south Sulawesi that lasted for almost two and a half centuries. During the 19th century the Bugis-Dutch relationship became increasingly embittered.

»» *La Pawawoi Karaeng Segeri with followers on board the ship that brought him to Batavia to spend his last days in exile. His foot is bandaged. Standing in the back are the Dutch civil servants J. Tideman (left) and J.A.G. Brugman (right). (Bintang Hindia 4, 1906, p.66).*

By 1905 the Bugis were defeated by the Dutch at Bone. The Dutch managed to capture entire south Sulawesi by 1911, and remained in control until 1942. The map shows the Dutch control over the different areas in southern Sulawesi.

Nineteenth Century South Sulawesi

Between 1825 and 1905 four wars were fought between the Bugis and the Dutch. The last one meant the end for Bugis political independence; the Dutch became the direct rulers of the land until they in turn were ousted in 1942. The Bugis never again regained political autonomy, although even today the traditional aristocracy is still powerful and respected, and district borders still follow the borderlines of the former kingdoms.

In the 19th century, there were three significant players in the power game of south Sulawesi: the Dutch, the Bugis of Bone, and, weakest of the three, the Makasarese of Gowa. While in many circumstances there is an obvious difference between Bugis and Makasarese culture and identity, it should be noted that on a political level the two became blended to a large degree. From the 17th century there has been a policy of extensive inter-marriage between the nobilities of all major kingdoms in south Sulawesi. These networks of kin ties in the area contributed to the notion of south Sulawesi as a political entity. To keep the noble 'white blood' pure, it should mix with other white blood of the south Sulawesian aristocracy. There were large and small Bugis kingdoms, in a continuously changing pattern of alliances. Apart from Bone, the mightiest, most influential of them, other large kingdoms included Luwu, the 'cradle' of

Bugis culture, Wajo, home of the entrepreneurs and seafarers, Soppeng, and Sidenreng, the second most powerful Bugis kingdom.

Bone and the Dutch

From the beginning of the 19th century onwards, as a consequence of a broader policy, the Dutch tightened their control over the area. Already in 1825 they tried forcefully to push Bone into a new alliance. In particular from the middle of that century onwards when the scope of Dutch colonial policy widened to the Outer Islands, mutual suspicion and irritation increased. The ruler of Bone, Queen We Pancaitana Besse Kajuara, perceived the imperialistic motives behind Dutch moves and resisted. She showed her hostility in several ways. Among other actions, she ordered that the Dutch flag be carried upside down on trading vessels from Bone. For the Dutch this provocation in particular formed the justification for two military expeditions against Bone in 1859 and 1860. The queen was deposed and replaced by a nobleman more loyal to the Dutch. He bore, as did his famous predecessor, the title Arung Palakka. He, in turn, signed a contract that would reduce Bone's power in many ways. It was in particular the enormous loss of territory that was damaging for Bone; all territories south of the Tangka river, including the island of Selayar, passed into Dutch hands.

Although the territory of Bone became partly Dutch property and partly a Dutch dependency, Bone retained its own administration. Dutch involvement in internal affairs limited itself to formal approval of the ruler (*arung*) and the prime minister (*tomarilaleng*) after their election by the ruling council of seven kings (*ade pitu*). This situation continued when Arung Palakka died in 1871 and was succeeded by his daughter Fatima Banri.

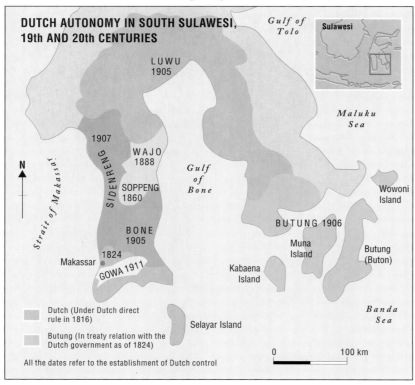

DUTCH AUTONOMY IN SOUTH SULAWESI, 19th AND 20th CENTURIES

Gulf of Tolo

Sulawesi

LUWU 1905

Maluku Sea

1907

WAJO 1888

Gulf of Bone

SIDENRENG

SOPPENG 1860

Wowoni Island

Strait of Makassar

BUTUNG 1906

BONE 1905

Muna Island

Butung (Buton)

1824

Makassar

GOWA 1911

Kabaena Island

N

Banda Sea

Dutch (Under Dutch direct rule in 1816)

Selayar Island

Butung (In treaty relation with the Dutch government as of 1824)

0   100 km

All the dates refer to the establishment of Dutch control

La Pawawoi Karaeng Segeri (seated in the centre) at the height of his power, c. 1900. The other seated persons are members of the ade pitu. Standing behind them are their followers. This is the only known photograph of La Pawawoi Karaeng Segeri before his arrest (Weekblad voor Indie 2, *1905–06, p.568*).

House of the rulers of Gowa.

Towards the End of Bugis Power

After the death of Fatima Banri in 1895 things, however, changed. A power struggle followed in which all major parties of south Sulawesi were involved, Makasarese, Bugis and the Dutch. The Makasarese were represented by Karaeng Popo from Gowa, who, as the husband of the deceased queen, had accumulated considerable power during her reign. In that period too, he had clashed a number of times, not only with the Dutch, but also with the Prime Minister of Bone, La Pawawoi Karaeng Segeri, who was to play a decisive role in Bugis politics. The Dutch experienced him as a friend who turned into an enemy; he was perceived as exemplary for the Bugis attitude towards them. It heralded the end of the Bugis kingdoms.

The Fall of the Bugis

At first sight La Pawawoi Karaeng Segeri did not appear to be an opponent of the Dutch. During the war in 1859 he had taken sides with the Dutch and was awarded by them with the rule over Sinjai. After a while he returned to Bone, where he was appointed commander-in-chief (*punggawa*) by his father, Arung Palakka. In that position he proved a good ally for the Dutch, who rewarded him in 1877 with a gold medal for good services. In 1889 La Pawawoi became Prime Minister under the reign of his half-sister Fatima Banri and had a prominent influence on the Dutch decisions. He played it masterfully. The election of his Makasarese contender Karaeng Popo should be avoided. It was easy to convince the Dutch of this because he knew they were not fond of Karaeng Popo either. So when the *ade pitu* appointed the 13 year old daughter of the deceased ruler, he knew that the Dutch would reject this, since it would only increase the power of her father, Karaeng Popo. And so they did. The Dutch decided to put La Pawawoi Karaeng Segeri on the throne instead, their ally of over 30 years and also of noble white blood.

Not long after the installation of La Pawawoi Karaeng Segeri in 1896, signs of growing mutual irritation became visible. In hindsight much of the blame could be put on the contract concluded between Bone and the Dutch in 1896. In the interpretation of this contract two worlds clashed: the bureaucratic, formalistic view of the Dutch against the loose, conceptual world of the Bugis. The tensions culminated eventually in the last war between Bone and the Dutch in 1905. It was a bitter war, in which many Bugis and a small number of Dutchmen died. The old ruler La Pawawoi Karaeng Segeri and a small group of adherents fled and were only captured after a long hunt, in many ways embarrassing for the Dutch. During the fight preceding his arrest, La Pawawoi's son, who was the Bone *punggawa*, was killed. When La Pawawoi Karaeng Segeri died six years later in exile in Bandung, the last autonomous Bugis ruler had passed away. It also marked the beginning of the end of a centuries old, independent, civilisation of high standards.

Put in a broader perspective, this final war against the Bugis was the conclusion of a long development, in which economic motives played a prominent role. As part of the policy that used imperialism as its base for colonial state formation, the suppression of the Bugis by the Dutch was simply inevitable.

GENEALOGY

Two pages from a genealogy of the rulers of Suppa and Sidenreng. The text is written in the Bugis language. The genealogy is read from top to bottom, starting on page 68, which mentions the first rulers, who 'descended from heaven'. A red triangle indicates a female ruler; a black hexagon a male ruler. A red T-shaped symbol marks a Suppa ruler; a Y-shaped symbol a ruler from Sidenreng. At the bottom of page 69 two 19th century rulers of Bone are indicated with a red flag. One of them is We Pancaitana Besse Kajuara; apparently she was ruler of Suppa as well. On the same line is a red star on the hexagon, indicating a ruler of the Makasarese kingdom of Gowa. The manuscript is kept at the Library of Leiden University (Or.22.018) and was completed around 1981.

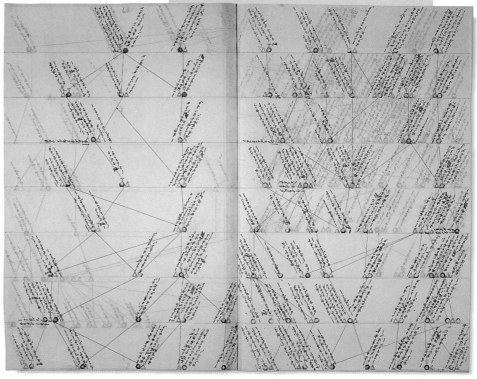

Transformations in Upland Eastern Indonesian Societies

*L*ong before their descendants set eyes on merchants or soldiers, administrators or missionaries from beyond the Archipelago, the upland inhabitants of eastern Indonesia felt the effects of changing trade relations taking place on the coasts and sea-lanes of the Archipelago. The creation of coastal trading centres had an impact on the way of life of uplanders.

A Dayak feast celebrating the return from head-hunting, by Schwaner (1853).

Burning of corpses by the Dayak of Koharingan, by Schwaner (1853).

Inhabitant from Timor, by Temminck (1839-47).

The Effects of Coastal Trading Centres

As elsewhere in the Archipelago, there may have been little ethnic differentiation between coastal and highland peoples in ancient times. Expanding regional and inter-regional trade promoted the development of regional systems of wealth and power. Over time, interior populations became subordinated to, and marginalised from, their outward-looking and increasingly cosmopolitan coastal neighbours.

As European interest in spices increased, the islands of eastern Indonesia became important nodes in long distance trade networks. One consequence in the early modern period was the rapid formation of centralised kingdoms of the sort that had emerged centuries earlier in Sumatra and Java. In eastern Indonesia, however, these kingdoms were framed as Islamic sultanates rather than as Indic polities. Through trading relations controlled by coastal rulers, remote populations gained access to new goods, including woven cloth, iron tools, weapons, gongs, jewellery, mirrors, Chinese porcelains, and eventually guns.

New Foodstuffs

From farther distances still came new foodstuffs. With European ships travelling between Asia and the Americas, a variety of new foods began to penetrate the Archipelago. Over the last four centuries, the diets of most upland swidden farmers in Southeast Asia have become increasingly diverse with the addition of food such as maize, cassava, sweet potatoes, squash, onions and tomatoes. New crops had ecological consequences for Timor and Sumba, where over-dependence on maize, rather than swidden farming practices themselves, has made subsistence difficult.

Exposure to Diseases

Invisible but lethal were pathogens that travelled along the trade routes. For many isolated populations, exposure to unfamiliar diseases came late in the 19th and early in the 20th century when the Dutch administration established direct control over remote areas, and forced relocation of uplanders to coastal settlements. Early in this century deaths from smallpox, for example, and other diseases drove people back to the highlands from resettlement villages near Ampana in central Sulawesi.

Stratification of Wealth and Power

The growth of coastal economies prompted stratification of wealth and power in some upland regions. By forging ties with coastal rulers, upland leaders enhanced their own authority and wealth. Many adopted titles and other symbols of power from stratified coastal polities. Upland chiefs sometimes married their daughters to coastal rulers, thereby establishing prestigious ties to power in the eyes of their associates. Often, they were charged with special responsibilities by their coastal patron. For example, they were often expected to present first fruits of the harvest or other forms of tribute to the ruler. Differences in wealth within upland communities created various forms of dependency, including debt-slavery. In some areas, slaves became an important commodity in inter-island trade. In defence against slave traders, interior peoples in many areas took refuge in fortified settlements built on hilltops. Upland elites were often implicated in the export of slaves. An estimated 12,000 Torajan slaves, for example, were sold at the end of the 19th century in response to coastal labour shortages and fluctuations in the coffee market.

Relations Between Coastal and Upland Populations

The authority of coastal rulers over their upland subjects varied in form and effectiveness. Certain interior populations served as fighting forces for coastal rulers. The Tobaru of Halmahera, for example, fought bravely on behalf of the Sultan of Ternate. Other interior groups, such as the Wana of central Sulawesi, found themselves victims of headhunting raids authorised by lowland lords. The highlands served as a refuge for people escaping from warfare, slave-raiding, and domination. Over the centuries, people would locate closer to or farther from the lowlands, depending in part on prevailing economic and political conditions. The imposition of direct Dutch rule in the first decade of this century, for example, sent residents of the coastal lowlands and foothills deep into the interior of large islands such as Sulawesi.

The Effects of the Dutch Presence

The Dutch did not establish direct rule over most of the interior regions of the eastern Archipelago until the beginning of the 20th century. The effects of the Dutch presence, however, were experienced far from the VOC fortresses that sprung up across the island chain. As the Dutch pressured local sultanates to submit to their authority, the relations of rulers and subjects altered.

In Maluku, for example, the power of the ruler was strengthened. The Sultan of Ternate was able to expand his dominion, with consequences still remembered by uplanders and lowlanders alike in eastern Sulawesi. One dramatic effect of the competition among the VOC and the powerful trading principalities of eastern Indonesia was the dislocation of population from south Sulawesi. In response to Arung Palakka's military campaigns of the 1600s, for example, Makasarese and Bugis 'took to their ships like marauding Vikings in search of honour, wealth and new homes'. Successive waves of adventurers, entrepreneurs, and would-be 'port sultans' established themselves along the coasts of Sulawesi, Kalimantan, and other islands in the region. The creation of coastal elites with ethnic ties to south Sulawesi contributed to the development of a *pesisir* culture and increased the social distance between uplanders and their lowland neighbours.

The Spread of Islam

The spread of Islam eastward through the Archipelago came to influence coastal-upland relations in significant ways. Prompted initially, some claim, by warnings of the Catholic Portuguese advance, Islam spread quickly along the trade routes of the eastern Archipelago in the 15th century and thereafter. Upland populations shared with their coastal neighbours common cosmological assumptions and ritual practices; the introduction of Islamic elements into courtly ritual enhanced, rather than supplanted customary practice. Over the centuries, however, the consolidation of an Islamic coastal culture had profound implications for interior populations who were marginalised as kaffir. Religion became the basis for drawing ethnic lines between closely related populations of uplanders and lowlanders. In the 19th and 20th centuries, these lines were further sharpened by colonial ideologies of race and primitive backwardness, and by more orthodox observance of Islam, resulting from increased contact with Islamic centres in the Middle East.

Pagan uplanders were profoundly affected by Islam and, later, Christianity. Unable to make headway among Muslim populations, European missionaries targeted upland Pagan populations. Conversion to Christianity further accentuated the divide between many interior populations and their coastal neighbours. Elements of world religions permeated ritual language and practices of Pagan uplanders, who tapped these foreign sources for their spiritual powers. Uplanders' notions of religion were shaped through their exposure to Muslims and Christians. To uplanders in central Sulawesi, for example, religion appeared to be importantly about diet (due to Muslim prohibitions on pork and other popular upland foods), hygiene (due to Muslim prayer practices), and funerary practices.

❶ *Soldier from Ambon (Nieuhof, 1732).*
❷ *Warrior of Savu, c.1800 (Temminck).*
❸ *A Dayak in war dress (Temminck).*
❹ *Sakai Dayak of southeast Borneo*
❺ *Orang Bukit from Amontai, South Kalimantan.*
❻ *Long-Wai woman, central Kalimantan.*

Dance of the Dayak of the Kapuas, chromolithograph from Borneo, by C.A.L.M. Schwaner (Amsterdam, 1853).

« *Two Alfur (Upland) warriors from Maluku, from F. Valentijn (Amsterdam, 1726).*

Puputan: End of the Kingdoms of Bali

*F*or a Balinese ruler faced with defeat, surrender was never an option. Traditionally, the only honourable course of action was to end his life and set aside his temporal power in a fight to the death, a ritual of self sacrifice known as puputan. Literally puputan means 'ending' or 'finish' but symbolically it also encompassed the proper display of courage and loyalty that was inherent in Balinese kingship.

AFTERMATH OF THE PUPUTAN IN BADUNG

In an eyewitness account of the massacre, H.M. van Weede described the scene: 'After the artillery fire stopped, the prince went there with his followers, women and children totalling around one hundred people, and there hidden from our view, they stabbed each other with kris. We found them together in a heap, the prince buried under the bodies of his faithful followers, as if to show that they wanted to protect him to the death, and the most beautiful young women we had seen in Bali lay lifeless next to their children. The gold sedan chair and other valuables lay there in the middle of the corpses...' (Arsip Nasional, Jakarta).

The only remaining part of the royal palace of Klungkung.

The royal palace of Klungkung was destroyed during the puputan in April 1908, and the ruins demolished afterwards by the Dutch colonial government. Only a door, water pavilion and Kertagosa or Hall of Justice remain of the pre-colonial centre of power. (Inset) Nagas at the entrance to the stairway of pavilion.

Dutch Encroachment

As the Dutch began to sweep through the remaining independent pockets of indigenous authority at the end of the 19th century, three Balinese kingdoms chose to end their independence in this dramatic way. Part ritual, part bravado, the Balinese armed with traditional weapons and dressed in ceremonial finery, followed their rulers into the face of Dutch gun and cannon fire, then turned their kris on themselves in order to die with their king. It was necessarily an uneven contest as traditional Balinese weapons such as spears, pikes and krises were pitted against the artillery of the Netherlands Indies armed forces.

The incorporation of Bali into the Netherlands Indies was a long and bloody process that brought about the annihilation of each of the Balinese royal lineages whose rulers opted for honour through the ritual of the *puputan* rather than peaceful concessions. In Bali this process of conquest had begun 60 years earlier with the signing of the Kuta Peace Treaty in July 1849. At the conclusion of this first major military encounter between the Balinese and Dutch, the north and western parts of Bali, Buleleng and Jembrana, had already lost their independence. Coming briefly under the governorship of the tiny landlocked kingdom of Bangli, north Bali had been administered by Dutch officials from 1854, and was placed directly under colonial authority when the Residency of Bali and Lombok was established in 1882.

For much of this period the Dutch were content to allow the rulers of south and east Bali to remain independent. Their efforts to control Bali were actually assisted by the strong rivalries that existed between many of Bali's kingdoms. The ambitious ruler of Lombok had gained control of the eastern kingdom of Karangasem in 1849 by allying himself to the Dutch, and the small kingdoms of Bangli and Gianyar had both recognised the advantages of concessions to the Dutch presence. In 1891, the same intense Balinese rivalries put an end to the once important kingdom of Mengwi when Badung, together with its close ally Tabanan, defeated its king and incorporated all his lands into Badung.

The Fall of Mataram in 1894

The first *puputan* took place in Mataram, when Dutch-Lombok relations, which for much of the 19th century had been cordial and mutually advantageous, reached an impasse. A Sasak uprising gave the Dutch the excuse they needed to intervene. Following the sacking of the royal palace at Cakranagara, the Lombok ruler, Agung Gede Ngurah Karangasem, took refuge in the village of Sasari. He was eventually persuaded to surrender with his son and grandson. Despite the king's capitulation, many of his relatives led by his nephew Anak Agung Nengah refused to surrender and chose instead to fight to the death advancing in the face of the enemy fire. Most were killed and those who escaped, including Nengah himself, were eventually rounded up and captured. The king was exiled to Batavia where he died on 20 May 1895.

The defeat of the Lombok dynasty, also brought the kingdom of Karangasem on Bali under Dutch control. In 1900 Gianyar, beset on all sides by its neighbouring rival kingdoms, sought refuge from Klungkung led aggression by seeking to become part of the colonial

administrative system. At the turn of the century, only Badung closely allied to Tabanan, Klungkung and Bangli retained their independence. With a number of changes in colonial personnel in Bali and in Batavia, particularly the appointment of J. B. van Heutsz, the victorious military leader of the Aceh War as Governor General in 1904, the Netherlands Indies government took a harder line on the remaining independent kingdoms.

PUPUTAN IN BALI AND LOMBOK IN THE 19th AND 20th CENTURIES

Map legend:
- --- Frontiers of Balinese Principalities
- Areas which signed treaties with the Dutch
- Areas where the Dutch established direct rule
- **Places and dates where puputan took place**

Map labels: Buleleng, Jagaraga, Singaraja, BULELENG, JEMBRANA, Jembrana, TABANAN, MENGWI, BANGLI, Bangli, KARANGASEM, Karangasem, GIANYAR, KLUNGKUNG 1908, Tabanan, Gelgel, Mengwi, Gianyar, Badung 1906, BADUNG, Nusa Penida Island, Ampenan, Mataram 1894, Labuhan Haji, Praja, LOMBOK, BALI, N, 0 25 km

Puputan Badung in 1906

The first confrontation took place in Badung, the immediate cause being the same as had prompted the three military expeditions over half a century earlier, salvage rights. On 27 May 1905, the *Sri Komala,* flying the Dutch flag, was stranded off the coast of Sanur in Badung. The Chinese owner claimed the Balinese had stolen the cargo in violation of Clause 11 of the Treaty of 1849 and the government demanded compensation of 75,000 guilders. When the ruler of Badung, Gede Ngurah Denpasar refused to pay, the Dutch blockaded the coast and demanded further compensation. The blockade was ineffective as supplies were brought through to Badung from Tabanan. Months of negotiation failed to achieve any compromise and on 14 September 1906, Dutch troops landed at Sanur.

On the morning of 20 September they reached Denpasar and marched on the palace of Gede Ngurah Denpasar. Having set fire to the palace, the king at the head of 300 followers emerged from the palace and came to a halt a few hundred metres from the Dutch ranks. Eye witness accounts state that the women had their hair loose and were dressed in white cloaks and all carried a kris. As the Balinese advanced to within metres of the Dutch lines the order to fire was given. The ruler was amongst the first to fall. Later the same afternoon the Dutch troops advanced on the co-ruler of Badung, Gusti Gede Ngurah Pamecutan where the scene was repeated. Again the Balinese men, women and children marched into the Dutch fire. The official number of Balinese casualties was put at 400 but was probably far greater. The Dutch then marched on Tabanan, whose ruler Gusti Ngurah Agung agreed to surrender. Both he and his son killed themselves on 29 September, the night before they were to be exiled to Lombok.

The Fall of Klungkung in 1908

The two remaining independent rulers, the Dewa Agung of Klungkung and Dewa Gede Tangkeban of Bangli were persuaded to sign new treaties with the Dutch on 14 October 1906. For a little over a year, relations between Dutch colonial officials and the Dewa Agung remained cordial. The imposition of the opium monopoly in Bali in 1908, though, led to riots in Klungkung. The Dutch declared the riots to be in breach of the contract of 1906 and sent in their troops. During a skirmish in Gelgel on April 16 1908, a Javanese opium dealer was killed and his opium store razed. Over 100 Balinese were killed or wounded and one Dutch official was killed. The Cokorda of Gelgel fled to Klungkung to take refuge with the Dewa Agung. The Dutch marched on the palace and demanded the Cokorda be surrendered. This was refused and on 28 April, in a repetition of the 1906 *puputan*, the Dewa Agung and his followers marched towards the Dutch lines and were killed. With this, the royal house of Klungkung came to an end and Bali finally became part of the Dutch colonial empire.

KRIS

The kris in Indonesia is thought to have a spirit of its own. This spirit may have a positive aspect: the form of certain weapons may invoke protection. This Balinese state kris for ceremonial use invokes talismanic protection through the raksasa (demon) figure. Balinese kris were strongly associated with the ritual self-sacrifice known as *puputan* in the late 19th and early 20th centuries.

The Raja of Buleleng commits suicide with his subjects during the Dutch invasion, from Le Petit Journal.

A TALE FROM BALI

This book by Vicki Baum provides a fictional account of the 19th and early 20th century Balinese-Dutch interactions that led to tragedy-the deaths of thousands of Balinese.

When the Balinese villagers loot a shipwreck off the coast of Sanur in 1906, the Dutch use the incident as a pretext for taking complete control of Bali. The rajas refuse to give way to Dutch demands, and with hundreds of their retainers and other followers, clothe themselves in white, and armed with their krises they march out of the *puri* to their deaths. Those not killed by Dutch gunfire commit suicide having first slaughtered their families. The Dutch, who believe themselves the victors, can only look on in horror as men, women and children choose honour by death. Their deaths symbolise *puputan*, 'the end' of an old way of life.

Glossary

ABBREVIATIONS:

Malay/Indonesian except where indicated. (Ar.) Arabic, (Bal.) Balinese, (Bug.) Bugis, (Ch.) Chinese, (D.) Dutch, (Jav.) Javanese, (Mak.) Makasarese, (Per.) Persian, (P.) Portuguese, (Sp.) Spanish, (Sun.) Sundanese

A

ade pitu: (Bug.) the ruling council of seven kings.

alang-alang: *Imperata cylindrica*, a tall grass. It is usually found covering areas where forest has been repeatedly burned.

alun-alun: (Jav.) the public square to the north of a Javanese palace.

arung: (Bug.) a ruler.

B

babad: (Jav.) a Javanese traditional chronicle.

bafta: (Per.), also *basta*, meaning 'woven'. In the Indian context (Gujarati) in the 17th century, it referred to a calico woven in Gujarati, 15 yards long and 25 inches wide. It later evolved into a more generic term in the textile trade, encompassing many different grades of cotton cloth.

bahar: measure of weight (three **pikuls**), varying from place to place, but approximately 180 kilogrammes for pepper and 272 kilogrammes for cloves.

bait: a couplet, verse.

Bate Salapang: (Mak.) the 'nine banners', or the nine communities which formed the core of the kingdom of Gowa.

belukan: (Jav.) Javanese boat with a shallow draught

designed fo river transport.

Bhairawa: in Buddhism a being who embodies negative impulses.

bupati: (Jav.) a regent, a government officer in charge of a regency.

bundu pammanakang: (Mak.) a term for 'civil war', or literally 'war within family'.

C

cahaya: a radiance, glow.

candi bentar: 'split candi', a gateway consisting of two separate, symmetrical parts flanking the entrance to a temple or tomb complex. If placed together, these two parts would form the outline of a *candi*.

cannekin: pieces cut from **bafta**, usually dyed black or blue, and sold on the Asian market.

casados: (P.) Portuguese settlers in Timor and Flores, and other islands in eastern Indonesia.

ceppa: (Bug.) a treaty. (cf. *cappa* Mak.)

D

Dabogong: (Ch.) or Toapekong, god of earth and riches.

dangau: a small, temporary hut in fields used to guard the crops.

daulat: (Ar.) sovereignty.

F

fardhu'ain: (Ar.) the individual obligation of a Muslim.

fikh: (Ar.) the study of laws pertaining to ritual obligations.

G

gaga: (Jav.) field for dry rice

cultivation.

gaharu: Indonesian word for eaglewood (*Aquilaria*) which produces resin used as a perfume.

gaukeng: (Bug.) /*gaukang* (Mak.), spiritual object which is considered the palladium of the community.

guilder: (D.) a Dutch silver coin; about 10 grams of silver.

H

Heren Zeventien: (D.) 'the Gentlemen Seventeen', 17 lords, or Directors of the **VOC**

hikayat: a Malay prose form, similar to a historical romance.

halus: refined, cultured.

huma: (Sun.) a field for dry rice cultivation.

haji: one who has made the pilgrimage to Mecca.

J

jihad: (Ar.) a holy war.

K

kaba: a tale, story.

kabupaten: a regency, the area headed by a **bupati**.

kadhi: (Ar.) a judge in Islamic law.

kafir: an infidel, an unbeliever.

kakawin: (Jav.) an Old Javanese verse form.

Kapitan China/Cina: a representative of the Chinese community who was recognised by the Dutch authorities.

Kapitan Melayu: a representative of the Malay community (sometimes including Javanese), and recognised by the Dutch authorities.

kapthay: (Ch.) from *kapitan*, a headman or captain, *dai*, Chinese for 'great'; a title recognised by the Dutch for a **kongsi** head.

kaum: a religious official in charge of the mosque.

kongsi: a loan word from the Chinese (*gongsi*, company). Miners formed *kongsis* to share work in the mines, the revenue farmers used them to spread the risk of running the tax farms.

kyai: (Jav.) a term of address for a venerated scholar, teacher of Islam.

L

labuhan: a harbour.

ladang: an unirrigated, dry rice field.

Laksamana: an admiral.

lurah: a village chief.

M

mancanegara: foreign countries.

maulana: a title used for Islamic scholars.

mesjid: a mosque.

N

nabi: a prophet.

nakhoda: a ship's captain.

O

orang kaya: a 'rich person', an aristocrat, generally with wealth from trade.

P

pangreh praja: (Jav.) the civil service.

pasar: a market.

paseban: (Jav.) a courtyard in front of a palace or in a noble's compound.

patih: a governor, vice regent, chief minister to a king.

penghulu: a village chief, Muslim leader.

petak: compartments under the deck of a Malay junk, separated by bamboo matting in which merchandise was carried.

peranakan: locally born Chinese Indonesians, usually the descendants of Chinese fathers and Indonesian mothers.

pendapa: (Jav.) from South Indian *mandapa*, a 'pillared hallway'; in Indonesian, a term for an unwalled pavilion.

pesantren: a school of Koranic studies for children and young people, most of whom are boarders.

pikul: the weight a man can carry; two sacks; taken as 60 kilogrammes for pepper.

prahu: a sailing vessel.

priyayi: (Jav.) the aristocracy.

puputan: (Bal.) 'ending' or 'finish'; in particular the suicidal attack by which Balinese rulers acknowledged final defeat.

puri: a Balinese temple.

pusaka: heirlooms.

R

ratib: repeated, chanted recitation of prayer.

Ratu Adil: (Jav.) The Just King, a legendary figure.

real: (Span.) *Peso de och* or piece of eight; 25.5 grams of silver.

rijksdaalder: (D.) the Dutch equivalent of Spanish *real*; 2.5 *guilders*.

S

santri: a student at a traditional Muslim school; a strict adherent of Islam.

sawah: a wet rice field.

selamatan: a ceremonial meal. These may be held on numerous occasions associated with the bestowing of luck and blessings on individuals or undertakings.

shari'a: (Ar.) the code of Islamic law.

sumping: (Jav.) a decoration covering the ear, used for noble, ceremonial dress.

surau: a prayer house, a communal building suitable for any devotion except Friday prayer.

syahbandar: the harbour-master.

syahid: (Ar.) a martyr or warrior killed while fighting for Islamic principles.

syair: a story related in verse form, a poem.

T

tambo: a traditional Minangkabau literary genre which focuses on genealogies.

tarekat: the religious path followed by mystics, especially of the Sufi school.

tasauf: (Ar.) a form of mysticism practised by the Sufist school.

tauhid: the unity of God, the acknowledgement of the oneness of God.

tuanku: a title of royalty.

tegal: a dry field used for vegetables and other secondary crops.

tomanurung: (Mak.) a 'being who descended [from the Upperworld]', progenitors of the royal families in south Sulawesi.

Tupassi: 'Black Portuguese' or Topaz. A mestizo community who developed from the mixed marriages between Portuguese settlers in eastern Indonesia (particularly in Timor and Flores) and local women.

U

ulama: (Ar./Mal.) Islamic scholars.

ulubalang: a military leader or commander; also, head of a *mukim* (administrative district) in Aceh between the 1790s and 1870s.

V

VOC: (D.) 'Verenigde Oost Indische Compagnie', the Dutch East India Company.

W

wahyu: a divine revelation, vision from God to man.

wali: (Ar.) a representative (of God), a saint; especially the 'nine *wali*' to whom the conversion of Java is traditionally attributed.

Bibliography

GENERAL WORKS

Lombard, D. 1990. *Le Carrefour Javanais. Essai d'histoire globale.* (3 vols.) Paris, Editions de l'Ecole des Hautes Etudes en Sciences Sociales.

Tarling, N. (ed.) 1992. *The Cambridge History of Southeast Asia.* (2 vols). Cambridge: Cambridge University Press.

Reid, A. 1988-93. *Southeast Asia in the Age of Commerce 1450–1680.* (2 vols.) New Haven: Yale University Press.

Reid, A. (ed.) 1983. *Slavery, Bondage and Dependency in Southeast Asia.* St Lucia: University of Queensland Press.

Reid, A. 1993. *Southeast Asia in the Early Modern Era.* Ithaca: Cornell University Press.

Ricklefs, M.C. 1993. *A History of Modern Indonesia since c. 1300.* London: Macmillan.

Sartono, K. 1987. *Pengantar Sejarah Indonesia Baru: 1500–1900. Dari Emporium Sampai Imperium.* Jakarta: Gramedia.

EARLY EUROPEAN ACCOUNTS

Graaf, H.J.de. 1958. *De regering van Sultan Agung, vorst van Mataram, 1613–1645, en die van zijn voorganger Panembahan Seda-ing-Krapyak, 1601–1613.* The Hague: Martinus Nijhoff for KITLV.

Graaf, H.J.de. and Th. G.Th. Pigeaud. 1974. *De eerste Moslimse vorstendommen op Java: Studien over de staatkundige geschiedenis van de 15de en 16de eeuw.* The Hague: M. Nijhoff.

Marsden, W. 1966 [1783]. *A History of Sumatra. Reprinted 1966.* Kuala Lumpur: Oxford University Press.

Raffles, T.S. 1978 [1817]. *The History of Java.* (2 vols.) Kuala Lumpur: Oxford University Press.

Pires, T. c.1515. *The Suma Oriental of Tomé Pires,* (trans. Armando Cortesão). London: Hakluyt Society, 1944.

MATERIAL CULTURE

Adhyatman, S. 1981. *Antique Ceramics found in Indonesia.* Jakarta: Ceramic Society of Indonesia.

Bellwood, P. 1985. *Prehistory of the Indo-Malaysian Archipelago.* Sydney: Academic Press.

Brown, R. 1988. *The Ceramics of Southeast Asia: Their Dating and Identification.* Singapore: Oxford: University Press.

Gittinger, M. 1985. *Splendid Symbols: Textiles and Tradition in Indonesia.* Singapore: Oxford University Press.

Guy, J. 1986. *Oriental Trade Ceramics in Southeast Asia: Ninth to Sixteenth Centuries.* Singapore: Oxford University Press.

Jessup, H.I. 1991. *Court Arts of Indonesia.* New York: Asia Society Galleries.

Maxwell, R. 1990. *Textiles of Southeast Asia: Tradition, Trade and Transformation.* Melbourne: Oxford University Press.

Niessen, S.A. 1993. *Batak Cloth and Clothing: A Dynamic Indonesian Tradition.* Kuala Lumpur: Oxford University Press.

POPULATION, AGRICULTURE AND ENVIRONMENT

Boomgaard, P. 1989. *Children of the Colonial State: Population Growth and Economic Development in Java 1795–1880.* Amsterdam: Free University Press.

Elson, R.E. 1994. *Village Java Under the Cultivation System.* Sydney: Allen and Unwin.

Fox, J.J. 1977. *Harvest of the Palm: Ecological Change in Eastern Indonesia.* Cambridge, Mass.: Harvard University Press.

Geertz, C. 1963. *Agricultural Involution: The Process of Ecological Change in Indonesia.* Berkeley: University of California Press.

ISLAM AND CHRISTIANITY

Abdullah, T. (ed.) 1983. *Agama dan Perubahan Sosial.* Jakarta: Rajawali.

Dobbin, C. 1983. *Islamic Revivalism in a Changing Peasant Economy: Central Sumatra, 1784–1847.* London/Malmo: Curzon Press.

Kumar, A. 1985. *The Diary of a Javanese Muslim: Religion, Politics and the Pesantren 1883–1886.* Canberra: Faculty of Asian Studies Monographs, Australian National University Press.

Reid, A. 1993. *The Making of an Islamic Political Discourse in Southeast Asia.* Melbourne: Monash University Papers on Southeast Asia.

Schurhammer, G.S.J. 1977. *Francis Xavier: His Life, His Times,* vol 2, India (1541–1545). Rome: Jesuit Historical Institute.

ISLAMIC PORT STATES

Andaya, B. 1993. *To Live as Brothers: Southeast Sumatra in the Seventeenth and Eighteenth Centuries.* Honolulu: University of Hawaii Press.

Andaya, L. 1981. *The Heritage of Arung Palakka: A History of South Sulawesi (Celebes) in the Seventeenth Century.* The Hague: KITLV.

Andaya, L. 1993. *The World of Maluku: Eastern Indonesia in the Early Modern Period.* Honolulu: University of Hawaii Press.

Drakard, J. 1990. *A Malay Frontier: Unity and Duality in a Sumatran Kingdom.* Ithaca: Cornell University Southeast Asia Program.

Gould, J.W. 1956. *Sumatra: America's Pepperport, 1784–1873.'* Essex Institute Historical Collections 92. pp. 83–152, 203–51, 295–348.

Guillot, C., Ambary, H. and J. Dumarçay. 1990. *The Sultanate of Banten.* Jakarta: Gramedia.

Kathirithamby-Wells, J. and Villiers, J. (eds.) 1990. *The Southeast Asian Port and Polity: Rise and Demise.* Singapore: Singapore University Press.

Lombard, D. 1967. *Le sultanat d'Atjeh au temps d'Iskandar Muda, 1607–1636.* Paris: Ecole Française d'Extrême–Orient.

Meilink Roelofsz, M.A.P. 1969. *Asian Trade and European Influence in the Indonesian Archipelago between 1500 and about 1630.* The Hague: M. Nijhoff.

Pigeaud, Th.G.Th. and Graaf, H.J. de. 1976. *Islamic States in Java 1500–1700.* The Hague: M. Nijhoff.

LITERATURE

Carey, P. (ed.) 1981. *Babad Dipanagara: An Account of the Outbreak of the Java War (1825–1830).* Kuala Lumpur: Malaysian

branch, Royal Asiatic Society.

Drewes, G.W.J. and Brakel, L.F. 1986. *The Poems of Hamzah Fansuri.* Dordrecht: Foris.

Florida, N. 1995. *Writing the Past, Inscribing the Future: History as Prophecy in Colonial Java.* Durham: Duke University Press.

Gallop, A.T. and Arps, B. 1991. *Golden Letters: Writing Traditions of Indonesia Surat Mas: Budaya Tulis di Indonesia.* London: British Library.

Pigeaud, Th.G.Th. 1967–1970. *Literature of Java: Catalogue Raisonné of Javanese Manuscripts.* (3 vols.) The Hague: M. Nijhoff.

Raja Ali Haji ibn Ahmad. c. 1850. *The Precious Gift [Tuhfat al-Nafis].* Edited by V. Matheson and B. Andaya (1982). Kuala Lumpur: Oxford University Press.

Ricklefs, M.C. 1978. *Modern Javanese Historical Tradition: A Study of an Original Kartasura Chronicle and Related Materials.* London: School of Oriental and African Studies.

Ras, J.J. (ed.) 1968. *Hikayat Bandjar: A Study in Malay Historiography.* The Hague: M. Nijhoff.

THE CHINESE ROLE

Butcher, J. and H. Dick. (eds.) 1993. *The Rise and Fall of Revenue Farming: Business Elites and the Emergence of the Modern State in Southeast Asia.* London: Macmillan.

Reid, A. (ed.) 1996. *Sojourners and Settlers: Histories of Southeast Asia and the Chinese.* Sydney: Allen and Unwin for ASAA.

Remmelink, W.G.J. 1990. *Emperor Pakubuwana II, Priyayi and Company, and the Chinese War.* Leiden University Dissertation.

Rush, J.R. 1990. *Opium to Java: Revenue Farming and Chinese Enterprise in Colonial Indonesia.* 1860–1910. Ithaca: Cornell University Press.

Somers-Heidhues, M. 1992. *Bangka Tin and Mentok Pepper: Chinese Settlement on an Indonesian Island.* Singapore: Institute of Southeast Asian Studies.

THE RISE OF EUROPEAN POWER

Blussé, L. 1986. *Strange Company: Chinese Settlers, Mestizo Women and the Dutch in VOC Batavia.* Dordrecht: Foris for KITLV.

Boxer, C.R. 1965. *The Dutch Seaborne Empire 1600–1800.* London: Hutchinson.

Glamann, K. 1981. *Dutch–Asiatic Trade, 1620–1740.* The Hague: M. Nijhoff.

Houben, V.J.H. 1994. *Kraton and Kumpeni: Surakarta and Yogyakarta, 1830–1870.* Leiden: KITLV Press.

Kathirithamby-Wells, J. 1977. *The British West Sumatran Residency: Problems of Early Colonial Enterprise.* Kuala Lumpur: Penerbit Universiti Malaya.

Reid, A. 1969. *The Contest for North Sumatra: Atjeh, the Netherlands and Britain.* Kuala Lumpur: Oxford University Press.

INDONESIAN STATES IN THE 17th - 19th CENTURIES

Anderson, B. 1990. *Language and Power. Exploring Political Cultures in Indonesia.* Ithaca: Cornell University Press.

Geertz, C. 1980. *Negara: The Theatre State in Nineteenth Century Bali.* Princeton: Princeton University Press.

Geertz, H. 1979. *Bali. State and Society.* Leiden: KITLV Press.

Lee Kam Hing. 1995. *The Sultanate of Aceh: Relations with the British, 1760–1824.* Kuala Lumpur: Oxford University Press.

Remmelink, W.G.J. 1990. *Emperor Pakubuwana II, Priyayi and Company, and the Chinese War.* Leiden University Dissertation.

Ricklefs, M.C. 1974. *Jogjakarta under Sultan Mangkubumi, 1749–1792: A History of the Division of Java.* London: Oxford University Press.

Ricklefs, M.C. 1993. *War, Culture and Economy in Java, 1677–1726: Asian and European Imperialism in the Early Kartasura Period.* Sydney: Allen and Unwin for ASAA.

Wiener, M. 1994. *Visible and Invisible Realms: Power, Magic and Colonial Conquest in Bali.* Chicago: Chicago University Press.

Index

Photo Credits

Pictures not credited here were supplied by Antiques of the Orient.

The Publisher acknowledges the kind permission of the following for the reproductions of photographs.

Chapter openers: The Island World and its People, Diversity of people and batik making by EDM, Bugis boats by Photobank, and Stadhuis by Leo Haks. Islam and the Port Sultans, Map by Anthony Reid. A Crisis and Change of Direction, Dutch attack on Makasar by Anthony Reid. Living Without Strong States, Kora-kora by Yu-Chee Chong Fine Art, London. The End of Autonomy, Gun and kris by kind permission of the National Museum of Jakarta, and Indigenous soldiers by kind permission of the KITLV.

Reproduced by kind permission of the Arsip Nasional, Jakarta. p. 140, Aftermath of puputan.

Reproduced by kind permission of The Bodleian Library, University of Oxford. p. 64, Hikayat Nur Muhammad; and p. 85, Letter from Iskandar Muda.

Reproduced by kind permission of The British Library. p. 37, Hikayat Raja Raja Pasai; p. 42, Sultan Suleyman; p. 43, Acehnese seige of Melaka; p. 68, Colophon of Taj us Salatin, and Hikayat Muhammad Hanafiah; p. 69, Hikayat Banjar, Damar Wulan; and Diary of King of Bone, and Bugis Compendium of firearms; p. 80-81, Babad Mangkunagara; p. 84, letter from Sultan Muhammad Yasin (Ternate); p. 85, two Banten envoys; p. 110-111, Captain Thomas Forrest; and p. 112, seal of Sultan Jauhar Alam Shah.

Reproduced by kind permission of Koninklijk Institute voor Taal–, Land– en Volkenkunde, Netherlands (KITLV). p. 32, Chinese junk; p. 61, rumah gadang; p.72, print of Dutch ship; p. 82, coffee; p. 83, salt; p. 88, opium industrial technology; p. 94, Lombok slave; p. 100, Panglima Dalam; p. 105, Pendapa Agung; p. 112-113, Babad Dipanagara;

p. 114, Ratu Agung Agung Ngurah Karang-asem; p. 115, Anak Agung Jilantik Karang-asem; p. 121, female workers, and peasants; p. 124, Chinese officer; and p. 125, Tjong Yong Hian.

Reproduced by kind permission of the Leiden University Library, Netherlands. p. 78, Babad Dalem; p. 79, Bharatayuddha; p. 113, Dipanagara in exile; and p. 136, Bugis genealogy.

Reproduced by kind permission of the Ministry of Education and Culture, Indonesia. p. 48, Queen Nahrasiyah, and calligraphy of Surat Yasin; and p. 49, calligraphy of Queen Nahrasiyah.

Reproduced by kind permission of the Nasional Museum of Jakarta. p. 7, Balinese kris and kain simbut; p. 20, gamelan; p. 24, Cirebon batik; p. 32, Jiangxi plate; p. 33, Chinese plate; p. 66, Singhabarwang carriage; and p. 105, Nagasasra kris (Photograph byTara Sosrowardoyo).

Reproduced by kind permission of The Royal Asiatic Society, London. p. 65, Bustan al–Salatin.

Reproduced by kind permission of the Tropen Institute, Netherlands (KIT). p. 73, Chinese porcelain (photo graph by Anthony Reid).

Leonard Andaya, p. 57, Royal tiger; p. 92, ritual chant, and mosque in Makian; p. 93, interior of Church, and Fort Victoria; p. 106, Bugis courtier, and Arung Palakka's tomb; and p. 107, Dutch governor's residence.
Barbara Watson Andaya, p. 100, ka–ga–nga; and p. 101, Lemabang royal complex, and gold digging.
Peter Carey, p. 112, Dipa-nagara in 1807, and sketch of Dipanagara.
Paul Chesley, p. 14, chilies.
Bruce Coleman Ltd, p. 30, drying cloves.
Jane Drakard, p. 60, royal seal; p. 66, manuscript from Minangkabau, Riddell; p. 64, tomb of Syech Bachrin; and p. 65, Tarjuman al–Mustafid.
Jill Gocher, p. 17, modern selamatan.

John Gollings, p. 66, crown; and p. 67, fan and umbrella finial. By kind permission of Helen Jessup, Court Arts of Indonesia [New York, Asia Society].
John Guy, p. 22, kendi; and p. 23, Chinese jar.
Leo Haks, p. 9, map of East Indian colonies.
Rio Helmi, p. 107, Fort Rotterdam; and p. 140–141, Balinese kris.
Adolf Heuken, p. 81, death of François Tack, and p. 96, Chinese revolt, both courtesy of Times Books International.
Virginia Hooker, p. 98, library in Penyengat mosque; p. 99, Tuhfat al–Nafis, and pulpit.
Alfons van der Kraan, p. 114, Anak Agung K'tut Karangasem, and Lombok chiefs.
Ibrahim Alfian, p. 48, gold coins; p. 49, tombstone of Na'ina Husam al–Din; p. 133, Hikayat Perang Sabil.
Kathirithamby-Wells, p. 25, Palepei; and p. 34, pepper vine.
Khoo Su Nin, p. 118, Acheen Mosque.
Ruurdje Laarhoven, p. 24, Indian textile; and p. 25, samples of cloth.
Roy Lewis, p. 43, casket of Francis Xavier.
Pierre-Yves Manguin, p. 28, war galley; and p. 29, remains of ship.
John Miksic, p. 19, dammar; p.21, gold panners; p. 22, Viet-namese tiles, pottery, and firing straw; p. 23, earthenware/birdform, /four–footed animal, glazed lotus, minaret at Kudus, and Kudus ceramics; p. 36, Leran tomb complex; p. 38, tomb of Sunan Giri, Guardian of Tomb, Sunan Kudus, (carved stone); p. 39, Sunan Bayat, (tomb complex, tombstone associates Sunan G. Jati), Soko Tunggal, and (closeup); p. 49, tombstone of Malik Ibrahim; p. 54, Brantas river; p. 55, parang kusomo, gate-way to grave, decora tive carving on grave, and model; p. 56, fort Oranje; p. 61, sacred regalia; p. 64 pesant-ren; p. 66, Balinese ruler; p. 76, Fort Speelwijk; p. 99, grave of Raja Ali Haji; and p.99 Mosque Penyengat; p. 104, Taman Sari; p. 115, pleasure gardens at Narmada, and Lingsar; p. 116, mosque at Pariaman; p. 127,

Pendapa Agung; p. 134, Christian grave; p. 136, Bugis flag; and p. 140, palace of Klungkung, and Nagas.
Kal Muller, p. 106, Salakoa crown.
Luc Nagtegaal, p. 82, coffee plantation.
Sandra Niessen, p. 134, Toba Batak market, missionary Ginsberg, by kind permission of Vereinigte Evangelische Mission–Bildarchiv; and p. 135, Karo Batak women, Canoe, Chief Pa Mbelgah, and bride.
Anthony Reid, p. 24, spinning, and weaving; p. 29, ship cloth; p. 38, Mesjid Agung by kind permission of Helen Jessup, Court Arts of Indonesia; p. 42, Sultan Suleyman receiving a visitor, with his troops; p. 50, characters of Banten, by courtesy of Claude Guillot, and Great Mosque of Banten; p. 51, royal cemetary, Kenari, Ki Amuk cannon, and Ki Amuk inscription; p. 52, orang kaya, from Peter Mundy, 1667; p. 53, Iskandar Thani's funeral; p. 70, Dutch attack on Makasar; p. 91, Australian aboriginal drawing of a Bugis prahu; p. 95, Toba Batak slave; and p. 117; Tuanku Bonjol, Padris' style of dress, and Penghulu from Singkarak.
Willem Remmelink, p. 97, Chinese revolt, and map of Semarang.
Merle Ricklefs, p. 80, Captain Tack, Surapati; and p. 81, remnants of Sri Menganti, Old Dutch grave, and Susuhunan Pakubawana II.
Somers–Heidhues, p. 103, tablets of the dead, Toapekong, and Chinese Headmen.
Heather Sutherland, p. 94, slave auction; and p. 95, chained Toraja slaves.
Tara Sosrowardoyo, p. 127, royal procession.
Roger Tol, p. 136, La Pawawoi Karaeng Segeri on board; and p. 137, La Pawawoi Karaeng Segeri.

The following illustrators have also contributed to the book:
Domitille Héron, p.12, Indonesian Archipelago map.
Julian Davison, p. 19, Hornbill casques; and p. 29, remains of a 15th century ship.

The publishers have made every effort to ensure that all photographs and illustrations contained in this volume have been correctly credited, and apologise if any omissions or errors have occurred. These will be amended in the next printing.